D1229792

The View From Shanty Pond

The View From Shanty Pond

An Irish Immigrant's Look at Life
in a
New England Mill Town
1875 – 1938

Joseph P. Blanchette

The View From Shanty Pond:
An Irish Immigrant's Look at Life in a New England Mill Town
1875-1938

Shanty Pond Press
350 North Pasture Lane
Charlotte, Vermont

Published November, 1999
Printed in Canada
99 00 01 02 03 04 05 06 07 08 09   5 4 3 2 1

Publisher's Cataloging-In-Publication
(Prepared by Quality Books Inc.)

Blanchette, Joseph P.
  The view from Shanty Pond : an Irish immigrant's look at life in a
New England mill town, 1875-1938 / Joseph P. Blanchette. – 1st ed.
    p. cm
  Includes bibliographical references and index.
  LCCN: 99-90262
  ISBN: 0-9671537-5-1

    1. Cassidy, Peter. 2. Lawrence (Mass)—Emigration and
immigration. 3. Irish Americans—Massachusetts—Lawrence—
Biography. 4. American poetry—Irish American authors.   I. Title.

F74.L4B53 1999   974.4'5'04
                      QBI99-1273

        Design and Layout: Dawson Design
        Manuscript Editor: Rebecca Davidson
        Line Editor: Patsy Fortney
        Proof Reading: Jean Silveira
        Technology Consultant: Bruce Williamson

        This book is printed on acid-free paper.

To
Josh, Dan, and your children's children

Contents

Foreword
by
Kerby Miller

I first met Joe Blanchette a few years ago, when I was giving a public lecture at the old Hibernian Hall in Lawrence, Massachusetts, on the history of Irish immigration. In the course of explaining my own research in Irish immigrants' letters and memoirs, I mentioned that although historians knew a great deal from newspapers and census data about the formal history of the Irish in Lawrence and other American cities, we still knew very little about their everyday lives and feelings. At that time I didn't realize that among my audience was a man, Joe Blanchette, who in fact knew a great deal about the texture of Irish-American life in late nineteenth- and early twentieth-century Lawrence, because he had discovered a cache of marvellous evidence: the poems and songs of his great-grandfather, Peter Cassidy. Once locally famous as the Shanty Pond Poet, Cassidy was born in 1861 near Manchester, England, the son of Famine refugees from Co. Galway. In 1875 he immigrated to the United States with his widowed mother and siblings, and, except for the period 1882-90, he lived, worked, and composed poetry in Lawrence's Irish-American community until his death in 1938.

Now Joe is publishing his great-grandfather's poems and lifestory, and I am privileged that he has asked me to write this Foreword. For although Peter Cassidy's poems and songs may have dubious artistic merit, they provide a unique, personal window onto a world that we have lost: the world of Irish-America at the turn of the century, when ethnic life still centered on densely-packed tenements in tightly-knit neighborhoods, on parish churches and political machines, on taverns, ballparks, and fraternal organizations. It was a world whose inhabitants often had little material wealth (Peter Cassidy spent most of his life as a casual laborer) but who shared an intimacy, a spirit, and a sense of identity that rarely thrives among today's more affluent suburbanites. Not only through Peter Cassidy's poems, but also through Joe Blanchette's painstaking recreation of the urban and human contexts of those poems (the result of his admirably exhaustive research), we are now blessed with a glimpse of that vibrant and vanished community that was chronicled in Cassidy's compositions.

As a professional historian, I feel it incumbent to make a few analytical remarks suitable to my trade. First, the nearly total absence in Cassidy's poetry of words or references to the old Irish (or Gaelic) language is striking, for Cassidy's parents were almost certainly Irish-speakers in their native Galway, and although Cassidy himself was born and raised in England, Irish was probably the language of his childhood home. Furthermore, we know that in the late nineteenth and early twentieth centuries a very large number of the Irish immigrants who settled in Lawrence (as in Boston, Springfield, Holyoke, and other New England cities and milltowns) came from the western districts of counties, such as Kerry, Galway, and Mayo, that were still overwhelmingly Irish-speaking. There was a "hidden Gaelic world" in Irish America, about which we still know very little. Yet that world apparently disappeared very quickly and quietly—more thoroughly than in Ireland itself—and the absence of reference to the old language and its associated customs in Peter Cassidy's poems is an indication of the rapid rate of Irish acculturation in America—especially on the public (vs. the private or domestic) level, and nearly all of Cassidy's poems dealt with public events or were written for public, not private, audiences.

Second and despite the absence of the Irish language or of mention of traditional Irish customs in Peter Cassidy's poems, I am also struck by the remarkable similarity between the functions of both Cassidy and his songs on the one hand and those of the old Gaelic bardic poets and later ballad-singers on the other hand. Like Cassidy, the bards and the balladeers were public performers and entertainers as well as chroniclers of their people's history, and they depended heavily on the patronage of neighbors and, especially, of rich and powerful patrons who, in one form or another, paid them for their compositions. Equally remarkable, nearly all of Cassidy's poems and songs can be categorized by topic in precisely the same manner that scholars have categorized the poems and songs of the Gaelic bards and the ballad-singers. Thus, in modernized renditions, Cassidy composed praise-poems to honor and flatter his "chieftains"—the Irish politicians in Lawrence on whom he and the other working-class Irish in Lawrence depended so heavily for patronage—and poetic satires to ridicule those who failed to honor their commitments to their dependents. He also wrote eulogies of the glorious deeds of heroic warriors—who for Cassidy were the Irish-American soldiers who left Lawrence to fight in Flanders during World War I, and also the local Irish athletes who upheld their community's honor on baseball fields and in boxing rings. Again, like the bardic poems in honor of "Dark Rosaleen," many of Cassidy's songs were written in praise of Irish-American women—their stylized beauties and virtues.

Other of his compositions, like the songs the bards wrote after the English conquests of Ireland, lamented the departed glories of the past—in Cassidy's case, the decline of Lawrence's oldest Irish neighborhoods on "the Plains," and the disappearance of familiar landmarks, such as Shanty Pond itself, before the forces of progress. In a similar, nostalgic vein, a few of Cassidy's poems and songs lamented emigration as "exile" from Ireland, one of the bards' and the balladeers' most prevalent themes, while other, more rousing compositions urged his countrymen to sacrifice their money, if not their lives, to free Ireland from British rule, just as the seventeenth- and eighteenth-century poets had called on their listeners to expell the "foreigners" from Irish shores.

As my analogy suggests, few of Peter Cassidy's poems are what we might call "realistic," although in my opinion, those few include some of his most interesting and evocative works. These include compositions such as "My Daughter Has Me Most Crazy," a darkly humorous poem that reveals the generational conflicts that often raged between Irish-born parents and their American-born offspring; and "Not an Egg in the House," which exposes the bitter contrast between the spiritual promise of Easter and the pangs of hunger which families such as Cassidy's suffered in the Great Depression. However, what we might call Cassidy's "social protest" poems are rare: his vision, or the vision he put forth in his compositions, was one of a united, organic Irish-American community, one without profound or bitter internal conflicts shaped by class or ideological differences. Thus, his few poems that do touch on economic exploitation, such as "Keep the Home Fires Burning" and "An Appeal for the Strikers," blame "outsiders"—distant "coal barons" or unidentified "scabs"—as the source of the community's distress.

My last observation is that Peter Cassidy's poems and songs portray an Irish America in profound transition—in what Boston's late William Shannon, former U.S. ambassador to Ireland, once described as "an ambiguous, indeterminate state"—during the turn-of-the-century period. As the flood of new Irish immigrants receded, Irish-American communities such as Lawrence's were increasingly dominated by the U.S.-born second and third generations, for whom Ireland was largely a distant, inherited memory. Although a large number of Irish immigrants and their offspring remained impoverished (particularly in New England), growing numbers had joined the better-paid ranks of skilled, unionized labor, and a sizeable and increasingly suburbanized Irish-American middle class had already emerged. Finally, despite past and continued nativism, Irish-Americans had become powerful not only in organized labor but also in city government and in the Catholic church, and the patronage that flowed from both those institutions—for example, through construction contracts as well as jobs and charity— helped nurture the nascent Irish-American middle-class and shelter Ir ish-American workers' families from the frequent economic recessions that plagued the era. Yet Irish-Americans—again, especially in New England— were still conscious of their distinctiveness, still not quite certain they were "real" or "100% Americans." As Shannon put it, situated as they were between the Famine Irish refugees of the mid-nineteenth century and the millions of New Immigrants from southern and eastern Europe that flocked to America in 1890-1924, the turn-of-the-century Irish were "the closest to being in [the American mainstream] while still being out."

In my opinion, Peter Cassidy's poems and songs reflect the "ambiguous, indeterminate" status and identity of his Irish America, poised as it was between Irish memories and American loyalties, between working-class hardship and bourgeois respectability, between nativist prejudice and political power. For example, whereas some of Cassidy's compositions regret the loss of Ireland or, more often, the passing of Lawrence's old Irish neighborhoods, his compositions are more commonly characterized by the hyper-patriotic "boosterism" that was such a prominent feature of early twentieth-century American culture. Thus, in view of Protestant New England's traditionally-virulent nativism, it is somewhat ironic that Cassidy would boast, in his World War I poems, that "We are Yankee soldiers through and through." Even Cassidy's songs promoting Irish independence display the caution and restraint that marked the attitude of most "respectable," middle-class Irish Americans toward the early twentieth-century Irish struggle for freedom: Cassidy's predominant theme is that Irish-American sacrifices in World War I have earned Ireland representation at the Versailles Peace Conference; Irish independence will seemingly be achieved through united, peaceful means, while the angry and violent themes of the old Fenian songs, composed in the Famine's immediate aftermath, are almost entirely absent from Cassidy's compositions. Likewise, it may be revealing that Cassidy's only poem in honor of one of Lawrence's fraternal societies was dedicated to his inter-ethnic Moose Lodge, not to one of the many exclusively-Irish organizations, such as the Ancient Order of Hibernians.

Finally, as noted above, Cassidy's poems usually eschew controversial topics that might expose profound conflicts, as of class, within Lawrence's Irish community, or between the city's Irish Catholics and other immigrant groups. Thus, his portrayal of Lawrence is one that comported with and promoted the interlocking hegemonies of the Irish-American bourgeoisie and the Irish-dominated Catholic church over an ethnically diverse and sometimes rebellious mass of exploited mill-operatives and other workers. It is not surprising that Cassidy composed no poems about what was perhaps the most tumultuous event in Lawrence's history: the great 1912 Textile Strike, in which the city's Irish-American politicians, priests, and police joined with Yankee mill-owners to suppress an uprising of New Immigrant workers led by "godless" and "un-American" radicals. To be sure, Cassidy's poems heaped scorn and ridicule on Prohibition, but opposition to the Volstead Act united nearly all Irish Americans, and his song in support of the 1922 textile strike focused much less on the workers' plight or struggle than on the generosity to the strikers' families displayed by Lawrence's Irish-American policemen, firemen, and school teachers.

On the other hand, it may be that professional historians, such as I, have focused too much on conflicts and not enough on the social, cultural, and political bonds that held Irish-American (and American) society together—

vertically and horizontally—in spite of class, ethnic, and other differences. Ties of family, neighborhood, church, and political patronage—even the naive optimism and simple patriotism that characterized most people in that era—may have promoted a "false consciousness" that allowed the nation to survive the Great Depression without fundamental change, yet it is difficult not to regret their absence in much of American society today.

And so, in conclusion, perhaps Peter Cassidy provided a more accurate mirror for his community than even he knew. Singing for jobs, cash, or nickel beers, as the old Irish bards had sung for a place at their chieftains' feast tables, Cassidy embodied the ethos that linked Lawrence's Irish Americans to a sentimentalized vision of a vanished homeland, to be sure, but more importantly, to each other and to the broader American society which they would enter more fully after World War II.

Kerby Miller is professor of Irish and Irish American history at University of Missouri-Columbia and is an award winning author. Among his many books and articles, he is best known for co-authoring the PBS documentary film and book *Out of Ireland: The Story of Irish Emigration to America (1994),* and for *Emigrants and Exiles: Ireland and the Irish Exodus to North America (1985).*

Preface

In the summer of 1981, a year after the birth of my second son, I returned to my home in Lawrence, Massachusetts, to attend a family cookout. While chatting with cousins I hadn't seen since childhood, I first learned about my great-grandfather, Albert Blanchette, and his father, Nazaire Blanchet, who had emigrated to Lawrence from Warwick, Quebec, in 1885. That cookout triggered a nearly insatiable drive to learn about my French Canadian heritage, and within a year I had traced the Blanchet(te) name back to early fifteenth century France. A few years later I asked my father why he had never mentioned either Albert or Nazaire to me during the first thirty years of my life. He answered that he had never known about Nazaire and had little contact with Albert while growing up in Lawrence, despite living just a few blocks away from his grandfather.

"Why was that?" I asked.

"Because I was raised by the Irish side of the family," he replied. "The Cassidys."

"Irish?" I said in a startled voice, "I thought we were French." The spark had been lit again.

Over the next decade, many more questions followed. With each response, I began to look back differently on my early years growing up in Lawrence, searching for recollections that might help me make the link with my newly discovered Irish heritage. One of my earliest memories brought me back to a time when I was seven years old and singing in the St. Patrick's Day musical, an annual event at St. Patrick's Parish. I was playing the role of MacNamara in "MacNamara's Band." While on stage, each of my fellow band members shouted out his name and each met with applause. "Bobby Doyle, Patrick Qualters, Jimmy Lanigan, Timothy McGuire, Michael Mahoney,"—a fine sampling of Irish parishioners. When I belted out my name, however, the master of ceremonies turned to the audience in wide-eyed disbelief and cried in jest, "Blanchette! How did he get in here?" Everyone roared with laughter, including me. At that time, of course, I didn't really get the joke.

Though I had a French name, I attended an Irish school, an Irish church, and most of my classmates and friends had Irish names. As I got older, I did wonder occasionally why we didn't attend the "French church," Sacred Heart, which was not much farther from our house than St. Patrick's. Such socioethnic analyses never last more than a few seconds for an eleven-year-old boy, however. Ethnicity simply wasn't a topic of discussion around the dinner table. For the most part I just thought of myself as an American. For reasons I would not know until decades later, this Irish parish was more my home than I ever could have imagined.

Although raised by members of the Cassidy family for over two decades, my father didn't remember much about his life in an Irish home. He had shared the same house with his Irish grandfather, Peter Cassidy, for the first sixteen years of his life, but had little to offer about him. As I approached adulthood, I did learn that Peter was a poet—the Shanty Pond Poet—and my father later gave me copies of some of Peter's poems and songs, long hidden in the attic. Beyond this, I recalled little more.

So, I began the search for my Irish heritage. After ten years of research I learned that of my sixteen great, great-grandparents, eight were Irish, one was Scottish, one was English, and only six were from Quebec. So much for my French heritage. Unlike my research in Canada, where I had to rely solely on vital records, the quest for my Irish identity was enhanced by the writings of my great-grandfather. As I reread each of the poems, I became more intrigued about Peter and his world. What was he writing about? Why? Though I possessed but a fraction of his total work at the time, I did have his handwritten list of songs. From studying the titles, such as "The Shanty Pond Sewer," "My Daughter She Has Me Most Crazy," and "We Want That Free Lunch Back Again," I knew that Peter had to have some wonderful stories to tell, and that they would tell me not just about his life, but perhaps mine as well.

I read countless newspapers of Peter's day, researched various local records, and investigated Irish culture and the Irish-American experience. I became especially intrigued by the historic role of the Irish poet. Not seen as naive dreamers living at the edges of society, the Irish bards who lived over a millennium ago maintained a social rank second only to that of the tribal kings, and their influence within the community surpassed that of the ruler in many ways. For well over a thousand years the local bard was an integral member of society, who chronicled the happenings within the village and, in the eyes of some, actually shaped future events. The Irish poet-singer was honored by most and feared by many. To murder a poet was a crime cursed by God and mourned by all.

Although the role of the village bard has changed over the centuries, his central place was preserved well into the twentieth century, both in Ireland and within the Irish immigrant communities of America. One noticeable development in this evolution was the emergence of the earthy, hard-rhyming, "occasion" poet or songster, who would comment on the everyday events of the Irish village—or, as in Peter's case, the urban mill town of New England. He would write not only of births, deaths, war, politics and other "serious" happenings, but also of ball games, dances, good cigars, and boxing matches. Peter Cassidy straddled both worlds. Also known in Lawrence as "The Bard of Shanty Pond," he brought great enjoyment to his Irish contemporaries and left behind rich accounts of Irish life for later generations.

As I pieced together Peter's poems along with old newspaper accounts and interviews with people from the community, a fascinating picture began to emerge. It was like watching ripples from a pebble dropped in a pond. Each of his poems led me deeper into the history of Lawrence, its Irish immigrants, and eventually to the long and painful history of the Irish people, a saga about which I knew little. One story led to another and before long I had learned of Peter's friends and foes, his likes and dislikes, joys, and fears, his life as in Lawrence, and his passion for a free Ireland. Though my father had given me only about twenty of Peter's songs, I knew that the only way to really know my great-grandfather's world was to locate the rest of his work.

Starting in 1992, I traveled frequently to locations along the East Coast to conduct interviews and visit libraries. With each trip I would confirm a hunch and dispel another, bring back a few new pieces of information, and raise a handful of additional questions. But I found few additional poems or songs. In June of 1996, I met an elderly Irishman still living in Lawrence named Arthur "Dude" Regan. Born in 1903, Dude had known Peter Cassidy and fondly referred to him as the Shanty Pond Poet. When I mentioned names and places from Peter's songs, Dude smiled knowingly and recalled many of same details that were scattered throughout Peter's work. My earlier hunches were confirmed. Peter's poems and songs were not so much the whimsical musings of an aging Irishman as his historical account of the times. He was the bard of Lawrence.

In late summer of 1998, I returned to Lawrence once again, still hoping to locate Peter's missing work. I contacted a local reporter with a strong reputation as a writer, Kathie Neff Ragsdale, and we met for several hours to discuss Peter and his work. Six weeks later, the *Eagle Tribune* ran a large story on the Shanty Pond Poet with photos and excerpts from Peter's songs and poems. One day later I received the call I had been dreaming about for years. Ms. Ragsdale telephoned to say that she had heard from a gentleman named Jim Johnstone, Jr. "I think you're going to want to call him," she said. I did so immediately and the story he told left me nearly speechless.

"My father was one of Peter Cassidy's best friends," Jim started. "They knew each other from the Moose Club. Just a year before Peter died [in 1938], he gave my father a scrapbook full of his songs and poems. Years later, just before my father's death in 1956, he gave me the scrapbook and asked that I take care of it." Jim continued on for a few moments, recounting the details of his own life in Lawrence.

Then he added, "This past April, when my wife and I were packing for our move into the nursing home, I found the scrapbook and decided to throw it out. We would have very little space for storage in our new home. As I sat down to flip through it a final time, I came upon a note Peter had written to my father. It read, 'Jim, I hope U *(sic)* will keep this for old time sake. Yours, Peter F. Cassidy.' I realized that my father would want me to save the scrapbook, so I decided to take it with me."

When I asked if I could photocopy the book, he paused and said, "I have already thought that over. My father would want you to have it."

The following day after work I drove to Lawrence and met Jim Johnstone, Jr. As we shook hands and he handed me the scrapbook, we both felt a special presence. He said, "Peter and my father must be very pleased." I nodded. Sixty-one years later, Peter's scrapbook had come back into the family. For years it had lain in the darkened corner of a drawer, out of sight and all but forgotten. During the past decade, as I had been conducting my research, it sat tucked away on a bookshelf. Now, rather than being buried at the bottom of a landfill, it rested securely in my hands.

Jim and I sat down together and looked at its contents. A ledger book almost two inches thick and fourteen inches long, it was filled with Cassidy memorabilia: newspaper clippings pasted onto wallpaper, handwritten drafts, photographs, a small Irish flag about an inch and a half square, and yellowed copies of over one hundred of Peter's published poems and songs. Clearly, he had meant this book to be his final testament as he had penciled in notes, and scratched in missing words where newspaper clippings were torn or unclear.

Jim and I shared stories about our ancestors—each of us hoping to learn more about the men who had become such trusted friends. Jim even recalled his father introducing him to Peter. I knew I was reaching back to touch a different time. Jim Johnstone Sr. had kept his pledge to his friend and preserved the scrapbook "for old time sake." And so did his son. I now could understand more fully the life of my great-grandfather and his story of the Irish in Lawrence. As a new century approached, Peter's words could enrich and entertain yet another generation.

Acknowledgements

I wish to express my appreciation to the following individuals for their help in making this book possible.

Joe and Nancy Blanchette (Mom and Dad); Bill, Deb, Diana and Matt Blanchette; "Buddy" and Eileen Blanchette; Paul Blanchette, Dave Boulanger, Tom Caffrey, Rebecca Davidson, Frances Farrell, Patsy Fortney, Mark Hage, Jan Hubbard, Laurie Huse, Kathie Neff Ragsdale, Arthur "Dude" Regan, Joseph Sagan, Jean Silviera, Carolyn Thornton, Terri Thibault, Bruce Williamson, Jack Williamson, Linda Williamson, Susan Williamson, Leona "Toots" Villemaire, the fine staffs at the research and audio-visual departments of the Lawrence Public Library and at Immigrant City Archives.

Special thanks to:
Jim Johnstone for taking care of Peter's scrapbook all these years; Ken Skulski, who knows more about the history of Lawrence than any person alive today; Dave Burke, (no relation to the alderman in 1932) the heart and soul of the Irish community in Lawrence and beyond; and most importantly, to Peg—the love of my life.

Looking at the Lawrence mill district along the north shore of the Merrimack River, circa 1900. Courtesy Lawrence Public Library.

1

The Making of an Immigrant Family

For James Cassidy and his young wife Mary, the summer of 1845 was very much like others they had endured growing up as peasant farmers in County Galway. They were relieved that their second child, John, had survived his first year. Daughter Mary was now three and starting to help her mother care for her younger brother. Centuries of harsh government policies, including the Penal Laws, had left most Irish Catholics desperately poor and incapable of owning property. As their forbears had done, however, the Cassidys eked out their survival as tenant farmers who tilled and labored over a scratch of land, and paid taxes and rents designed to maintain their dependency. They had been taught by their parents how to endure such poverty. As Catholics, they had also learned how to survive the centuries of bigotry and hardship under the heel of the English monarchy. None of this would prepare them for the events of the next five years, events that would dramatically alter both their lives and that of another young woman from County Galway named Mary Egan.

The policies of the previous 250 years had left the majority of Irish men and women highly dependent on the potato for nutrition. For many, it was virtually their only source of food, with adults often consuming ten to fourteen pounds of potatoes each day. When a blight originating in the Americas finally crossed over into Europe and then Ireland in the fall of 1845, its destructive effects were not cause for alarm. County Galway had suffered and survived famine before, including several thus far that century. The summer of 1846, however, saw the beginning of a more destructive and widespread crop failure with far deadlier results than that of the previous year. Bitter cold, heavy snows, and an inept government response made matters even worse during the following winter, the start of "Black '47."

The crisis in Ireland reached its apex that year with the majority of the population, poor Catholics, suffering from a host of devastating hardships. Agricultural disaster led to economic disaster throughout Ireland. Starvation and unemployment were widespread. Dysentery, diarrhea, typhus, "the fever," and scurvy quickly overwhelmed the starving masses. Soup kitchens were established, but those who came for food and other forms of relief were required to work for it first. In 1847 County Galway employed over 33,000 impoverished people each day, second only to County Cork. Throughout Ireland over 700,000 heads of families were participating in some form of poorly organized "make-work" relief projects—building roads to nowhere.

Most land owners were oblivious to the suffering and insisted that rents be paid, no matter the human cost. All of the relief projects were to be funded by higher taxes on those already suffering the devastation of the Famine. Those tenants with a few remaining farm animals for ongoing food production either ate their stock, sold them to buy food, or had them seized by landlords to pay back rent. Once their paltry sums of money were spent, their few animals gone, and their meager crops destroyed by the blight, tens of thousands of starving and sickly families were evicted. From 1849 to 1854, over fifty thousand families were permanently ousted.[1] For many, the slow, lonely death from starvation was preferable to the more immediate and public humiliation brought on by eviction and life in the poor house.

Pestilence and horror were found everywhere, especially in the western counties of Clare, Mayo, Sligo, and Galway. Desperate to live, neighbor stole from neighbor, and family members were forced to choose between feeding their young or their elderly parents. Thousands of old men, women, and children lay stiffened and half naked by the roadside, their lips stained green from eating weeds in their final days. Packs of starving dogs feverishly patrolled the countryside seeking out the unburied.

While some argue that much of the death and hardship caused by the blight was unavoidable, it must be said that, through acts of omission and commission, the British government, the local Protestant ruling class, and their underlings were most responsible for what became such an horrific catastrophe. Government-run poor houses, work programs, and soup kitchens proved inadequate and even counterproductive. Those renting more than a quarter acre of land were excluded from any relief programs as they were not considered to be destitute.

Worried that desperate peasants would assault Protestant landowners, Queen Victoria urged Parliament to pass the Coercion Bill, which prohibited anyone from "being out of his house" between sunset and sunrise. The penalty, up to fourteen years' "transportation," was often a blessing to tens of thousands of wandering skeletons evicted from their homes. Parliament also passed the Labour Rate Act, which further taxed the Irish people in order to create low-paying employment opportunities. To receive assistance, desperate farmers first had to surrender all but one quarter acre of land. Still blaming poor farming practices for the food shortages, the government sent teams of agricultural lecturers into the countryside to teach better farming techniques. Those assigned to the western counties reported finding no one to whom they could lecture.

Most troubling was the fact that throughout the Famine years, when millions of Irish were dying of starvation, large quantities of food were being exported to England from Irish ports. John Mitchel, a leader of the Young Irelanders, wrote that a relief ship bringing food to the starving Irish would be "sure to meet six ships sailing out with a similar cargo."[2] British store houses held countless bushels of potatoes and corn for speculation on the commodities markets.

The result of this Famine was the near death of a people. From 1845 to 1851, Ireland's population declined by over two million people, almost one quarter of the population. About half died, while the remainder left Ireland forever. The massive flight first began as a trickle late in 1845. During the spring and summer of 1846 and the years immediately following, it became a flood. Those better off were able to board ships for the four-to-eight week passage to America, but even then there was no guarantee of safety or relief. It was not unusual for upwards of 20 percent to die during or immediately after passage to America on these "coffin ships." The poorest had to settle for a less expensive and more hostile exile in England where they worked in the mills or the coal mines or as domestic servants, laborers, or farm hands.

By June of 1847 an estimated 300,000 Irish had emigrated to Liverpool, doubling its size, overwhelming its citizens, and triggering a surge in anti-Irish, anti-Catholic hostility. Some waited a decade or more before they could earn enough to leave for America with their families. Although tens of thousands of Irish had come to the United States prior to the Famine, hundreds of thousands would arrive over the next fifty years. The Famine would prove to be a defining event, not only in the history of Ireland, but also in the history of the United States, and particularly in the history of Lawrence, Massachusetts.

Located in northeastern Massachusetts, about thirty miles north of Boston, the city of Lawrence was carved out of farmland previously considered part of two adjoining towns, Andover and Methuen. Unlike many cities located in New England, Lawrence did not enjoy a two-hundred-year-long history dating back to pre-Revolutionary times. Its development was swift. Since the early nineteenth century, Yankee businessmen had been striving to transform the Northeast into the world's dominant manufacturing center by taking advantage of the region's good harbors, plentiful streams, and powerful rivers. The establishment of Lawrence was a continuation of that trend—a strategic business proposition by a small group of Boston Brahmins. With a well-ordered plan that anticipated most facets of the city's evolution, these business-men hoped to create one of the world's premiere textile centers. While much of the original vision for a model city was achieved by its Protestant founders, the subsequent domination of city government by Irish Catholic immigrants a half century later could never have been part of their wildest dreams.

Prior to 1845, a traveler heading north along the Essex Turnpike as it reached the Merrimack River would have noticed only a couple of farms on either side of the road and perhaps 100 residents living over a several-square-mile area. This pastoral setting was about to change quickly. The Merrimack already had proven to be a reliable source of water power for the cities of Newburyport, Haverhill, and Lowell. A manufacturer named Daniel Saunders wanted to establish yet another manufacturing center along its banks, unri-valed in New England. In 1843 Saunders teamed up with Samuel Lawrence and others to form the Merrimack Water Power Association. They decided that a great dam should be built at a location known as Bodwell Falls, just north of the spot where the Andover Bridge crossed the river. Soon thereafter, several prominent Boston-area merchants joined them to form the Essex Company. With the dam as its heart and the river its lifeblood, a great city was about to spring to life, but first they needed cheap labor and lots of it.

It was into this setting that the Irish first arrived in Lawrence, or the "New City" as it was first called in 1845. Lawrence was coming to life as millions of Irish were starving and dying across the Atlantic. Many fled to the United States in the years that followed and found the situation in Lawrence as good as reasonably could be expected. It was certainly much better than the one they had left. The majority of newcomers hoped to find work as farmers, but found they lacked the skills necessary to manage large tracts of land, let alone start-up money. Unskilled in the trades or the professions, they soon realized that hard, manual labor in urban settings offered the only realistic opportunity to earn a living.

As the years passed greater numbers of penniless Irish immigrants came to Lawrence looking for work. They came by train or wagon, and most arrived on foot from Boston and as far away as Canada. From a rural settlement prior to 1845, the city's population shot up to over 6,000 inhabitants by 1848. While some 3,900 were native to the region, almost 2,250 were foreign-born and of these, fully 95 percent were Irish. The large work force needed to accomplish the aggressive development goals of the Essex Company was now in place. Irish laborers would build the great dam, the canals, and the textile mills.

Once work began on New City it continued at a remarkable pace. In August of 1845 excavation began on the dam with the first granite stone being laid on September 19, 1845. Three years to the month later the great dam, the most massive in the world at the time, was completed under the guidance of Charles Storrow and Charles Bigelow and on the backs of Irish immigrants. At about this same time, the Boston and Maine Railroad began a project that would build another bridge across the river, just south of the site of the dam, and lay tracks connecting Lawrence with Lowell, Haverhill, and Boston. That project would be completed in February of 1848. The old Andover Bridge, which also crossed the river just south of the new dam, was replaced by a wooden trussed bridge in 1846. During this same time a canal paralleling the north side of the river was built along with the first mills and boarding houses on Canal and Methuen Streets. By 1855 eleven mills had been built, six cotton and five woolen, making Lawrence one of Massachusetts' foremost textile centers almost overnight. At every turn and on every construction site, the Irish were present.[3]

Securing shelter proved challenging for most of these Irish workers. In the earliest years of the city's construction, many workers huddled together in areas immediately surrounding the different construction sites found along both sides of the river. They lived in "shanty" huts (shantee or shantie) made of wood scraps, tin, sod, and other discarded construction material, and were built on land rented from the Essex Company. The term shanty comes from Gaelic words meaning "old house." Cold, damp, and drafty, the shanties were heated with primitive stoves, and the floors usually consisted of dirt and packed sawdust. No two looked exactly alike. Their size varied from relatively small, about seven feet by ten feet, to larger structures that housed upwards of one hundred people.

By 1847 it was estimated that over 120 shanties were located north of the Merrimack River, above the dam and west of the Turnpike, the main north-south road through the city that later became known as Broadway. Scores more were located between Canal and Essex Streets, just north of the mill district. Several dozen more shanties were scattered downstream from the dam. They were quickly relocated across the river by the Essex Company. By 1848 over ninety shanties were found on the south side of the river just above the dam and reaching out a quarter of a mile west of the Turnpike to a small water inlet of the Merrimack River.[4] Still other Irish settlers built their shanties below the dam, adjacent to the area where the south canal would later be built, or farther to the southwest near the Dream Ledge and Carpenter's Ledge. Built on property rented from the Essex Company or one of the mills for about two dollars a month, these structures were intended as temporary housing, although many were used for decades.

With each passing year the rate of growth in the city increased. This was especially true in North Lawrence where the basics of city life, no matter how crude, soon were in place: schools, churches, police, fire, waste removal, banks; housing, and businesses. The city exploded in all directions on the north side of the river, starting with the downtown area on Essex Street, the mill district along the river, spreading north onto the Plains, west on Tower Hill, and east on Prospect Hill. Many Irish immigrants not living in the shanty towns settled in company-owned boarding houses located along the north side of the Merrimack near the mills. These structures often accommodated about 200 residents and were generally well kept. Most had rules about personal appearance, the use of liquor or profanity, and "unfaithfulness." For newly arriving immigrants, these mill-owned rooms offered a welcome and secure housing alternative to run-down shanties or the rough-and-tumble world of overcrowded and filthy tenements.

The largest of the Irish settlements, known as "the Plains," was located in the north-central part of Lawrence. While some inhabitants of the Plains lived in shanties, many more lived in tenement units. This area eventually became one of the most densely populated regions of the entire city, and proved to be the heart and soul of the Irish community in Lawrence for the remainder of the nineteenth century.

By 1855 Lawrence was a textile center to be reckoned with. While successful to a large extent in controlling the city's structural development, Essex Company planners were fighting a losing battle in their plans for long-term development. Lawrence simply was growing too fast to maintain a healthy and ordered environment. Public health and safety problems, directly related to the growth rate and overcrowding, continued and even worsened into the next century. From 1845 to 1855 few immigrant Irish lived in conditions that would be considered acceptable by the native populations inhabiting the city. With rare exceptions, life for the Irish in Lawrence was harsh with poor housing, little food, and very difficult working conditions. Whether employed as laborers building the dam or the mills, men would work from dawn to dusk, six or seven days a week. Work days were quite long and arduous, and the pay ranged between seventy-five cents to a dollar a day. Women frequently worked as machine operatives in the textile mills and they, too, worked ten or more hours a day. Failure to report for work, no matter the reason, frequently resulted in the loss of one's job.

Sanitation was a serious problem. Drinking water was taken from polluted sources such as the Merrimack River, which was full of sewage waste from Lowell, a mill town located about ten miles upstream. This condition was further complicated by runoff from thousands of outhouses, polluted streams, and wells. For decades, "night soil" was collected by city sanitary personnel lest this human waste result in even more widespread water pollution and disease. From 1847 to 1849 over 50 percent of all Irish deaths in Lawrence were a result of typhoid fever and consumption. In 1850 the Lawrence Sanitary Commission sounded an alarm about these deplorable public health conditions, placing blame on the victims. The commission stated that the "habitations, habits and peculiar modes of living of the Irish" were a threat to all inhabitants within the city. Despite coordinated city efforts to address ongoing water and sewage problems, it was decades before conditions improved.[5]

From 1845 to the end of the Civil War, the Essex Company carefully mapped out and managed the city's growth, section by section, street by street, and even building by building. Almost overnight a large, bustling city rose up

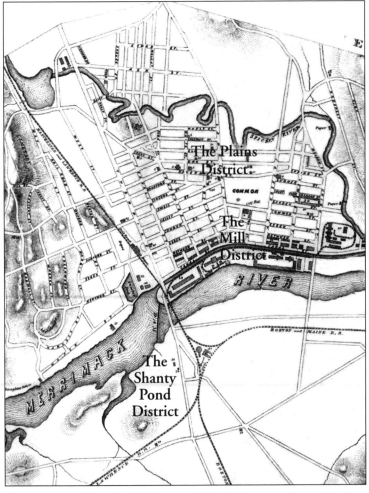

This 1850 map shows the development of North Lawrence about a decade after the city's birth. Two primary Irish settlements existed at this time, the Plains district north of the river and the Shanty Pond district to the south. Courtesy Immigrant City Archives.

from once pastoral farmland. In 1847 alone, in addition to mill projects, the Lawrence City Directory reported the construction of over 450 buildings, scores of tenements, boarding houses and business shops. During the summer months the city's dusty streets were crowded with activity: horse-drawn wagons and carts hauling construction materials and workers moving about, loading materials, reshaping the land, digging foundations, and laying bricks. During the height of construction season, it was reported that upwards of 200,000 bricks were delivered to the city every day.[6] Anyone able to get a bird's-eye view of this Merrimack valley area in 1845 and then again twenty years later would have been left in awe by the extent of the development.

G rowth in South Lawrence, or the "South Side" of the Merrimack, was not nearly as dramatic as that north of the river. As work began on the dam, a small grocery store was erected along the Turnpike just south of the bridge, and a steam lumber mill was also built in response to the need for construction timber. Most of the residents living on the South Side during the city's first decade were Irish laborers housed in the shanty district above the dam. This section of the city was first known as "Dublin," "the Shantee district," and later as "Shanty Pond, or the Shanty Pond district."[7]

The early establishment of the B&M Railroad Station, just east of the Turnpike, brought about the start of this area's transition from being a shanty town to one with permanent housing, its own business center, a church, and residential community. Beginning in the early 1850s, the Essex Company started selling plots of land to employees of the B&M Railroad, such as Edward Matthews, John Caldwell, and George Copp, who built residences on the west side of the Turnpike between Kingston Street and Dover Street.[8] At about the same time, many of those living in shanties began to buy the plots of land they had been renting from the Essex Company. Over the next few decades, most of the shanties east of the pond were destroyed to make way for permanent homes and tenement buildings.

With the end of the Civil War in 1865 and the return of several thousand veterans, settlement in this part of the South Side grew at a more rapid pace, so much so that the Irish church in North Lawrence began a mission church in 1868 for the residents living around Shanty Pond. By 1875 this entire area was covered with residences and businesses. Within the Shanty Pond district, a second residential development grew and became known to the Irish as "the Patch." While the terms "Shanty Pond" and "the Patch" were often used interchangeably during the mid- to late nineteenth century, some residents in the early twentieth century identified the Patch as a distinct part of Shanty Pond.[9] Residents of the Patch saw themselves as being "one step above" those Irish still living in older parts of Shanty Pond. The next step up the social ladder for the Irish was the "lace curtain district," located east of Union Street in South Lawrence. The lace-curtain Irish were a sure sign that the American dream was starting to work.

With each passing decade the word spread of the growing prosperity of this great new city, known as Lawrence. It spread not just through the north-eastern portion of the United States, but all over the East Coast and across the Atlantic. Masses of Irish men and women, put off their land and craving the basics of a good life, continued to flood into the United States. They came by the shipload, some hoping just to escape death, others with dreams of gold and great prosperity. Soon they realized, however, that the American dream was really about freedom and opportunity. For most Irish immigrants, that was more than enough reason to risk flight across the sea.

The Green Fields of America

(Traditional Irish Ballad)

So pack up your sea-stores, consider no longer,
Ten dollars a week is not very much pay
With no taxes or tithes to devour your wages,
When you're on the green fields of America.

*Formal portrait of Peter Cassidy, often used in newspaper articles.
Circa 1910. Courtesy the Cassidy Collection.*

2

Coming Over

While large events in Ireland and Lawrence were being interwoven from 1845 to 1875, another story was unfolding on a much smaller scale. Among the estimated one million deaths resulting from the Irish Famine was that of James Cassidy's wife, Mary. After her death, James knew that he had to leave Ireland if he and his children were to survive. At the height of the Famine, large land owners found it cheaper to pay for steerage out of Ireland than to provide assistance programs for their starving tenants. Being among the poorest of emigrants, James and his two small children were able to secure passage to Liverpool, England. It is likely that he hoped to follow the course of so many Irish emigrants and continue on to America and the prosperity it promised. But unable to afford steerage costs, he traveled inland in search of work until reaching the small village of Ashton-under-Lyne, just outside of present-day Manchester.

At about this time he met a young Irish woman from County Galway named Mary Egan, who had also lost her spouse to the Famine. She was childless. On November 9, 1851, they married and began a new life together. One year later, Mary gave birth to a son, Martin, followed by daughter Bridget about 1857. On April 29, 1861, they celebrated the birth of another son, Peter, and shortly thereafter, their last child, Thomas, was born.

While in England, James worked as a laborer and a farmhand. Mary was a washerwoman when they first married, but six children and chores kept her at home. Though they no longer had to confront the prospect of famine, life for the Cassidys was still very hard. Too many Irish Catholics had flooded into this area where jobs were already scarce and pay extremely low. As a result, the native English were openly hostile toward these immigrant "papists" for taking away their jobs. Violence frequently erupted. Despite the turmoil, the Cassidys persevered.

By 1861 James' first son John had turned seventeen and was working in the textile mills as a cotton spinner. His older daughter Mary was now nineteen and worked as a machine operative in the cotton mills. While the jobs secured by the older children provided critical income for the family, they also provided employment skills and important information about opportunities available in the mill towns of the northeastern United States. News had spread among the mill workers about a new textile power in America: Lawrence, Massachusetts. It often was referred to as the "Bradford of America," an allusion to the city of Bradford, England, which had been a prominent manufacturing center for woolen and worsted products for over five centuries. The Cassidy family discussed their future living in England and decided that they would again become emigrants.

From 1865 to 1875 England saw a marked increase in emigration to America, primarily out of the port of Liverpool. It was during this period that the members of the Cassidy family began coming to the United States. The first of the older children left for New York late in the 1860s. In 1875 fourteen-year-old Peter Cassidy boarded a ship with his mother and brother Thomas for the journey to America. The experience made an impression on young Peter. As a child he had heard of the pain such parting had caused his parents and older step-siblings when they left Galway during the Famine. In his poem, "Coming Over," written later in his life, Peter described the inner thoughts of an Irish immigrant, very much like himself, making passage to America. The poem describes the scene Peter witnessed on his trip across the Atlantic, the same one played out hundreds of times each day as ships headed toward New York or Boston.

Coming Over

He was only a young Irish lad, to America coming o'er,
Standing on the deck he was looking back to Ireland's receding shore.
His lips they moved in silent prayer; tears down his cheeks did pour.
As the evening screen shut out the scene of Kerry's rockbound shore.

I could not help but notice as beside him I did stand,
With his face towards the Irish coast, his rosary beads in hand.
I saw him kneel, he said a prayer, while others knelt and cried
As he blessed himself and kissed the cross on which his Savior died.

A sight like this I ne'er before saw in my travels around the globe,
I ne'er was on a ship before with such a pious load.
Two soggarths watched o'er them, like shepherds o'er their flocks,
Preaching the word of God since leaving Cobb till we reached the New York docks.

'Twas a pleasant trip on board that ship till tied up at the wharf,
Tears in our eyes, kisses and good byes, we parted in New York.
I bade Godspeed to that Irish lad as we parted for to go,
He bound for a village in the old Bay State, and me for Ohio.

By 1870 Lawrence had a population of 28,921 individuals. Almost overnight it had become one of the fifty principal cities of the United States, ranking forty-fourth in total population. When comparing the size of its Irish population with Irish from these same cities, its 7,457 Irish residents placed Lawrence twenty-third among the nation's fifty largest cities. Most significant, however, was the fact that Lawrence ranked first among these same fifty cities when comparing Irish populations as a percentage of the total population. Just under 26 percent of all Lawrencians were of Irish descent in 1870, greater than New York City's 21.4 percent or Boston's 22 percent.[1]

When Peter Cassidy emigrated to Lawrence, he, along with his brother Thomas and his mother, settled with older brother Martin who already had taken up residence in the city. There is no record of his father living with them at this time. In fact, city directories list Mary Cassidy as a widow. Perhaps it was James' death that precipitated emigration by the rest of the family. As was the custom, Irish immigrants new to the city immediately gravitated to the established ethnic enclaves. After a brief stay at 49 Hampshire Street, the Cassidys moved into a tenement at 203 Oak Street in the very heart of the Plains.

Lawrence was a bustling textile center by now, and the Cassidys quickly became enmeshed in city life. They attended St. Mary's Church, and Peter joined the Gilmore Guards, a drill team established by the pastor. He followed a traditional path of a young man at the time and went to work at the Pacific Mills, an experience that brought him face to face with the harsh, dawn-to-dusk work of a mill operative. The 1880 census indicates that Peter also tried his hand at becoming a life insurance agent. For a premium payment of ten cents a week, a poor Irish laborer or mill worker could buy a death benefit worth about one hundred dollars. Needless to say, Peter soon tired of selling insurance to fellow immigrants and before too long he returned to the Pacific Mills.

L iving on the Plains placed Peter and the Cassidy family at the center of Irish life in Lawrence. The Plains section of North Lawrence was unquestionably the hub of Irish activity. It was here that the greatest number of Irish immigrants lived. Bounded initially by the Spicket River to the North, Essex Street to the south, and Union Street and Broadway on the east and the west, the Plains was where the first two Irish churches were built: the Immaculate

Conception Church and St. Mary's Church. It was home of the Fr. Mathew Temperance Society, the Ancient Order of Hibernians Hall, and the Irish Benevolent Society, whose motto was "We visit our sick and bury our dead." The annual St. Patrick's Day parade wound its way up and down every street on the Plains during the 1860s and 1870s. It was here too that the first seeds of the local Fenian movement (1860s) flourished, and where Fenian leaders from Lawrence met to plan their role in the unsuccessful invasion of Canada in 1867.[2] On the Plains the local chapter of Charles Stewart Parnell's Land League had its birth, as did many of the Irish politicians who would eventually run city government.

In 1875, when Peter and his family were emigrating to the United States, Lawrence was witnessing the beginning of the second great wave of immigration. This time it was the French Canadians who migrated into the city looking for work. Over time, dozens of other ethnic groups moved into the city, though in smaller numbers. The 1910 census showed that forty-one different nationalities resided in Lawrence. Each nationality that arrived caused a reshuffling of the ethnic centers. Catholic immigrants, such as the Canadians and the Italians, gravitated to areas adjacent to where Irish Catholics had been able to "get a rent." The native-born residents had long since moved to the outskirts of the city to avoid the Irish riffraff, establishing developments on Tower and Prospect Hills. The Irish, in turn, had established a second settlement in the Shanty Pond area on the South Side, which began to grow at a tremendous rate. They also moved even farther north across the Spicket River. While always considered part of the Plains, this area had been predominantly farmland until the expansion that took place during the 1880s and 1890s.

The view looking southwest across the Spicket River into the heart of the Plains, circa 1897. The steeple off in the distance is the Immaculate Conception Church. Courtesy Immigrant City Archives.

By the end of the nineteenth century, the Plains had become one of the most densely populated and poorest immigrant centers anywhere in the United States. In some city blocks in and adjacent to the Plains upwards of 600 people per acre were crammed into tightly packed, wooden tenement buildings. By way of contrast, when Peter first lived in the Plains, the average population density in Lawrence was ten people per acre, with the worst crowding found near the city center with about 120 people per acre.[3] Not surprisingly, along with the overcrowding came tremendous poverty, crime, and disease. Though once solely an Irish area, the Plains Irish were now joined by a scattering of poor Italians, Syrians, French Canadians, Armenians, and a host of other ethnic groups. As has happened many times in the past, there was often resentment of newcomers. Upon their arrival in Lawrence, the Irish felt hostility from the native inhabitants. When other immigrants began to arrive, however, some Irish began to act like the native population and dealt out a bit of it themselves.

When Peter wrote his poems about the Plains and the Spicket River just prior to World War I, he was living in the Shanty Pond area of South Lawrence. While conditions there were not luxurious, they were far superior to those throughout most of the Plains. Obviously, Peter was troubled and confused by the changes that had taken place in his old neighborhood. He longed for the days he had first encountered upon his arrival, when the Irish dominated this part of the city. As many of us would do when dreaming of our youth, Peter's recollections warmly remember the good times. He chose not to recall the poverty and squalor that was also characteristic of some parts of the Plains, even when he lived in its midst. This notwithstanding, he did provide firsthand insight into those features of community life around which so much Irish myth was later built.

Beautiful Spicket

You have got to go to Ireland, where the shamrock's ever green,
If you want to see Killarney's Lake, on the Shannon Stream.
All the beautiful sights ain't over there, we have one here you know,
In all this land there's no place so grand as where the Spicket flows.

Evenings in the summer time you can see a lad and lass,
Walking arm and arm along its banks, or sitting on the grass.
Enjoying the breeze, coming through the trees, where the wind does blow.
There's no perfume like the bees in June, where the Spicket flows.

You can see the cattle grazing, as you pass there any time,
Every neighbor owned a cow, clothes ain't safe out on the line.
The beautiful dumps, trees and stumps, along its banks do grow,
And goats eat their fill of the neighbors' swill where the Spicket flows.

The place ain't like it used to be, they have made a change of late.
The swill house and the brewery's gone, they've made the Spicket straight.
There now are houses in the fields, where the flowers used to grow,
No more the smoke, the bull frogs choke, where the Spicket flows.

I could sing its praises for nights and days, stories I could tell,
Of the good times the boys and girls had around the old spring well.
If you want to see a beautiful spot, some time you want to go
From the Arlington Mill to Prospect Hill where the Spicket flows.

When the Irish Owned "the Plains"

I oftimes wander thru the streets, where as a boy I used to play,
Though its many years ago, it seems like yesterday.
The friends I knew, there's just a few, in Irish town remain,
It don't look to me as it used to be when the Irish owned "the Plains."

From Essex Street to Spicket Bridge, Union Street to Broadway,
North and South, East and West, the Irish they held sway.
On every ship that made a trip, some one from Ireland came,
And settled down in Irishtown, when the Irish owned "the Plains."

Sure every part of Ireland, it was represented there,
Limerick, Cork, and Kerry and Dublin, Wicklow and Kildare,
Cities and towns from County Down, Bantry and Coleraine,
From Maltown Bay and sweet Galway, there was Irish on "the Plains."

The Hannagans and Flannagans, McCartys and O'Briens,
Hogans and Brogans, Carneys, Sheehans, and the Ryans,
Caseys, Connors, McCormicks, Finnigans and McShanes,
These are a few of the ones I knew when the Irish owned "the Plains."

Every night there'd be a party, or something going on,
Perhaps a new born, or a greenhorn come across the pond,
A raffle for a stove, a clock or else a watch and chain,
We'd have shindigs, with reels and jigs, when the Irish owned "the Plains."

On Sunday morns 'twas a grand sight, when the bells they rang for prayer.
To see them all, the big and small, for church they would repair.
The throngs you'd pass going to Mass, in sunshine or in rain—
The Lord felt proud of that pious crowd of Irish on "the Plains."

I never thought it could ever be, or it would ever come to pass,
The Irish, they would e'er give way to any foreign class.
Now they've gone, there's something wrong, I don't know what's to blame.
I know it is true, the Italian and Jew drove the Irish from "the Plains."

I often take, for old time's sake, and view the scene around;
I find a change has taken place, in what was once Irishtown.
The old folks are gone to the great beyond, I'll never see them again,
Or the times I had when I was a lad, when the Irish owned "the Plains."

Peter wrote one more poem that gave a wonderful glimpse of a very special day in the life of the Irish on the Plains during the 1870s and 1880s: St. Patrick's Day. "An Old Time Patrick's Day" look backs at a time when celebrating St. Patrick's Day was as much a political statement by the Irish as a demonstration of their love for the old country and its holy saint. The first formal Patrick's Day parade in Lawrence occurred on March 17, 1864, under the sponsorship of the Irish Benevolent Society (Peter frequently omitted the saint from St. Patrick's Day). For the Irish, this public celebration of heritage was a bold move for a people so despised throughout the United States for their race and their religion. It reflected their confidence in their faith, their newly acquired political standing, and their defiance of the anti-Catholic "Know-Nothing" movement. Winding its way through the streets on the Plains, the parade also provided politicians the chance to display their power, their ethnic pride, and their unbounded American patriotism.

An Old Time Patrick's Day

We don't see Patrick's Day parades as we did in days of old,
We don't see Ireland's banners of green with Tara's harp of gold.
No Irishman a-marching with green sash white cockade;
Will we ever again see Irishmen in a Saint Patrick's day parade?

At early dawn Saint Patrick's morn each little lad and lass
Sure felt proud being in the crowd with parents going to Mass;
Every one seen had a ribbon of green or shamrock from the old sod,
To begin the day they were on their way to offer prayers to God.

Service o'er, outside once more, they were a happy throng,
With a "Good morning, Dan," shaking of hands and a bit of an Irish song.
Then to the Hibernian hall they would proudly make their way,
Their brothers join and to be in line for the Patrick's day parade.

Oak Street and White were a grand sight with Erin's colors of green,
With U.S. stars, red and blue bars, and the eagle shield between.
Every building was decorated, sure was a grand display,
The red, white and blue and Erin's flag too entwined on Patrick's day.

The crowds that would gather there! There would be scarcely room to stand;
They would listen to the Irish airs played by the cornet band.
They would set the old folks dancing. Oh! Boy, how they could play
The "Red Haired Boy," "Pat Malloy" and "Glorious Saint Patrick's Day."

All cops then were Irishmen, and each was glad to leave his beat
To be in advance, and get the chance, to lead the parade along the street.
Suits cleaned and pressed, they looked their best, each one carried a stick,
I now remind that was the time when every cop was called "Mick."

Crowds would part for the parade to start, cheers would rend the air
When the honorable John came along, Lawrence's first Irish mayor.
With sword and sash, shiny tall hat, on his breast a sprig of green.
That Hibernian crowd sure felt proud of Grand Marshal John Breen.

John brought his smile from Erin's isle and a heart as big as a spud,
You would always find him doing something kind for others if he could.
Everyone had a liking for John, and he loved his people all;
From whence they came, they were all the same, from Cork to Donegal.

A Patrick's day parade I'm much afraid we will never see again.
The times aren't like they used to be since the Irish left "the Plains."
They now have crossed the Spicket and gone over to Back Bay;
Those days are past, we have seen the last of the Patrick's day parades.

The first St. Patrick's Day parade in Lawrence wound its way through the Plains and then to the Immaculate Conception Church where Father Taafe celebrated Mass. As was custom, a lengthy oration was offered by the priest on the history of St. Patrick, the Celtic race, and England's seven hundred year reign over the Irish people. This opportunity to educate each generation became a key component of Patrick's Day celebrations in the years that followed, whether or not a parade was held. Over the next dozen years, parades continued as the focus of St. Patrick's Day festivities in Lawrence. During the greatest of these processions, onlookers would see over 1,000 participants from the numerous Irish societies and marching bands demon-strating their loyalty to their new country while remembering the land of their ancestors. American and Irish flags were carried and displayed all along the parade route.

Regardless of the weather conditions, the Irish societies would meet in the morning around 9:00 and begin their lengthy procession through the Plains section of the city to St. Mary's Church for Mass. Normally, the parade route was four to six miles in length, and it often took five or six hours to complete the march. So many Irish children would skip school that the public schools usually closed for the day rather than hold classes with half-empty classrooms. Reflecting the growth of the Irish community in the South Side of the city, the parade route sometimes crossed the bridge along Broadway and passed through the parts of the Shanty Pond area: Crosby, Newton, Kingston, and Durham Streets. This first occurred in the 1871 parade and was repeated in 1874 and 1876.

At the parade held in 1872, the grand marshal was Captain Timothy Deacy, a Fenian who played a role in the famous Manchester Martyr incident of 1867 in England. The 1874 procession typified the best of the Patrick's Day parades. In order, the marchers were: Captain A. K. Currier, two platoons of police, Chief Marshal Peter Davey; Chief of Staff James W. Joyce; Aids Michael Rinn, James Lane, John Ford, Charles Bradley, Benjamin Farrell; Knights of St. Patrick, mounted; St. Jean de Baptiste Society; Manchester

Cornet Band; Irish Benevolent Society; Andover Cornet Band; Lawrence Cornet Band; Ancient Order of Hibernians, Division 1; Father Mathew Cadet Drum Corps; Fr. Matthew Temperance Society; Ancient Order of Hibernians, Division 2; and the Association of Prayer. Each society was accompanied by "barouche" wagons, banners, Irish and American flags, and lots of shamrocks and green sprigs.[4]

In 1875 the Irish societies began to question the parade's value. In Ireland, the plight of the tenant farmer was becoming worse each year. Over the next four years the value of the potato crop would plummet by about 75 percent and there would be a dramatic increase in the never-ending ritual of tenant evictions. Charles Stewart Parnell and Michael Davitt were in the process of leading the Land War among the Irish peasants. Given this political climate, most of the Catholic charitable and benevolent societies felt that the money spent on the outward show of Irish and American patriotism would be better spent to "more practical and benevolent uses" in Ireland. On March 18, 1880, *The Lawrence Daily American* reported on the growing trend among Irish societies: "March 17th . . . was observed in a very commendable manner in this city, by successful efforts to raise funds for the relief of the famine stricken inhabitants of Ireland. . . . As in most places throughout the country, the several Irish Societies long ago decided to omit the usual parade, and appropriate the money which such a display would cost to the aid of the Irish peasantry."[5]

On March 1, 1884, *The Lawrence Daily American* noted that "a small representation of the Irish societies met at Fr. Mathew Hall on Oak Street . . . to take action relative to celebrating St. Patrick's Day . . . Daniel Murphy presided. It was voted to dispense with the parade and to leave the matter of celebrating the day to the option of the several societies."[6] Apparently, previous gatherings by leaders from the many Irish societies tended to be rambunctious affairs. Reflecting the earlier controversies about holding the parade, that same article closed with this bit of understated editorial comment: "The proceedings were unusually tame." Thereafter, Patrick's Day was celebrated in a more limited fashion with church services, evening dinners, presentations, and social gatherings.

The early years of the Patrick's Day celebrations were often characterized by much drunkenness, rowdiness, and frequent brawls in city streets and taverns. Over time, parade leaders and parish priests persuaded the revelers to tone down their celebration. On March 18, 1871, *The Lawrence Daily American* publicly complemented the Irish community, stating, "It was pleasant to see such cordial feeling existing everywhere. The most perfect order and sobriety prevailed during the day, and our Irish residents have done themselves lasting credit by the manner in which they conducted themselves."[7] On March 18, 1878, *The Lawrence Daily American* again reported with some relief, "St. Patrick's Day passed off with very little drunkenness, and there were fewer arrests than usual after a monthly pay day. The anniversary occurring on a Sunday gave less opportunity for dissipation, and the closing of the liquor saloons on Sunday made it somewhat difficult to get the ardent."[8]

During the 1880s only one parade was held in Lawrence, but it was a spectacular event. In 1887, the twentieth anniversary of the Manchester Martyr incident, some 1,400 Irish men and women wearing symbolic green sashes, carnations, sprigs, and shamrocks marched in the Patrick's Day parade as all the local Irish organizations once again joined to honor their patron saint. Former Mayor John Breen was the grand marshal. Breen was one of Lawrence's first great Irish politicians who regularly marched in Patrick's Day parades. Daniel McCarthy, another influential Irish politician of this period, served as chief-of-staff. Hibernian divisions from Haverhill, Andover, Groveland, and North Andover joined their brothers and sisters from Divisions 1 and 8 of Lawrence. Interestingly, many of the textile mills declared the day a holiday and closed down. Ten years later in 1897 the Irish came out in force for what proved to be the last of the great Patrick's Day parades in Lawrence for decades. Once again, John Breen was seen parading down the streets, this time mounted upon a magnificent steed draped in green.

John Breen marching in a parade behind a row of Lawrence's finest. Courtesy Immigrant City Archives.

Most likely, Peter Cassidy saw several parades during the first years after his arrival in Lawrence in 1875. The celebration of Patrick's Day showed him and the rest of the city the best that the Irish and the Plains had to offer. Such celebrations were brief, however. On most days life was hard and resources scarce. Peter continued to work to help provide for his mother and younger brother. In 1882 he was twenty-one years old and employed as an operative at the Pacific Mills along with his older brother Martin. They still lived on the Plains at 203 Oak Street with their mother. Located just a few blocks south of their home, the Pacific Mill was a massive textile enterprise that regularly employed young Irish men and women looking for their first job. Like many before them, Peter and Martin learned firsthand that the hours were long, the wages were low, and the working conditions were atrocious. Later that winter Peter experienced yet another side of life in a mill town that proved to be a turning point in his life: the first major labor strike.

On March 14, 1882, people throughout the city were shocked when the mill owners announced an unexpected wage reduction and locked the factory doors. Thousands of workers were suddenly without work, out on the street, and unsure of how to resolve the stalemate. The labor movement was in its infancy at the time. Over the next two months, the Irish community and the city as a whole argued over how to settle the dispute. The newly elected mayor, Irishman John Breen, openly supported labor and urged striking workers to "head west" rather than return to the mills and accept the reduced wages imposed by the owners. That's exactly what Peter decided to do. He left Lawrence and spent the next several years engaged in a variety of life experiences. For a time, he toured Canada with a traveling one-night show called "The Scenery of Ireland." An Irish version of Buffalo Bill Cody's wild west shows, it offered paying customers a glimpse of the old country through story, songs, readings, and theatrical vignettes. Peter also worked on cargo ships traveling between Detroit and Cleveland, and toiled in the steel-rolling mills and shipyards along Lake Erie. While working as a loftsman for a bridge-building company, he narrowly escaped death after falling from construction staging into the river below. A close friend died during the same incident.

By 1885 Peter turned up in Archbald, Pennsylvania, a small bustling coal town located about ten miles north of Scranton. This region was located just north of the area where, less than a decade earlier, the secret society known as the Molly McGuires led its violent and ultimately doomed campaign for better pay and working conditions in the mines. Like Lawrence, a large proportion of Archbald's residents were Irish. Also like Lawrence, it was a new town created to advance a business proposition, mining coal. The twenty-four-year-old Cassidy took a job working in the mines for Jones, Simpson and

Company. By year's end he also married a thirty-year-old widow named Maggie Coughlin.

It is very likely that Peter and Maggie had a friendship that reached back to Lawrence. Originally from County Galway, Maggie Devine was one of several children born to David Devine and Catherine McGuire. Like Peter, she came to the United States in 1875 and settled in Lawrence. On January 17, 1878, she married a twenty-four-year-old Irishman from Galway named Thomas Coughlin, who lived on Valley Street and worked in the Pacific Mills at the same time Peter did. By 1881 the Coughlins had two young daughters, Kate and May. When the Pacific Mill strike began the following year, they also headed west to Wyandotte, Michigan, a steel producing town just south of Detroit. Thomas hoped that he would secure a better wage in the steel mills than he had in the textile mills. In December of 1882 Thomas and Maggie had a third daughter and named her Margaret. Their last child together, Delia, was born in Archbald in January of 1885. Just nine months after Delia was born, Maggie Coughlin, now a widow, married Peter Cassidy on September 30, 1885.

Although it is only speculation, Peter Cassidy and the Coughlins probably had been friends since he arrived in Lawrence. This would certainly explain how Margaret ended up in Archbald and why she married Peter so soon after the death of her husband. All had roots in County Galway and lived on the Plains in Lawrence, and Peter and Thomas worked in the Pacific Mills up until the 1882 strike. The Coughlins and Peter also left Lawrence at about the same time, and within a few years all had moved to the Wyandotte/ Detroit area. While employed at the Pacific Mills, Thomas and Peter had probably shared their dreams of heading west in search of adventure and better pay. It is likely that Thomas was the friend who died after a fall from a bridge with his Peter. Peter must have known that Maggie was pregnant when the accident occurred, and we can only surmise that this is how they came together in Archbald.

Life in a coal town was challenging enough for a man and woman raising a family together. It would have been nearly impossible for an illiterate widow trying to raise her four small girls alone. Digging for coal wasn't an option for her. Peter came to her aid, though, and faithfully helped raise Maggie's daughters along with three more girls born of their union. The Cassidys lived on Hill Street, which steeply climbed the side of the Number 5 Hill, the mine belonging to the Jones, Simpson and Company. While Peter no doubt had found his earlier work experiences difficult, he must have found mining coal punishing. Six days a week he would head down into the mines to work ten or more hours among the cold, dark, damp, and rat-infested shafts tunneled below Archbald. During the winter months he would not see sunlight until his day off on Sunday.

A newcomer to the mines, he probably started out as a laborer who partnered with a miner in one of the chambers where coal was being dug. Eventually, he moved into a miner's position. For three cents an hour, young boys of ten or eleven also worked in the mines picking slate, tending doors, or driving mules. During lunch the miners would arrange fights among the boys for all to watch and wager upon. It was at the bottom of the Archbald coal mines in 1889 that Peter wrote his first poem. It was about the spectacular bare-knuckled championship fight between John L. Sullivan and Jake Kilrain. Several decades later, it would become a favorite of Peter's loyal following in Lawrence.

Maggie and Peter spent five years trying to earn a living in Archbald. In February of 1888 they had their first child together, Tess, and two years later Loretta was born in April of 1890. Now there were six young mouths to feed on a miner's salary, and Peter became more concerned about their life in Archbald. He had fully experienced life at the bottom of a mine, with cave-ins, explosions, and accidents being common occurrences. It was not something he wanted for the rest of his life. Beyond these hazards, however, Peter knew that there would be few positive opportunities for his six daughters in a mining town as they grew older. Mining wasn't a woman's job and that's all there was in Archbald.

Maggie and Peter both had relatives still living in Lawrence, and they were well aware of the city's continued prosperity. There were lots of jobs for women, and Peter also would have a good chance for employment above ground. Ten years earlier, as an independent young man in search of adventure, Peter had headed west. Now, having seen the Midwest, the Great Lakes, and Canada, and experienced a host of backbreaking jobs, he boarded a train for Lawrence accompanied by his wife and six daughters, ages one to twelve years. Upon his return, he would move to the South Side of Lawrence where the shantytown once known as "Dublin" had evolved into a large new Irish community called Shanty Pond.

3

Returning Home: A Sense of Place

In 1845 the city of Lawrence had several streams and three major bodies of water within its boundaries: the Spicket River to the north, the Shawsheen River to the east, and the Merrimack River, the largest of the three, running west to east through the center of the city. After the completion of the great dam across the Merrimack in 1848, there was another sizable body of water within the city limits that would become known as Shanty Pond. Located one quarter of a mile upstream from the dam, this large fingerlike inlet stretched into the southern shore of the river for almost two thousand feet. Prior to the dam's construction, this area was the site of a lowland streambed that ran from the hills south of the city all the way to the river. While this area occasionally flooded during high-water periods, the dam significantly raised the upstream water level and transformed this wetland into a permanent body of water. The new pond averaged fifty to seventy feet wide, but was almost two hundred feet across at its widest point. Shanty Pond's depth varied, but it was deep enough for swimming, sailing, and logging activities.

As the dam was being built, and in the years immediately following its completion, Irish laborers on the South Side scattered their shanty huts all around the area between the Turnpike and the pond. This section of the city quickly developed as a community, just like the Plains on the north side. The shanties located east of the pond and near the dam were built on land rented from the Essex Company, arranged in orderly rows, and assigned lot numbers. Before long, not only the pond but the area adjoining it to the east became known as "Shanty Pond."[1]

While the transition from shanties to permanent residences in this Shanty Pond area or district began in the early 1850s, the pace quickened from 1857 to 1869 when over five dozen lots were sold along a strip of land between Kingston Street and Dover (now Salem) Street.[2] In the years that followed, the development spread for several blocks to the north and south. By 1875 the entire area between South Broadway and the pond was settled. Over 250 permanent structures were clustered into an area one quarter of a mile square, with about 90 percent belonging to Irish owners. Many owners of the old shanties built their new homes adjacent to their decrepit huts, which they kept as storage buildings or animal shelters. Far fewer in number, some shanties still housed their Irish residents. The last of these shanties remained standing into the twentieth century.

The original characteristics of Shanty Pond had changed during the two decades since Peter first arrived in Lawrence. In the early years, virtually all the residents of Shanty Pond were poor, and most had small gardens and several farm animals grazing on their small tracts of land. Virtually every resident was Irish, and they maintained an intense loyalty to one another. Shanty Pond provided them with the same sense of security they had felt back home in the villages and parishes of their native land. It had a church, variety stores, a blacksmith, recreational sites, and most everything else they needed. When not working in the mills or as outdoors laborers, neighbors would meet while tending farm animals in their yards, and they would gather regularly to share a drink, enjoy a dance, or swap a bit of gossip. The nearby B&M Railroad station, on the east side of South Broadway, made it easy for residents to greet new arrivals from Ireland and welcome them into their special community. For decades the pond itself remained a focus of activity for the inhabitants of the area. Adults and children would swim and fish in it and sail their boats, canoes, or homemade rafts. Outings often were held along its shore, especially in the areas on the west shore know as "the Pines" and "the Grove." On the South Side, Shanty Pond was a body of water, an Irish community, and a way of life.

Peter first experienced Shanty Pond when he arrived in the city in 1875. Though he had lived on the Plains at that time, he certainly spent time with Irish friends on the South Side, perhaps selling insurance. During his ten years away, the city had seen tremendous change due to the continued influx of immigrants, especially throughout North Lawrence. Upon his return around 1891, he and his family decided to avoid the overcrowded and more impoverished Plains area. They wanted something better for their children. They sought out the more relaxed and traditional Irish life-style still to be found in Shanty Pond.

Their first home was an apartment at 134 South Broadway, near the center of travel, commerce, and social activity on the South Side. Peter was able to secure a job as a laborer for the B&M Railroad, whose tracks and station were less than a minute's walk from his doorstep. The couple quickly

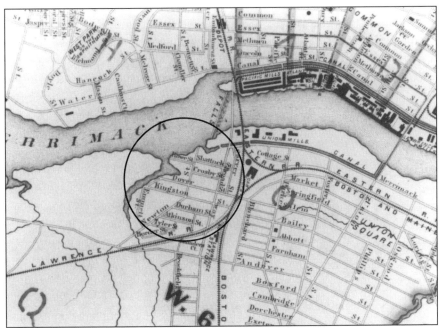

This 1896 map of Lawrence shows the development along the south side of the river. The Shanty Pond community (circled) is bounded by the river to the north, the railroad tracks to the east and south, and the pond itself to the south. Courtesy Lawrence Public Library.

settled into the community fabric and joined St. Patrick's Church, located just a few hundred feet from their apartment. Peter became one of the organizing members of the Hibernian Rifles, an Irish fraternal organization, and he also enlisted in the local militia. On December 26, 1892, Maggie gave birth to her sixth daughter, Frances Patricia, and one year later to her first boy, also named Francis. This baby boy, who had been so long in coming, died soon after his birth. Shortly thereafter, Peter started to sign his name using the middle initial "F" for "Francis." Although Peter and Maggie found their familiar surroundings comforting, their financial situation would remain precarious for quite some time. They always struggled to pay their rent and were forced to move quite frequently. In fact, from 1891 to 1914, they lived in nine different apartments throughout Shanty Pond.

Peter loved the old way of life in Shanty Pond that he first experienced when he came to Lawrence in 1875. He often wrote of the early days, when life was simpler and more like an Irish village than an urban American mill town. Two poems written in his later years offered Peter's warm and unique reflections on the lives of Irish immigrants who lived in the tightly-knit Shanty Pond community from about 1860 to 1880.

Good Old Days on the Patch

My mind often wanders back to my boyhood days,
And to the boys with whom I used to play.
The girls are all women, the boys are all men;
Those good days are gone, I'll ne'er see them again.
When school would be over, I often would stroll
Down by the ledge to the old swimming hole.
No wonder I sigh for the good times that are gone;
When I used to go swimming in the old Shanty Pond.

The old folks weren't rich, but they owned their own cot
In a place called "the Patch"—'twas a beautiful spot.
Sure each neighbor had chickens, a pig and a cow.
The place has since changed; they can't keep them there now.
We had a small piece of land which we'd plant in the spring;
And raise for the winter the good things it would bring.
Sure neighborly and friendly, we all got along;
When I lived in the Patch near the old Shanty Pond.

Evenings in winter all the young folks would join
In some neighbor's house and have a good time.
It was fours right and left, no two-step or glide.
T'was balance your partners and refreshments besides.
The fiddler in the corner would strike up a tune;
The boys and the girls they would dance 'round the room.
Oh, the days of the shindig in the Patch are now gone;
And the good times we had near the old Shanty Pond.

Shanty Town of the Old South Side

Let them sing of old Wyoming, or roaming in the gloaming
And the beauties of the park in Yellowstone;
They can praise the Swanee River, I've seen no place ever
Where once we had our old dear Shanty home.
'Twas a Michael, Jon and Pat, first built up the patch,
In their little shacks they sure took pride.

They were small but neat and clean, fit for any king or queen
Were those little shanties on the old South Side.

There the Irish settled down and called it "Shanty Town,"
When they came o'er here from the old sod;
That's why they crossed the foam to make themselves a home
In the land of full and plenty. With their trust in God.
They left that Irish shore, for America they sailed o'er,
Landed safe in Boston at high tide,
Taken on a train o'er the Boston and Maine
To get off in Lawrence at the old South Side.

When at their destination, those emigrants arrived,
Never was a happier lot—or one more surprised.
Friends they had not seen in years, folks they never knew,
Received them at the station and bade them welcome, too.
Hand shakes, kisses and laughter, mingled in with tears;
Fathers, mothers, sons, and daughters that hadn't met for years,
In each other's arm they wept. Softly sobbed and cried;
United again, they'd all remain on the old South Side.

When the greetings were over, each one filled with delight,
Every home in Shanty Town had a "greenhorn time" that night.
Plenty to eat and drink, dancing and fun galore,
Beer and wine, a real good time—one couldn't ask for more.
When they set the table it sure was a grand spread;
Pretees boiled and baked; pie and cake; good homemade bread.
The old folks had rum in their tay; the punch was passed around,
No such affair ever took place there again in old Shanty Town.

We all dispersed, some to go to work; coming on twilight,
To be at the mill at six and stay till six at night.
If the gates were locked one got docked if not there on time,
'Twas only on Sunday we enjoyed God's sunshine.
It would be afternoon. When we came from Mass
Mothers would take their babes to play on the grass.
Through the grove couples would roam, many a man chose there his bride
and settled down in old Shanty Town on the old South Side.

What's the need to talk again about the days of old—
The stories of the shanties have very often been told
By grandads and grandmas—children know it like a book;
In their imagination they know how the old shanties looked.
There's rose and lilac bushes where once weed and shrub,
You see two and three deckers where once shanties stood.
There are only a few old timers left; they'll soon cross the Great Divide—
Should they read this, they're the ones that miss the old South Side.

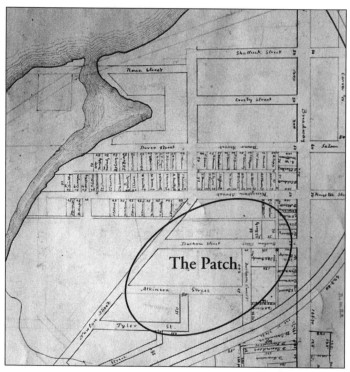

This Essex Company map of the Shanty Pond District, circa 1868, shows the pattern of permanent development within Shanty Pond. A number of shanties still remain around the pond, but are not indicated. The new development within Shanty Pond, the Patch, (circled) is just beginning to take shape. Courtesy Immigrant City Archives.

Interestingly, the demise of the pond itself resulted directly from the growing prosperity of the Irish in the Shanty Pond area. With a surge in population and the construction of new homes and tenement buildings came the associated problems of waste disposal and water pollution. Sewers that were built during the 1870s were unable to handle the discharge levels of the 1890s. According to *Lawrence City Documents* (LCD), sewers throughout the city frequently became full and overflowed "on account of the large number of water closets that empty into them at present, and which will be increased each year. A great number of the sewers were built over twenty years ago and were chiefly designed for carrying off waste water and drainage from sinks, and are inadequate to the future demands."[3] The 1892 and 1893 reports cite 2,184 new water closets, and more than a 50 percent increase in the loads of cesspool waste from "the large number of houses in the outskirts. . . ." The report also mentions, "Many cases of sickness have been caused by this want of sewerage, as the cesspools are exposed to the air, and the foul odors and germs."[4]

Development south of Andover Street also resulted in sewage waste being discharged into the stream feeding the Shanty Pond. The existing sewer lines along Newton Street could no longer handle the increased discharges, and before long the pond was turned into a large, foul-smelling, waste-strewn cesspool. The Lawrence Canoe Club, which had recently begun to relocate on the south side of the river near the outlet for Shanty Pond, complained that the stench and water quality restricted their recreational activities. Those who lived near the pond, all complained about the smell and the filth of the pond. Year after year, the health board pressed city government for money to build what was to become known as the Shanty Pond Sewer.

These pollution problems, the lack of waste capacity, and one other event, resulted in the end of the Shanty Pond. For two decades, stone paving blocks had been used on some city streets, and each year the demand for paved roads increased. The 1894 *Lawrence City Documents* noted that a large ledge deposit existed at a location near the future site of the Wetherbee School (1897), called the Blue Ledge, which was being used to provide stock for macadam roads. Soon it was discovered that another ledge adjoined the existing ledge but was covered by a "heavy bank of earth backing the ledge we are now working. Its close proximity to 'Shanty Pond,' so called, suggests the idea that the material might be used in partially abating the nuisance now troubling the residents of that section."[5] After repeated petitioning, board of aldermen and the common council finally agreed to act. A new sewer would be constructed.

In the fall of 1895, the first phase of the sewer project was begun with a contract awarded to A. W. Bryne. In September of 1896 James Chambers, a private contractor, undertook construction of the next section of the sewer to a point near the mouth of the pond. The December 1897 edition of the

Lawrence City Documents reports the unique sight observed by the residents of Shanty Pond. "[T]he pond has been drained into the manhole built at the end of the Chambers contract. . . . the winter has been cold leaving the bottom of the pond bare." By July 22, 1898, the Shanty Pond Sewer was almost completed. "All sewers which have discharged into Shanty Pond have been connected into the main sewer. . . . The nuisance caused by the discharge from the Newton Street sewer into the river close to the Canoe Club building was abated by the connecting of the Newton Street sewer to the Shanty Pond sewer."[6] One final section was needed to connect the Salem Street leg of the sewer to Andover Street. Construction began in the winter of 1899 and was completed by the end of the year.

Though the pond once surrounded by shanties was gone, the entire area continued to be called Shanty Pond for the next thirty or forty years. It was about this time that Peter became known throughout Lawrence as the Shanty Pond Poet. The demise of the pond symbolically marked the end of an era. Progress had taken its toll not only on the physical characteristics of the Shanty Pond District, but also on its rural, old-country feel and life-style. In the last two decades of the nineteenth century, extraordinary growth took place throughout the city, including the start of the third large wave of immigrants into the city: the Italians. Though Peter was prepared to move into the twentieth century and face all the changes it had to offer, he would do so reluctantly and never would be able to leave behind completely the life he knew in old Shanty Pond.

This is the only known photo showing the Shanty Pond community and Shanty Pond itself. Taken in the mid-1870s from atop a smokestack in North Lawrence, the Shanty Pond residential area makes up the top third of the photo. The Shanty Pond can be seen in the far, upper right hand corner, separating the houses from the wooded section, the Grove. Courtesy Immigrant City Archives.

4

The Irish Political Ascendancy

The social and economic success of the Irish in America can be linked in part to the strength and unity they found in their faith, the solidarity gained from labor unions and benevolent societies, and most important, to politics. The Irish plied the political trade more successfully than any other ethnic group in the Northeast during the late nineteenth and early twentieth centuries. Indeed, it could be argued that they displayed greater political acumen than any other immigrant group ever to come to America. Centuries of social and political struggle against the British had made the Irish very aware of the power of government policies. Thanks to Daniel O'Connell's grassroots campaign for Catholic Emancipation in the 1820s, and the Repeal Movement of the 1840s, their political instincts and skills had been sharpened. They also had learned the power of collective action.

In Lawrence, the Irish rise to political power can be divided into three distinct periods, each lasting about thirty years. The first occurred from 1845 to about 1875, when they had little political influence and were subject to the harsh policies of anti-Catholic, anti-Irish, nativist politicians. The second, from 1875 to 1911, saw the Irish inserting themselves into city politics, establishing a large political base, and starting to win high-level government seats. The third period occurred from 1912 to about 1940. During this period, the Irish dominated every aspect of city politics. They consistently held key elected and appointed offices. Peter was a witness to the Irish rise to power in Lawrence from the John Breen era during the 1870s and 1880s up until his death in 1938. His songs and poems gave testament to these events, and to the people who made Lawrence an Irish city.

After arriving in Lawrence, the Irish received a quick and harsh introduction into the sociopolitical realities of their new homeland. While their strong backs were welcomed by the owners of the Essex Company, not all of the native population embraced these Catholic newcomers. They were subjected to fierce attack by nativist forces who undertook strident measures in hopes of forcing them to leave American shores. Signs reading "No Irish Need Apply" were only the tip of this iceberg of bigotry. Known nationally as the Know-Nothing Party, its members, mostly Yankee Protestants, were virulently anti-Catholic and blamed the Irish for the filth, disease, gambling, prostitution, and crime found throughout Lawrence, and especially on the Plains. Tensions heightened in the 1850s when the Irish population had grown to such an extent that the Democrat and Whig parties started vying for Irish votes. While jobs had always been plentiful in Lawrence's brief and robust history, a serious statewide depression from 1854 to 1855 and a decline in the number of massive construction projects resulted in intense competition for an ever-shrinking number of jobs. As "outsiders" and Catholics, the Irish were easy targets to blame for the bad times.

The Know-Nothing Party found fertile ground in Lawrence in 1854 when their candidates were quite successful at the polls. That summer bands of nativist rowdies marched onto the Plains with placards, brick bats, stones, and guns. Violence erupted in the streets. Not surprisingly, Irish mobs roamed the city looking to retaliate. On November 15, 1856, the *Lawrence American,* a nativist-leaning newspaper, reported on one political rally with harsh, anti-Irish tones: "A procession composed of the most noisy Irish rabble . . . comprising of some 500 ragged, dirty-faced, filthy urchins culled and dragged forth from the rum-holes, grog cellars and shanties of 'the plains,' with a goodly delegation from the underground mud huts of the 'City of Cork,' upon the south Side . . . started directly for the Irish settlements of Oak and Elms streets, making the night hideous with their yells and outcries. . . ."[1]

With time, attitudes slowly changed. The antislavery movement and the nation's march toward the Civil War dampened the Know-Nothing Party's appeal to the masses. The patriotic response and brave performance of Irish troops at Gettysburg, Antietam, Fredericksburg, and dozens of other battle-fields doused the most extreme conduct of the nativists. Their movement was not dead, however. It repeatedly threatened the Irish during the final decades of the century.

Up until the 1870s city government was not representative of the large Irish population that lived in Lawrence. According to its charter, the city government was modeled after the bicameral structure of state and federal government. The voters elected a mayor and two governing bodies: the common council, which consisted of three representatives from each of the city's six wards, and the board of aldermen, made up of one representative from each ward. While the Irish had the raw numbers necessary to seize significant political power, it wasn't until after the Civil War that they would secure their first seats on the common council and board of aldermen. In 1868 John Kiley was elected to the board of aldermen, followed by John Hart in 1870, Michael Carney in 1873, and Mathew Carney in 1874. That same year, John Dolan was seated as the president of the common council. Four different Irishmen reached the same political plateau during the 1880s. By now, the Irish had moved into the second phase of their rise to political power.

Once in these positions of power, the Irish began to take care of their own. With newfound influence over hiring practices and appointments to the police, fire, and other municipal departments, Irish politicians steered jobs to their friends and supporters. Newly employed workers, in turn, remained loyal supporters to their benefactors at election time. With each election victory, more Irishmen were put to work. By the end of the century, as increasing numbers of Irish moved into professions such as teaching, law, and the skilled trades, their influence and respectability grew even more. Thanks to politics, the Irish would no longer be relegated solely to jobs as unskilled common laborers.

One promising and dynamic Irish politician whose presence characterized this second period was John Breen. Born in Tipperary, Ireland, in 1842, he came to Lawrence in 1853. He was a well-known member of the Fenian movement and volunteered for dangerous service in Liverpool, Manchester, and Dublin on behalf of Irish patriots planning an insurrection against England. Upon his return to Lawrence in 1868, he started an undertaker's business and later won a seat on the common council in 1876 and again in 1877. Breen felt the Irish had the ability to assert their considerable influence on city government, so he ran for mayor in 1881 against Henry Webster. It was the first Irish bid for the mayor's seat, and Breen lost by just a few hundred votes. One year later he ran again and secured a stunning victory.

Just thirty-five years after its founding by the Brahmin elite, Lawrence and New England had its first Irish-Catholic, Irish-born mayor. His election electrified the Irish population within the city and throughout the Northeast.[2] More importantly, John Breen's rise to power marked the beginning of serious machine politics in Lawrence. Through his connections in the business world and as a member of the Washington Fire Steamer Company, Breen created a sizable bloc of loyal supporters who got out the Irish vote. He promised a sympathetic ear to those in trouble, a helping hand when needed, and most importantly, he promised jobs. He ran again in 1883 and 1884 and was reelected both times by comfortable margins.

Once out of the mayor's office, his popularity ebbed and flowed with the political tides, yet his stature and reputation within most of the Irish community remained landmark. For several more decades he continued to help shape the direction of the Democratic Party in Lawrence and trained many of the next generation of Irish politicians. By the end of his tenure, the patronage system was starting to pay dividends for the Irish, but wouldn't reach its pinnacle for several more decades.[3]

After Breen left the mayor's office in January of 1885, the Irish were unable to maintain control of the top spot in city government during very difficult times. Breen's handpicked successor was defeated, and over the next fifteen years the mayor's seat switched back and forth between Irish Democrats and native Republicans. Resentful of Irish loyalty to the Democrats, city Republicans attempted to "gerrymander" voting districts in hopes of securing more seats on the common council. A new nativist movement, known as the American Protective Association (APA) also reared its head. Its members leveled serious attacks against Irish Catholics and their desire to have parochial schools. More troubling, however, was a split among the Irish themselves. Breen and another noted Irish leader and Fenian, John Sweeney, found themselves on opposite sides of the embarrassing scandal involving the collapse of an Augustinian Father's bank which resulted in hundreds of Irishmen losing their life savings. They confronted each other again during the 1884 presidential election when Breen supported Grover Cleveland while Sweeney came out for Republican James G. Blaine. Repeated defeats by Irish candidates brought Irish voters back together by the end of the century. Soon, Irish politicians began to capture the mayor's seat with regularity.

At the turn of the century, Irish politicians continued to hone their skills. They knew full well that getting elected and running city government was dependent on taking care of their constituents, especially their Irish ones. The typical Irishman in Lawrence learned that a victory for an Irish politician would mean jobs and income for him and his fellow Irish workers. It was not just the police and fire forces that depended on politicians for their step up the social ladder. So too, did the common laborer, though perhaps he had more interest in paying the rent and providing food for his family than improving his social status. Everyone knew that getting out a bloc of voters at election time meant security, at least for another year when elections were held again.

No one knew this better than Peter Cassidy. In the winter of 1899 he wrote a song about the debate over the final stage of the Shanty Pond Sewer. It was his first known venture into political comment. It was also the first time he was known to refer to himself as the Shanty Pond Poet. In his later years, Peter frequently wrote about men seeking work and the politicians who provided it. Of all the issues he cared about, jobs was the most important.

Shanty Pond Sewer

Did you hear the latest, boys, the news is out today,
On the street each one you meet, this is what they say;
The aldermen met last night, work we'll get I'm sure,
Of course you know, they gave MO, the Shanty Pond Sewer.

Chorus:
The cry was all Mahoney. Some called him a turk.
Many a man was loafing, then Mahoney gave him work.
His foreman, Johnny Connors, no better man I'm sure
Could handle men and the quicksand, on the Shanty Pond Sewer.

Mayor Eaton told the Aldermen, when they met last week,
Hannon had money enough to look after the streets.
Towle, Logan and Carney, were all good men I'm sure;
They had no show with MO, on the Shanty Pond Sewer.

(Chorus)

The way the Aldermen did it sure made the public click;
It was first Alderman Caffrey, then Alderman Dick,
Lane and Lynch will have a cinch, with the public next year, sure,
With the mayor's veto, they give MO the Shanty Pond Sewer.

(Chorus)

The cry was all Mahoney. Some called him a turk.
Many a man was loafing, then Mahoney gave him work.
His foreman, Johnny Connors, no better man I'm sure
Could handle men and the quicksand, on the Shanty Pond Sewer.
                    The Shanty Pond Poet

On Thursday, January 12, 1899, the mayor of Lawrence and two other city aldermen voted to authorize an independent contractor, Michael O'Mahoney, to complete the fourth and final leg of the Shanty Pond Sewer from Sanborn Street to Andover Street. Peter put pencil to paper the following day to announce the good news to his fellow working men in the Shanty Pond area. At the time he was living at 15 Ellis Street, in the Patch, and it is clear that his interest in the sewer project has little to do with the value of the sewer itself or the demise of the pond. Instead, he was pleased by the support of the aldermen for continuing the sewer project and especially for insisting that local labor be used by the new contractor, Mr. O'Mahoney. It may well be that this project was one of the many that Peter worked on as a laborer.

During his inaugural address one week earlier, Mayor James Eaton had voiced concern that the cost for construction of the Shanty Pond Sewer had become excessive under the direction of the superintendent of streets, John Hannon. "Had the sewer been built at the same prices paid to James Chambers under his agreement with the city of Lawrence, the cost would have been but $26,893, a saving to the city of $12,132."[4] It was Mayor Eaton's position that taxpayers would be better served if sewer construction was returned to private contractors who had the experience of numerous sewer projects, rather than street department employees and engineers who had very limited experience in these areas. The mayor added, "Men who are skilled in this kind of work know how to perform it at less cost than cities that have but one such sewer to build. There can be no objection to completing the Shanty Pond Sewer by contract, and restricting the contractor to employing only Lawrence men and paying them city wages for city hours. The laborer is worthy of his hire."[5]

One week later on January 9, the board of aldermen voted unanimously in support of Mayor Eaton's proposal to take construction of the Shanty Pond Sewer out of the hands of Superintendent Hannon. By unanimous vote the aldermen moved to annul their previous order authorizing Hannon to construct the final quarter mile of the sewer, and instead to have the sewer completed by "some competent person." Two days later the committee of sewers met and approved the appointment of a private contractor, Michael O'Mahoney, to complete the remainder of the sewer. O'Mahoney, considered one of the best known contractors in New England, had built numerous large sewer projects. He previously had served as superintendent of streets in Lawrence. When O'Mahoney offered to provide one of his foremen to oversee the project at no charge to the city, the committee refused the offer and voted to pay Mr. O'Mahoney five dollars a day to run the project himself.[6]

By year's end "MO" (O'Mahoney) had completed the sewer and tied it into the line along Newton Street and Andover Streets. For Peter Cassidy, the mix of politics, patronage, and sewers would come together again twenty-five years later when another Irish politician, Pat McNulty, would run for alderman promising to build another extension to the Shanty Pond Sewer and provide jobs for the workingman.

At the turn of the twentieth century Lawrence was in the midst of a period of tremendous growth. From 1890 to 1910 the population almost doubled, to 85,892, with most of the newcomers cramming into areas already stressed by overcrowding. This included the center section of North Lawrence from Essex Street north to the Spicket River, including much of the Plains where southeastern Europeans were moving into the homes vacated by Irish who had moved across the Spicket River. A 1911 survey of the area indicated that this section of Lawrence was overrun with humanity; one third of the city's population lived on one thirteenth of its area. Packed into three-and-four tenement buildings, between three hundred and six hundred people inhabited the average acre. This section of Lawrence was more densely populated than the most crowded sections of Harlem.[7] Such overcrowding was perhaps the most visible sign of the demise of the Essex Company's ordered plan for a model city.

Politics had always been an effective means for social change, and in 1911 this again proved to be the case. For years there had been growing concern that the old form of government, the common council and the board of aldermen, was too large and unwieldy to deal with the needs of the city in a timely manner. In addition, all elected officials held terms of just one year, making it nearly impossible to plan and implement meaningful change. In order to improve the overall operation of city government, a streamlined "commission" form of government was proposed, much like that adopted by many neighboring municipalities.

For several months leading up to the November 1911 charter vote, the electorate was treated to an extensive campaign with much debate and considerable partisan finger-pointing. With proponents promising lower taxes, better streets, new schools, a more beautiful city, less waste, and more jobs, the voters approved the new charter. In the future there would be only one governing board made up of five seats: a mayor and four aldermen, all of whom would be elected at large by the voters for two-year terms. Also commonly referred to as directors or commissioners, each alderman would manage one of four city departments: public safety, health and charities, parks and properties, and engineering. Aldermanic elections were staggered so that only two positions would be up for election at any one time. Though known to everyone, party affiliations were no longer formally designated during campaigns or on ballots, nor were they used to limit potential candidates at the primaries, held the second Tuesday in November, or the formal election, held the first Tuesday in December.[8]

The new charter, which went into effect on January 1, 1912, marked the beginning of a thirty-year period of Irish domination of Lawrence politics. It was the height of the Irish political ascendancy, even though the city's Irish-born numbered less than 10 percent of the total population. Factoring in second- and third-generation Irish, it is doubtful that they constituted more than 20 percent of the city's inhabitants. Nonetheless, it was the rarest of occasions when someone other than an Irishman held the mayor's seat or one of the aldermanic posts. While Irish success at the polls can be attributed in part to low voter turnout by other ethnic blocs, it is more likely the result of a half-century of learning and mastering basic principles of political success: build a large and loyal base, reward friends and punish enemies, and get out your vote. Finally, it was easier now. Irish politicians needed to secure and maintain a majority of only five governing positions, rather than twenty-five under the old charter.

——————

O n January 1, 1912, newly elected mayor Michael A. Scanlon met with the first board of aldermen chosen under the new charter. Its members were all seasoned officeholders, the next generation of Irish politicians: Paul Hannagan, Cornelius Lynch, Michael O'Brien, and Robert S. Maloney. They realized that while the city charter was new, little else about the city and its politics had changed. Elected officials confronted the same problems that most of them faced just a year earlier under the old form of government. The city's economic challenges were still daunting, as were the high rates of drunkenness, prostitution, and gambling. Taxes were difficult to raise, city spending continued to be a source of criticism, and the local papers kept up their nearly constant scrutiny of each politician's every move. While controlling the seats on the new city council may have been easier due to its smaller size, its members were now much bigger targets for criticism. They would need all their political skills to survive.

Two weeks into office the members of the city council confronted their first major crisis: the famous Textile Strike of 1912. Its repercussions would be felt years later, by key politicians at election time. For almost three months the strike crippled the city. About a dozen mills shut down operations, and 40,000 workers were off the job. Picket lines and soup kitchens were set up while massive marches and huge public rallies whipped up passions. The local police were called in along with several hundred "special police" (mostly Irish) to quell the strikers. Strike leaders, primarily Polish and Italian mill workers, quickly sought organizational help from the Industrial Workers of the World (IWW), an openly socialist union that had perhaps 300 members working in the mills. The IWW's presence in the strike engendered a great undercurrent of mistrust and fear among many Lawrence residents, and especially in the minds of city officials. Many felt that the socialist leaders of the IWW were using the workers to foment a wider revolutionary agenda. Indicating that he would break the strike or the strikers' heads, Mayor Scanlon called for the state militia, which faced down protesters in violent confrontations with horses, guns, and water hoses. Two people were killed: a female striker and a teenage boy. The strike proved to be a bad omen for city officials. The road ahead never got much easier.

Peter Cassidy remained fascinated with the personalities on the city council. He knew them all and was quick to offer comment, in public or private, about whom he liked and disliked, who was for the workingman and who wasn't. For over twenty-five years he wrote and published over one hundred songs about the goings-on in Lawrence. Many of them focused on the city's department commissioners, usually urging voters to support the incumbents from whom he and his friends were likely to get work. But not always. In his poem "The Paving Expert," Peter poked fun at the commissioner of the engineering department, who was facing an election challenge in the fall of 1915. Interestingly, Peter was a street department employee at the time.

The Paving Expert

My name it is O'Harragan, I'm a paving
    expert by trade;
All my friends can recommend the good
    streets I have made.
I have a scheme, it is no dream, I'll pave
    no more highways;
I'm the only man that made the plan
    for paving the waterways.

I'm going to pave the Atlantic to keep
    down the submarine;
They want me in Andover, just to pave
    the old Shawsheen.
The governor of New York would have me
    to pave Long Island Sound,
Wilson will try to get me to pave the sky
    if the world turns upside down

I'm going to pave the South Canal, and the
    the Merrimack above the dam;
When I get through I'll pave the Suez
    and the Tokyo River in Japan,
I'll pave the Rhine, also the Boyne, the
    Shannon and the river Lee,
The Graney in Clare, the gap at Delaware,
    the Wabash and the old Swanee.

I'd like to pave the Behring streets, the
  weather out there's too cold,
Captain Cook would have had luck, if I
  had paved the North Pole.
Carranza did say to the U.S.A. at some
  time he'd like to go,
If I'd pave from land to land across the
  Rio Grand—Texas to Mexico.

I'm going to pave the old canal, where they
  used to load Medford rum,
Then I'd pave the Charles River, 'neath the
  Harvard Bridge; when I've that done,
I'll pave over Castle Island
  away out in Boston Bay,
After that I'll pave South Boston flats,
  where Clancy dug clams at say.

I have to pave the Allegheny from Pittsburg, Pa.,
  to O-High-O,
And from Arlington Mills to Prospect Hill,
  where the smelly water flows.
Finnegan wants me to pave the reservoir;
he said it might keep off the rain,
If I ever do I'll pave the filter gallery,
  While I have paving on the brain.

The O'Harragan mentioned in Peter Cassidy's poem is actually Alderman Paul Hannagan, one of the more colorful and successful political characters in Lawrence at the turn of the century. "Paully," as he was known, grew up on the Plains of North Lawrence and served as a member of the Lawrence Police Department. He was often referred to as one of John Breen's "young turks" in the 1890s when he became a growing force in the Democratic Party.[9] The first government office Hannagan held was as assistant to the Lawrence city assessor, and from there he quickly gained influence and notoriety within the Democratic Party. In 1898 and 1899 he served as alderman, and from 1904 to 1907 he held the post of superintendent of streets. In the fall of 1911 he was elected alderman under the newly adopted commission form of government, which he had fought to establish. He was soon appointed to the post of director of engineering by the new mayor, Michael A. Scanlon. Two years later he was easily reelected. When Mayor Scanlon died suddenly in August of 1914, Hannagan was selected by the city council to serve as acting mayor for the remainder of the year.

Throughout his political career, Paully had a reputation as a firebrand. He was sharp tongued, decisive, quick to say what was on his mind, and seemingly unconcerned about the fallout from his actions. At a Democratic Party gathering held in December of 1896, Paully gave an impassioned speech, attacking the current Republican officeholder: "I shall not rest till that despot Bailey is removed from the city marshalship." At the same meeting, a local paper described Hannagan as having "bloodshot eyes" and a "threatening attitude" as he "hurled venomous epithets" at a fellow party member, Jeremiah "the Sliver" O'Sullivan. During an argument for the soul of the party, Paully declared himself the better of the men, a more loyal and more aggressive Democrat when campaigning for the party's interests in Lawrence. Speaking figuratively, Hannagan shouted, "When I carry a knife I carry it openly, not up my sleeve. Put that in your pipe and smoke it."[10]

Paully's bravado did eventually catch up with him. On February 23, 1915, while seated in the city engineer's office, he was shot three times by a disgruntled citizen, Dennis H. Finn. Finn was a veteran of the Spanish American War and a member of the old common council in 1897. One week before the shooting incident, he had publicly petitioned Hannagan and the other aldermen to offer more jobs to the unemployed who were native born, like himself. In classic Hannagan style, Paully dismissed "Din" Finn, telling him that he had "delusions of grandeur" and that even if he [Hannagan] had work available, he would not give it to Finn because "he was not worth ten cents a day." One week later, that same phrase echoed in Paully's ears as Din Finn fired three bullets into the alderman at point-blank range, while shouting "not worth ten cents a day?" Despite having one shot lodged in his throat, Hannagan wrestled Finn to the ground as help arrived. He was said to be sitting up and smoking his pipe two hours later. Paully recovered fully from his injuries, and Finn was sentenced to serve nine years in jail.

The first roads were paved in the 1870s. Hannagan was known far and wide as a master at building and maintaining block paved roads. Dirt roads in Lawrence were first replaced by cinders and later by cobblestone, macadam, and finally granite block paving, a Hannagan specialty. During Paully's tenure in office, "he had the distinction of installing more paved streets in Lawrence than was ever laid in the city's history and his specifications were sought by many municipalities while the streets themselves were the cynosure for the eyes of street builders. His paper on granite-block paving at the 'Good Roads Congress' in Atlanta, Georgia in November of 1914 attracted widespread interest. . . ."[11] In 1914 Mayor Curley of Boston tried to entice Alderman

Hannagan to leave his post in Lawrence and take control of the Boston Street Building Department for $5,000 a year, twice his current salary. Paully toyed with the idea for a time but chose to decline the offer. He did agree, however, to consult with the Boston Engineering Department as its "paving expert."[12]

Even aside from Din Finn, not everyone admired Paully Hannagan. He was his own best promoter and was resented for it. He plied the patronage business better than most and was disliked for that as well. But his extraordinary capacity for paving roads of granite and cement got him into the most trouble, not because people didn't like his roads, but because they cost so much and were seen as political gifts for friends and business interests.

On April 28, 1914, the *Lawrence Telegram's* lead headline read, "Is Lawrence Becoming Paving Mad?" Just a few weeks earlier, Paully's request for an additional $300,000 for paving had been reluctantly approved by the city council. His paving exploits were the talk of the city. Hannagan was the object of near constant and sometimes merciless criticism by editorial boards of *The Leader* and other papers for his spending patterns and heavy-handed tactics. The following year, election forces lined up to defeat Lawrence's "paving expert." It was about this time that Peter Cassidy wrote his poem. Though light in tone, his poem mirrored the growing criticism that centered on Commissioner Hannagan. It is unclear, however, whether Peter was poking fun at his boss or joining in *The Leader's* call for his ouster. Odds are it was the latter.

The political opposition in Lawrence mounted a broad assault against Hannagan during fall elections of 1915 as eight candidates challenged the incumbent in the primaries. Day in and day out, local papers quoted each candidate's attacks on Hannagan. One article in *The Leader* summarized the mood of the electorate: "'Hannagan Must Go' is the slogan from Prospect Hill to the Shanty Pond."[13] In late November the primary was held and the field was narrowed to Paul Hannagan and relative newcomer John F. Finnegan. Finnegan was a native-born Lawrencian of Irish descent who had worked on the street department for about ten years before deciding to challenge his boss. Almost immediately after the primary, Hannagan's opponents lined up behind Finnegan as the December 14 election approached. The same themes were pounded over and over again: favoritism, wastefulness, extravagance, and arrogance. Firing its final salvo the Sunday before the election, *The Leader* concluded in characteristic form, "We are told that Hannagan's reputation is made; and [we] agree that it is, for the high cost of paving and general extravagance; for browbeating people who have business at council meetings; excluding citizens from examination of public records; bombast and brag; catering to special interests and utterly ignoring the interests of the majority of the people, we have never had his equal. The dignity of the people, their rights, liberties and interests demand his defeat next Tuesday."[14] The people apparently agreed. Finnegan defeated Paully Hannagan, 5,956 votes to 5,201 votes.

Lawrence's Irish powerbase seen posing at a 4th of July parade, circa 1912. Left to right, Alderman Paully Hannagan, Mayor Michael Scanlon, Aldermen Robert Maloney and Cornelius Lynch as Uncle Sam. An unknown man. Courtesy Immigrant City Archives.

As the newspapers also had predicted, Hannagan would not soon fade from the political scene in Lawrence. Two years later he was back on the stump trying to reclaim his former seat from John Finnegan. Right from the start, Hannagan found himself under attack as aggressively as he had been in 1915. In early December of 1917 Finnegan took out large newspaper ads that effectively presented the voters with stark comparisons between Paully Hannagan's tenure as director of engineering and his own. One ad pointed out that Hannagan had 454 men on the city payroll the week before the election in 1915, while Finnegan had but 193 men employed during the same period two years later. During the entire election period from mid-November to mid-December 1915, Finnegan claimed that Hannagan wasted $13,703 of the taxpayers' dollars trying to buy men's votes with work. Finnegan also attacked Hannagan for putting down streets of cinder and grease throughout much of South Lawrence east and south of the B&M tracks that ruined homes, created "cinder bogs," and squandered almost $680,000 of the taxpayers' dollars. The voters had had enough of Paully, and Finnegan easily won reelection.

For the next several years, Paully Hannagan remained a powerful figure in the Democratic Party, serving as a member of the state central committee. In addition to political savvy, he also possessed a keenly inventive mind, which he had put to use as the director of engineering and as an inventor. Among his more notable creations were the Hannagan catch basin, a combination snow plough, leveller, and ice cutter; the Hannagan gutter plough; and an automatic traffic police officer that attracted attention in places as far away as Shanghai, China.

In 1919 Paul Hannagan began to succumb to throat cancer. His condition worsened and on January 6, 1920, while on his deathbed, he dictated a letter to his sister, Mary Brackett, asking that Dennis Finn be pardoned from jail after serving almost five years for the 1915 shooting incident. Many people from Lawrence, including previous employers and leading politicians, supported Paully's request for leniency. On Monday, January 19, 1920, just days after Hannagan's sixty-seventh birthday, the local newspapers announced that Paul Hannagan had died at his home on Arlington Street from throat cancer complicated by pneumonia. Two days later Dennis "Din" Finn had his sentence commuted by the parole board and was immediately released from jail.

———

While Peter Cassidy occasionally wrote songs that were critical of politicians, he usually wrote them in support of particular candidates. One of those was James Cadogan, who first won election as alderman in December of 1913, and who served on the city council with Paully Hannagan for several years. Cadogan was an Irishman who had clawed his way up the ladder of the police force and finally into city politics. As the commissioner of public safety, he was responsible for the operation of the fire and police departments. Peter had firsthand experience working for the police department for a short time, and was also an "on-call" member of the fire department, probably serving at the station located just a few paces from his home on South Broadway, Engine House #3, also known as "Tiger Three." Clearly, his loyalties rested with these men and the commissioner who supervised them.

In his poem "The Central Fire Station," Peter applauded the bravery of the men who risked their lives fighting fires for the Lawrence Fire Department (LFD). He identified by name thirty firefighters from the Central Station and added individual compliments whenever possible. He focused special attention on Fire Chief Dennis Carey and the role he and his men played in fighting a massive fire in Salem, Massachusetts, on June 25 and 26, 1914. Peter closed his poem with a glowing endorsement for Alderman Cadogan. As with many of his poems, however, there was more intended by this work than first meets the reader's eye.

The Central Fire Station

How many men we meet, as we go along through life,
In this world of sorrow, trouble, toil and strife,
I've seen many good fellows, both on land and sea,
But I've never met a better set than the boys of the L.F.D.

They always greet you with a glad hand; I've always found them square,
You never hear them knocking, with each other they play fair,
They seem to pull together, with each other they agree,
Do the boys of the Central Station, who belong to the L.F.D.

Acting Captain Gibson, I wish him all the health and joys,
That he can get in this world, for he's liked by all the boys;
He's a good lieutenant, And I hope soon to see,
That the time will come, when to fires he'll run, as a captain of the L.F.D.

Lieutenant Amos Ingham, a good fellow, tried and true,
A bigger or a better heart ne'er beat 'neath a uniform of blue.
Always a smiling countenance, when his fellow men he'd see,
He is one of the best among the rest of the boys of the L.F.D.

Lieutenant Sullivan and Billie Young, McCreadie, Reagan and Hayes,
Costello, Berry, Howard, Craven and Morrison, I give them praise,
With O'Reilly and Griffin, Keenan and Haigh and Dana you can see,
They belong to the fighters of the Central L.F.D.

Claude Morrell, Pete O'Loughlin and genial Dan O'Neill,
With Hopkins, Fraser, Kennedy and French, you're sure of a square deal,
Jim Burton, Seuss, and Collins, the last named are the three,
Who takes notes of fires that come o're the wires to the Central L.F.D.

Frank Morris, the Deputy, you will surely find him game,
He is always Frankie on the spot, when it comes to fighting flame.
You are sure to find him taking a risk, from danger he'll never flee,
He is never done, till "all out" is rung at fires with the L.F.D.

Lawrence should feel proud of Carey, he brought the city fame,
For the part he took at the Salem fire, all honor to his name.

The name of our Chief, I do believe, is in Salem's history
For the work he did with the help of some of the boys of the L.F.D.

Jim Cadogan, the alderman, they say he's some "Commish,"
And that his term will have no end, the fires laddies wish.
He's upright and fair, and does things that the citizens all agree,
There's no other like Cadogan for the head of the L.F.D.

Immediately following an early afternoon explosion at the Korn leather factory in Salem, Massachusetts, fire began to spread rapidly throughout the city. A combination of high winds and low water pressure made what would have been a difficult fire an impossible one. It took twenty-four hours to get the fire under control but not before much of the city had been destroyed, many citizens had died or were missing, and over 10,000 residents were made homeless. Early damage estimates exceeded ten million dollars.

On the afternoon of the fire's outbreak, Lawrence Fire Chief Dennis Carey rushed to Salem to assess the situation and offer assistance. Quickly realizing that a massive response would be needed, he contacted Deputy Chief Frank Morris and called for men and machines from Lawrence. Forty firefighters, some permanent but mostly "call men," were quickly transported to Salem by automobile. As part of the response, Hose Wagon #5 from the Central Station and Steamer Engine #2 from the firehouse on Garden Street were loaded onto flatcars in South Lawrence and shipped to Salem.

By 6:30 that evening Lawrence men were on the job along with their comrades from surrounding communities, trying to check the spread of this massive conflagration. Stationed at Buffam Street in North Salem, the Lawrence men were said to have mounted a "Herculean effort" and stopped the fire from passing their post. Sixteen hours later they returned to Lawrence blackened by smoke and soot, and exhausted from lack of sleep. For days Lawrence newspapers sang their praises along with the efforts of local police and militiamen, who also assisted their neighbors in Salem.

Peter's poem was published in *The Leader* in the summer of 1915, one year after the Salem fire. While Peter was undoubtedly interested in heaping public praise for his many firefighting friends, the timing of the poem is more appropriately linked to several political controversies swirling around Alderman Cadogan that were certain to become campaign issues that fall.

Jim Cadogan was born in Lawrence in 1871 and worked his way up through the police force before running for office in 1913. He was appointed patrolman in September of 1899 and he frequently experienced the ups and downs of the patronage system in Lawrence politics. He was promoted to plain clothes inspector in 1906 after just seven years of service. With a change in the mayor's office, however, he was demoted to patrolman by Mayor "Billy" White in January of 1909. In 1910, after White was forced to leave office and sent to jail, it was back to inspector for Jim Cadogan. On January 3, 1912, he was again reduced to patrolman by the newly elected director of public safety, Cornelius "Con" Lynch. As happened quite often, the man on the "outs" returned a year or two later to challenge the man who put him out of work. Cadogan and Lynch would come face to face once again.

When the strike during the winter of 1912 became violent, Mayor Scanlon called in the militia to support the Lawrence Police Department. In their efforts to suppress protesters and strikers, they employed a wide range of forceful tactics including the use of water hoses, horses, and rifles with bayonets. In the months that followed the end of the strike, the conduct of the local police underwent considerable scrutiny at the local, state, and national levels. Before long the Lawrence Police Department, Alderman Con Lynch, and the Scanlon administration were awash in a scandal that carried into the city elections of December 1913. Much of the criticism centered on political favoritism by the mayor and Commissioner Lynch, who had appointed the mayor's brother-in-law, John J. Sullivan, to the post of city marshal, or chief of police, in 1912. There also were accusations that some in the department had turned their heads away from illegal gambling and "objectional shows" that took place at the Elks Fair in July of 1913.

That fall, Jim Cadogan decided to run against Con Lynch, the man who had demoted him almost two years earlier. The election was hot with rhetoric, and in December Cadogan soundly defeated Lynch by a huge margin: over two thirds of the vote. The public expected their new commissioner to clean up the police department and to right old wrongs. One of Cadogan's first moves was to reappoint patrolmen Charlie Woodcock and Fred Thompson to their former duties as police inspectors. Like Cadogan, Woodcock and Thompson had been demoted by Con Lynch. In his own bit of political retribution, Cadogan demoted acting Inspector John J. Kelleher, a Scanlon appointee and loyalist, to the midnight beat, and City Marshal John J. Sullivan was replaced by Maurice McKenna.

The next two years were not easy for Cadogan. Controversy and his political opponents dogged him throughout his tenure in office from 1914 through 1917—the normal course of political life in Lawrence. One nagging problem was Cadogan's refusal to appoint a liquor squad dedicated to patrol the bars and enforce liquor laws. Feeling that it was a waste of manpower and city resources to dedicate a "spotter" to watch for liquor violations, he repeatedly rejected demands by local papers and political opponents stating, "I wouldn't put a dog on the liquor squad."[15] Another issue was pay raises. During the spring of 1914, city firemen circulated a petition to secure a twenty-five cent pay raise for the officers and permanent men in the department. Wages would have gone to three dollars per day for the permanent men. They eventually got their raise from Jim Cadogan, but it didn't come until early July of 1915. Soon thereafter, Cadogan gave raises to Inspectors Woodcock and Thompson. The rest of the police force hoped to be next in line for a raise, as one of their own was now the boss.

Cadogan took considerable heat for granting the raises. The press attacked him for the secrecy with which he made the pay decisions as well as for the impact that they would have on the department budget and future tax rates. They also criticized the fact that on-call firefighters had not gotten a raise and soon would be looking for more money. The lead editorial from *The Leader* read, "Alderman Cadogan made a great mistake when he yielded to the insistent demands of the permanent firemen for a pay increase. . . . The call men, too, are sore. They are as numerous as the permanent men and they wanted more pay. . . . Friends are grieved because he fell for those demands. . . . In antagonizing thousands of taxpayers . . . to please sixty firemen, in my opinion he has made many enemies to please three score men, many of whom will prove to be ingrates."[16] When election time rolled around, Cadogan's opponent was ready to attack.

Alderman Jim Cadagan, circa 1916.
Courtesy Immigrant City Archives.

Commissioner Cadogan entered the 1915 election facing stiff competition from a savvy young politician named Peter Carr. The challenger focused a strong attack on the incumbent alleging that widespread corruption existed in the city, especially with respect to gambling, peep shows, "immoral conduct," and drunkenness. According to Carr, the city was "wide open" to the forces of crime with full knowledge of the police and especially Cadogan. He also criticized the pay raises given to the firemen and the police, which contributed to the jump in the cost of running the department.

In response, Cadogan defended the overall performance of the police and fire departments, pointing out that arrests were up during his first term, including arrests for gambling and immoral acts. He did admit, however, that discipline within the fire department was "only pretty good . . . because there are a few incorrigibles around and there will always be some."[17] Cadogan issued a public challenge to Carr to come forward with "absolute proof" of the widespread corruption that he spoke of so often.

Just a few days before the December 14, 1915, election, Cadogan fired off his strongest and most effective volley. Speaking to an evening rally, he introduced public records showing that Peter Carr had been arrested, pleaded guilty, and was fined for being present at a gaming establishment on Essex Street in 1903. According to Cadogan, "Carr goes around with a prayer book in one hand and a pack of cards in the other according to his record." In his own feeble defense, a startled Peter Carr told voters at the rally that his presence at the gambling joint was an accident, and that he went in with a friend for only five minutes when the police raided and arrested the party. "I was the only one of that party who gave his correct name," he added meekly.[18] Hoping to change the tone of the rally, he began to tout the fact that he was the president of the Fr. Mathew Temperance Society and a member of the Holy Name Society. Four days later Carr lost the election to Cadogan, 5,716 to 5,312 votes. Though a victory for the incumbent, the vote totals indicated a significant loss in Cadogan's base of support in just two years.

In the days following the election, Cadogan began to take disciplinary action against members of the police department and fire department who had engaged in "pernicious political activity" during the election. Several heads rolled in the weeks that followed. The open opposition to his campaign by some of his men and the close election offered early warning signs that the political winds were changing for the incumbent. Over the next two years, the papers were filled with the same charges of police corruption and city-wide depravity.

By election time in 1917, Peter Carr was back on the stump hammering away at the same themes he had tried two years earlier. "The police department is shot to pieces. Discipline [is] thrown to the winds. How many prisoners have died in the new police station? Immorality is spreading to a startling degree in this city. . . . Doctors have told me that social diseases have never been at such a height as they are. . . . I will rid the city of this great evil if elected." Carr attacked the proliferation of gambling under Cadogan's watch, the "objectional shows, and drunkenness," calling Lawrence "the Mecca for the underworld."[19] This time it was Cadogan's defense that fell on deaf ears. On December 12, 1917, Peter Carr received 827 more votes than his opponent. [20]

O ne of the most popular and resilient political figures of this era was Jim Cadogan's nemesis and Peter Cassidy's friend, Peter Carr. Born in County Down on April 2, 1884, Carr came to Lawrence with his parents twelve years later and soon settled on the Plains. In the fall 1913 he successfully entered the race for the state legislature representing the Sixth Essex District and was reelected to a second term in the fall of 1914. One year later he turned his attention to city government and ran for Cadogan's seat on the city council. Peter Cassidy knew both men. As was his pattern, once the votes were counted and he and his friends had secured work, Peter's songs during the next election cycle would support the new incumbent, now Peter Carr.

Almost immediately after his election victory, Carr began to clean house by replacing Cadogan loyalists such as City Marshal Maurice McKenna, the head of the police force, and Fire Chief Dennis Carey. Chief Carey would come back within a year to haunt the new commissioner by making substantive charges that Carr was not a legal citizen of the United States.[21] After some embarrassment, Carr survived the controversy and soon was on his way to building one of the most effective political machines in Lawrence history.

Over the next fourteen years, Carr was reelected to the public safety seat on the city council each time he ran, and he often won by margins rarely enjoyed by other politicians. He was well liked and very visible, even having his own baseball and bowling teams, known as "the Peter Carrs." As with most politicians, he also was a member of numerous social and fraternal organizations throughout the city. These contacts helped win elections. One of his infrequent defeats at the polls occurred on December 11, 1923, when he ran for the mayoral seat against Walter T. Rochfort and lost by a mere 260 votes. He soon returned to the post of director of public safety where he managed not only the department but also a large and loyal bloc of supporters.

In his poem "Lawrence, Mass," Peter Cassidy followed his pattern of praise for city employees as well as the commissioner upon whose office so many depended for work. This time, it was the police force. This poem was likely written in the fall of 1921, while Peter was in New York City, probably attending a boxing match. That year Alderman Carr and incumbent Mayor

William White were each up for reelection for their respective offices. Carr would defeat his opponent, Henry Marshal, by less than 600 votes, while Billy White was handily defeated by Daniel Mahoney, a well-known city politician.

"Lawrence, Mass."

To Commissioner Peter Carr
From the Shanty Pond Poet
Dated, New York

Well, Pete, my boy, I'm away out here, in the city of New York;
I've seen those tall skyscrapers, and with some cops I had a talk.
When I heard them praise their finest, I then turned on my gas,
And I said that we had just as fine back there in Lawrence, Mass.

Is it true one said; "You have old men;" I said, "a few, of course.
But remember they were young when they first joined the force."
I said, "Your traffic cop don't try to stop, see how those autos pass;
They give preference first to those on foot, back there in Lawrence, Mass."

Just then a parade came marching by with the finest in the lead,
"Them cops," I said, "ain't got no pep, they don't show any speed."
You should see the line with Marshal O'Brien, cheered by the crowds they pass;
Eyes right, head erect, every cop in step, when they parade in Lawrence, Mass.

I started then upon my way, one said, "Just take your time,"
He asked "Is it true you've got stuff down there?" I knew he meant "moonshine."
I said, "My friend, I do not think you could get a pint or glass."
Then I knew quite well, I'd lied like h--- about old Lawrence, Mass.

They said, "Pete, old boy, give us a call the next time you come down;
We like to meet a man like you, that'll praise his own town hall.
I hear folks say you've a great white way." I said, "Not yet, alas!
If it's White's way it will come some day to good old Lawrence, Mass."

"Let me tell you what I say is true; you can travel near and far,
You could never wish for a better commish than my friend Peter Carr.
His captains and lieutenants I'm sure you can't surpass,
And a finer set you never met than the cops in Lawrence, Mass."

This poem dedicated to Peter Carr and his police force also hinted at one of the other more colorful characters in the history of city politics, William "Billy" White. He was described by friends and foes alike as quick witted, glib, flamboyant, verbose, bombastic, nimble-tongued, and highly controversial. His four terms as mayor were outdone only by his numerous criminal indictments, court appearances, convictions, and trips to jail. By all accounts he was a crowd pleaser, but no friend to Peter Cassidy or Peter Carr. He kept a high profile and flamboyant life-style, but never married and claimed not to drink. He died a pauper on November 28, 1938. His obituary accurately summed his life: "William P. White is gone, and his death marks the passing of a most unusual personality who gave Lawrence public life over a period of forty-five years color, dash and spice of the sort that it may never be known again."[22]

Peter Cassidy's allusion to Mayor White comes in the fifth verse of the poem when he mentions the "white way" and later "White's way." For many years in the early 1920s, a recurring political controversy focused on a proposal by the Lawrence Gas Company to install a new system of streetlights along Lawrence's primary commercial thoroughfare, Essex Street, as well as Broadway and other major streets. Referred to as the "white way project" because of its illumination of the roadways, the gas company proposed to absorb the entire cost of installation if it could pass along interest costs, depreciation, and taxes in the lighting rates it charged to the city.

When the white way project came to the fore in 1921, the political lines were drawn immediately. One side, supported by Peter Carr, argued that the common people should not have to bear the burden of such development. The rich property owners, businesses, and the gas company itself should take on the full cost of the project and not pass it on to the city through convoluted financing maneuvers. The other side, supported by colorful Mayor Billy White, felt that the gas company proposal would have little impact on the tax rate and was a great deal for the city and its people. For its part, the gas company framed the discussion quite starkly: "no pass-through onto rates, no white way."

This issue was the subject of political wrangling dating back to 1912, and it often came up during election season. Mayor White failed to secure the installation of the white way during his term from 1920 through 1921. His successor, Mayor Daniel Mahoney, also failed during the two years that followed. The matter came up again for a vote of the city council in February of 1925 during Mayor Rochefort's watch. This time, by a three to two margin, the council voted in favor of a white way provided it was paid for by abutting land owners, merchants, and the newly named Lawrence Electric and Gas Company. This policy would guide future white way projects. The debate continued and by September the white way project along South Broadway was completed. Soon after, Essex Street also got its white way.

Peter Carr's second defeat as a politician took place in December of 1931 when he lost his seat to Thomas F. Galvin in a sensational campaign. In the primary election several weeks earlier, Carr had garnered some 6,000 votes more than his closest opponent, Mr. Galvin. Throughout the city, all were confident of a Carr victory. Even the day before the December 8 election, the *Evening Tribune* confidently predicted Carr to be a sure winner. Unfortunately, a contentious labor dispute two months earlier proved to be his undoing at the polls. The impact of the strike on this election underscored how vulnerable even this longtime survivor of city politics could be during and after a highly charged labor dispute.

Alderman Peter Carr, circa 1917. One of Lawrence's most popular and skillful politicians. Courtesy of Immigrant City Archives.

Just two months before the election, on October 7, 1931, workers at the Wood, Ayer, Shawsheen, Pacific, Washington, Monomac and Arlington mills began walking off the job in response to a wage reduction imposed by mill owners. The owners returned to their constant theme from decades past: labor costs were too high to compete with other New England mills. So they did what they always had done—they reduced hours, wages, or both. In this instance they reduced the hourly rate from 41 cents an hour to 37.5 cents an hour. The workers responded quickly and forcefully. Police were called to the Pacific Mill, and ten men were arrested and brought immediately before a judge, who fined them five dollars each and warned others not to engage in similar instances of trespassing and intimidation. Not everyone paid heed to the warning. Rallies and demonstrations took place without permits throughout the city, and police were again called in to make arrests. As with the Strike of 1912, there were strong rumors that socialist influences were running the strike, which resulted in a significant drop in public and city council support.

From the outset it was clear that the strike of 1931 was going badly. The mill owners were holding firm and a citizens committee established to mediate the differences proved ineffective. More and more workers were ready to return to their jobs. In fact, 450 out of 575 workers at the Monomac Mill voted to end their strike and go back to work. Upon hearing the news, Peter Carr called in strike leaders from the United Textile Workers of America (UTWA) and asked their cooperation in allowing for a peaceful return to the mills by Monomac employees. Assured that only token pickets would be in place, Carr was outraged later that day when the union sent 2,000 men to picket at the mill. He insisted that union leaders not be allowed to terrorize returning workers. He had guaranteed the security of the workers and pledged to stand by his words. Police were sent in and the UTWA lost what little support was left from Carr and the other aldermen. Early on, local newspapers and city officials were hostile toward the strike as "red agitators" were very visible and assumed to be closely tied with the union leadership. Repeatedly, the aldermen denied the union a permit to rally on the city common and when 200 UTWA members marched on city hall to seek a meeting with the city council, they were refused an audience. Carr was very outspoken in his resentment of the union: "They abuse everybody, talk against the government and say this isn't a free country. No public park should be turned over to any group with such beliefs. No one agrees with them."[23]

On November 8, 1931 the strike was over and *Evening Tribune* editorialists were calling it "the flop of organized labor." The November primaries occurred shortly thereafter, and Carr easily outpolled a nine-man field. All appeared to go well for the incumbent in the weeks and days leading up to the December 8 election. On December 7, the morning before the vote, the Lawrence Central Labor Council, the Greater Lawrence Textile Council, and the UTWA distributed a handbill that attacked Peter Carr, his handling of the strike, and his loyalty to working people. Carr felt he had been blindsided and attempted to mount a last-minute defense in the papers. "The most unfair and unwarranted attack ever aimed at me during my entire political career made its appearance on Monday morning. . . . It is one of those cowardly, 'eleventh-hour' attacks perpetrated by some vindictive persons apparently hiding behind the names of respected organizations. My conduct . . . in the recent strike was as humane and liberal toward the protesting operatives as I could make it . . . I can look every mill operative square in the eye and hold my head up as regards to the part played by me in their recent trouble."[24] When the votes were counted, Thomas Galvin had overcome Carr's 6,000 vote lead in the primary, defeating him convincingly 14,946 to 12,826 votes.

Carr remained in the public eye for some time after his defeat. In November 1932, he was appointed to the state boxing commission where he served until his death in 1944. His attempt at a comeback in 1933 fell short when he lost his bid to unseat Galvin by thirty-five votes. Nonetheless, Carr was one of Lawrence's quintessential politicians who enjoyed unparalleled success spanning three decades. Over the years, Carr ran a coffee and tea store and an automobile supply business on Broadway and was an especially active supporter of boxing, baseball, and bowling events. As commissioner of public safety, he oversaw the revamping of the police department and the city's first use of automatic traffic lights. He also hired the first woman police officer in Lawrence, Miss Nora E. Herlihy of Avon Street. Under his supervision, the fire department fully implemented the "two platoon system" that was first proposed by Chief Dennis Carey, and during his tenure the department regularly placed near the top of the list of cities throughout the country with the lowest annual fire losses.[25,26]

D uring the early part of the twentieth century Peter Cassidy had his poems and songs printed in at least four different Lawrence newspapers. His work was most frequently found, however, in a very popular and often scandalous weekly paper called *The Leader.* First published in 1901, *The Leader* quickly developed into one of the city's most sought-after yet dreaded publications. The more traditional daily papers, such as the *Lawrence Telegram* and the *Evening Tribune,* focused on straight news with limited mix of editorial opinion. *The Leader* was almost entirely political commentary and local gossip. Its editorial bias was progressive in many respects, but it would readily take on anyone: elected or appointed officials, union bosses or judges, teachers or policemen, Democrats or Republicans. By 1912 the paper boasted the largest circulation base in the city with over 10,000 readers. Though under constant fire from political opponents, *The Leader* continued to publish until 1935. Known as the *Sunday Leader* in the 1930s, the paper's promotional material boasted: "It leads always. First in circulation in Lawrence and its suburbs. Sincere and consistent in its policy. It has acquired an influence that has given it the leadership of the Lawrence press."[27] While self-serving, there can be no doubt that *The Leader* gave its many readers a format that exposed the stark underside of politics in Lawrence. People couldn't wait to get their hands on it.

Over a period of four decades, *The Leader* blasted away at local politicians. Few escaped its scrutiny. For a time, it proudly and accurately posted the slogan, "The Politician's Nightmare" on its front-page masthead. Once locked in the sights of the editors, elected officials could expect their every word to be analyzed, every action questioned, and every appointment investigated. Paully Hannagan, director of engineering from 1912 through 1915, was one politician who suffered almost constant attack by *The Leader*, as did Mayor Michael Scanlon and Alderman John Finnegan. Frequently, local politicians would make their own backhanded and scurrilous comments about stories found in "a certain Sunday paper," and on several occasions they filed law suits against *The Leader's* publisher, William Sellers, and its editor, Valentine Sellers, his brother.

On May 6, 1914, the *Lawrence Telegram* reported that an angry, frustrated, and apparently sensitive Mayor Michael Scanlon brought a $1,000 lawsuit against Valentine Sellers and Leader Publishing for libellous articles alleging "that the mayor said that he considered $8 per week enough money for a man with a family to live upon."[28] This was not the first time Scanlon had sued Sellers. Just one year earlier, Mr. Sellers decided to plead guilty to charges filed by the mayor. He paid a $1,000 fine, but not before a host of witnesses paraded before the judge to encourage even stiffer penalties. One account of their testimony offers pointed insight into *The Leader's* reputation: "Charles Bradley, a real estate and insurance agent stated that . . . no man felt safe in Lawrence. If he had any flaw in public or private life, he was pretty sure to be seen by Sellers and unless he 'came across' he would be pretty sure to be written up. It created a feeling of cowardice in the community. He personally knew of no money being paid to Sellers to withhold anything."[29]

One of the city's liquor license commissioners and a frequent subject of *The Leader* editorial staff also testified against Mr. Sellers. John W. Duffy's testimony gave the court and the city a sense of the real fear that many had of the power of *The Leader* and its editors. ". . . Sellers had always been hand in glove with all the grafters and that he [Sellers] had scared the life out of the good citizens, their wives and children. . . . We can never have a good city as long as Valentine Sellers is allowed to run his paper."[30]

Even after this case was settled, little changed in the way *The Leader* did business. The lawsuits continued. In January of 1921 another lawsuit was filed against Valentine Sellers by James J. Wrinn, the manager of a competing newspaper, *The Sun American*. Mr. Wrinn asserted that he had been libeled when *The Leader* referred to him as "Peanut," and also exposed a petty theft complaint made against him twenty-four years earlier. According to Wrinn, it was his failure to purchase ad space in *The Leader* that triggered Mr. Seller's editorial vengeance.[31]

While elected officials most often suffered the wrath of this four-page political sledgehammer, average citizens could also expect to have their dirty laundry hung out by *The Leader* staff for all to see. On the front page of every issue was a picture of Ye Town Crier, who introduced the "I Wonder" section of the paper. Here could be found some of the juiciest bits of gossip and other curious offerings from around Lawrence and surrounding communities. In any given edition, *The Leader* would print four to six dozen rumors that had been submitted by anonymous sources from throughout the city. Affairs and romances were exposed, gambling and corruption uncovered, hypocrisy and favoritism highlighted, and vices of all kinds publicized. The politically powerful as well as the common laborer held their collective breaths each week in anticipation of each Sunday's release of *The Leader.* For quite some time, the "I Wonder" section was one of the most read columns in the city.

The following brief list represents a sampling of "I Wonder" contributions selected from copies of *The Leader* published prior to 1917. It's not surprising why so many anxiously read this Sunday morning tabloid.

> I wonder how many of the Essex Street lodging houses are as equipped as the one which one of the inmates boasted: "We don't have to go off the premises for booze, women or a game of poker. . . . All the comforts of home, so to speak.

> I wonder why the Titan-haired miss of the Ayer [Mills] . . . gets away with so much chewing gum? Is it because the prolific use of gum produces dimples? I don't see why anyone should want to raise dimples. A girl with a wart on her chin gets a husband of her own choosing.

> I wonder who is the farmer's wife from the suburbs that hangs around the engine house with a basket of eggs. Does she think any of the men need eggs?

> I wonder if that South Lawrence woman hasn't sworn off on canned salmon since she found a man's finger in the can she had opened. (Think of a little thing like that disturbing a south sider!) Evidently the digit had been chopped off . . . in the cannery . . . and little time was lost hunting for the thing. Time is valuable when the salmon are running.

> I wonder if the school teacher whom an anonymous neighbor accuses of going home at 4 a.m. shouldn't be more careful about her hours? Also the company she keeps if he really is a married man. I won't give the locality, for she might lose her position, but print the foregoing to put the young woman wise to the fact that she is being watched.

> I wonder if it's a fact that the entire street department and its collateral branches are to be shut down Tuesday? The law allows men a certain time to vote and this should be sufficient, unless the street department machine is to be used for booming certain candidates at the polls.

> I wonder if the Arlington Mills are satisfied with the city's drinking water? Can they see through it?

I wonder why it is almost impossible to get more than a handful of the permanent firemen out to a meeting of their association. It wasn't so before they got their pay raise. Now, they can't get a quorum together.

I wonder which Methuen policeman searched a prisoner and located only $8, while a Lawrence police inspector went through the same prisoner and dug up $65, three watches and several rings, all concealed in the fellow's shoes?

I wonder if the local pastor fancies that doing the sleuth act around barrooms at a late hour at night will benefit his flock or the cause of religion in general.

I wonder if the Broadway grocer, whose store was infested with rats didn't get a big surprise when he found the cat he had borrowed, with a high reputation as a rat killer, playing tag and fraternizing in the cellar with the rodents.

Interestingly, Peter Cassidy's work was usually found within the "I Wonder" section of the paper. He was a regular contributor of poetry and song lyrics. A typical editorial introduction by the paper would read, "I wonder if the following magnum opus by Lawrence's own Shanty Pond Poet isn't one of his very finest." On several occasions the "I Wonder" column would publicly encourage Peter to write a poem about a given topic. Sure enough, a week or two later, Lawrencians would read of his latest work, prefaced by: "I wonder if Peter F. Cassidy, the Shanty Pond Poet Laureate, hasn't done himself proud once again with these lines."

The Leader staff was clearly charmed by "old Pete," as was evidenced in this 1929 introduction: "The Leader's prize poet, the bard of Shantytown, whom this paper first presented to the public twenty years ago, comes to the front with a timely political ode, and answers the much asked question, 'What has become of Peter Cassidy?'" The editor was also quick to come to his defense when necessary. Once, when introducing one of Peter's poems, Mr. Sellers included this stern admonishment to an out-of-towner who apparently had caused Peter considerable upset: "I wonder if the querist who desired to know what has become of the Shanty Pond Poet isn't answered in the following verselets. (And, by the way, the Holyoke [Massachusetts] Democrat which the Shanty Pond Poet swears stole, plagiarized, mangled and mistreated Peter's famous lines on the 'Irish On The Plains,' is hereby warned to keep hands off.)"[32]

5

Icons of an Irish Community

I n 1914 Peter Cassidy was fifty-three years old and working as a laborer for the city street department. That year he and his family moved from their apartment at 48 South Broadway across the street to 57 South Broadway. Peter obviously loved this part of the city. From 1900 to 1925 he and his family always lived in apartments located on one of the four corners at this intersection of Shattuck Street and South Broadway. It was centrally located between the bridge crossing the Merrimack River and St. Patrick's Church, in the very midst of the commercial and social center of South Lawrence. By now, three of his stepdaughters, Kate, May, and Delia, had married local Irishmen and moved out of the house. Stepdaughter Margaret was still at home, but working in the woolen mills. Tess, who soon would marry baseball player Larry Mahoney, was employed at the Kimball Shoe Factory just a few blocks away from the house. Frances, now twenty-one, had finished "Evening School" and joined Tess at the Kimball Factory.

Peter was entering his golden years. With fewer mouths to feed and more money coming into the home, he became even more involved in the events of Shanty Pond and the city as a whole. He also settled down a bit, spending the next twelve years at 57 South Broadway, twice as long as he ever stayed at one location. Having been back in Lawrence for over twenty years, this proud and confident Irishman knew everyone who was anyone in the city. When not working, which was often months at a time, he would make the rounds of various establishments to drink, play cards, offer a tune on his concertina, and commiserate with his peers. He didn't have far to go. Frank McDonough's saloon was next door, Joe Bateman's was right across the street, and John Daly's bar was a short city block away. Anyone sitting next to Peter at a local tavern wouldn't have to wait long before hearing a song or a poem about the goings-on among the Irish of the city. In fact, no matter the topic, be it religion, sports, work, women, a good cigar or beer, Ireland, or politics, Peter was quick to voice his point of view, often in song or spoken verse. His opinions were often controversial, sometimes humorous, frequently nostalgic, and always on point.

Peter was a voice for his time. His songs provided great enjoyment to his contemporaries, who loved to hear or read his verse. He wrote in a manner that all could understand and embrace, and he touched upon subjects dear to those first- and second-generation Irish who inhabited the city. His scrapbook contained a yellowed newspaper article that must have made him very proud. A contemporary, but unidentified, literary critic had written an apt description of his poems. "Peter is not the meticulous, literary poet who polishes all the life out of his work. His poems are rough when held up against academic norms for comparison. . . . But as a reflection of the sort of life he has lived . . . the things [that] he writes find their audience among those who speak the same tongue as himself."[1]

The next collection of songs provides another glimpse of the Irish early in the twentieth century. They describe some of the events, institutions and

A view of South Broadway, looking south towards St. Patrick's Church circa 1900. In the foreground is the intersection of South Broadway and Shattuck Street. For a twenty-five-year period, Peter Cassidy lived in second floor apartments to the immediate right, at 57 South Broadway; to the immediate left at 46 and 48 South Broadway; and also at 64 South Broadway, the building just to the left of the carriage in the center of the photo. Courtesy Immigrant City Archives.

people within the community as Peter observed them—his view of the world from Shanty Pond. Through his verse, he visits Irish touchstones such as the local pub, the parish priest, the Irish colleen, fraternal organizations, labor unions, the cop-on-the-beat, and a simple, personable character who was probably like many of Peter's friends in Shanty Pond.

———

It should come as no surprise that tavern life held the same lofty perch in Lawrence that it did in Ireland. At times during Peter's years in Lawrence there were as many a 300 saloons scattered about the city. Along with the church and fraternal organizations, it was probably one of Peter's most revered institutions. Throughout most of his life in South Lawrence, Peter never lived more than a brief walk from a local saloon. It was a place where patrons would gather to drink, have a smoke, and engage in good conversation. For decades, the saloon was also a place where one also could enjoy a free lunch. Many enjoyed the free food that was often served at the bar along with their beverage. Others came to rely on the free lunch for their basic daily sustenance. In his song "We Want that Free Lunch Back Again" Peter publicly addresses a problem that distressed him greatly, and that nearly resulted in the downfall of Mayor Michael Scanlon's administration.

We Want that Free Lunch Back Again

Tell me lad why you aren't glad; what is it that makes you sad?
Come tell me now what makes you feel so blue?
I've always been your friend; stick to you I do intend
If there's anything wrong, tell me do.

He said, "Just listen here," as he wiped away a tear,
"I'll tell you I worry and have pain.
And the reason that I sigh and the tears come to my eye,
I'm looking for that free lunch back again."

Chorus:
I'm looking for the dish with the pickles and the fish,
The platters with the crackers and the cheese.
Those good hot frankforts too, and the big bowl of beef stew,
A hungry man's appetite would often please.

With a glass of beer it would oft give cheer
and drive away the hungry craving pain.
That's the reason I do sigh, and the tears come to my eye,
I'm looking for that free lunch back again.

Listen what I'm telling you, this story might come true.
The citizens are going to have some say.
They are going to right this wrong, and the time may not be long,
It may ere happen next election day.

On the ballot there's a place, for an X there is a space,
If men should vote "No," tell me who's to blame.
If the city should go dry, there are more than me would sigh
And wish the old free lunch was back again.

Chorus:
I'm looking for the dish with the pickles and the fish,
The platters with the crackers and the cheese.
All kinds of meat you like from balogna down to tripe
With beans, hot clams, sauerkraut and peas.
That pickled cabbage red, and a piece of baker's bread
Would drive away the hungry, craving pain.
It's the reason that I sigh, and you see tears in my eye,
I'm looking for that free lunch back again.

On February 3, 1914, the Lawrence papers shouted in their headlines: "Drastic Measures in the Liquor Business. License Commissioners Adopt Rules Against Free Lunches."[2] These "drastic" changes in how liquor would be sold were brought about by the three-man liquor commission chaired by John W. Duffy. The commission's report called for an end to the traditional free lunches, which for decades were offered to patrons: cheese, crackers, pickles, fish, sausage, and more. For many, the free lunch was the most important source of their daily caloric intake, nickel beers being the other.

During the latter half of the nineteenth century, the temperance movement had been a growing force in the United States. National prohibition would go into effect in 1920, but cities and states throughout the country continued to confront local temperance initiatives. It was especially strong among some members of the Irish community who viewed alcohol as an evil that destroyed individual lives and families. Since the Irish first set foot in Lawrence, there had been a growing concern about alcohol consumption.

Bartenders at Boehm's Café in Lawrence prepare to serve a free lunch to their clientele. Courtesy of Immigrant City Archives

From 1852 to 1875 there was a prohibition against the sale of most alcoholic beverages in the city. The decision to allow the sale of alcohol was then granted to the board of aldermen from 1875 to 1881 and left to popular vote until 1895. At that time the board of aldermen was charged with granting licenses through an appointed license commission. Each year thereafter, the public voted annually as to whether or not to continue to allow the granting of such licenses by the aldermen and the commission.[3]

For some critics, any consumption of alcohol was unacceptable. For others, concerns centered around whether alcohol was served, by whom, to whom, in what quantities, and/or in what manner. Prior to the new regulations by the license commission, complaints had been raised by the Catholic churches in Lawrence as well as other denominations about illegal trafficking of liquor, public drunkenness, and related sexual behavior. They were especially distressed by such behavior on Sundays, holidays, and after hours during the work week. In addition, concerns had been voiced about who should be allowed to sell liquor, as well as the clientele and the conditions of the inns and hotels in Lawrence where alcohol was being served.

Regular newspaper stories reported and editorialized about the growing social problems related to alcohol consumption. A "secret service man" visiting the city in 1912 described Lawrence as the "worst city in New England . . . even Boston will have to take a back seat." In great detail, he publicly listed the abuses relating to ongoing poker and crap games with three or more "lewd women on call" and the free flow of alcohol available for "entertaining girls" as young as fifteen lured into hotel rooms and lodges. He wrote, "intoxicants are purveyed openly . . . illegally on weekdays as well as Sundays, . . . as if there were no license law. . . . On Sundays, many of the drugstores, the dollar dram shops, do a land-office business in half pints of the made-while-you-wait stuff, or you can drink rotgut at the soda fountain with assorted sirups *[sic]* and soda water as a chaser. . . . Whatever the cause, the social conditions in Lawrence are frightful." Finally, he exposed the failure of police to enforce any of the curfew, gambling, alcohol, or prostitution ordinances, stating that "This is the only city where I ever saw policemen tipping their hats to . . . notorious women of the town."[4]

Shortly after the election of 1911, Mayor Scanlon responded to the pressure. He publicly admitted that "a deplorable condition of affairs" existed in the city's liquor business, and promised to appoint commissioners who would remedy the situation. The following August, Scanlon's newest appointee to the commission, John William Duffy, pushed through an ultimatum that required bar owners to close their side doors and stop selling alcohol to women. Within a short time, one saloon owner who failed to comply had his shop shut down for ten days. Years earlier, the pastor from St. Mary's Church, Father O'Reilly, succeeded in getting legislation passed that prohibited women from procuring liquor licenses. Apparently, it was one thing for men to distribute and consume alcohol, and something entirely different for women. Later, the commission put into effect mandatory licensing regulations that reviewed the location, equipment, furnishings, and "character" of all liquor establishments, as well as the character and fitness of saloon keepers.

Despite these efforts, Chairman Duffy and his fellow commissioners came under continuous criticism for the condition of the hotel and liquor businesses. To many in Lawrence, Mr. Duffy and at least one other commission member were considered beholden to a local brewmaster and to banking interests. They were even criticized by liquor wholesalers, who complained that first-class license establishments were allowing liquor to be purchased for off-premise consumption. Over the next year and a half, pressure continued to mount for the license commission and the police to get the situation under control. On February 2, 1914, in an effort to stem the chorus of criticism, the commission instituted sweeping regulations that included a ban on the free lunch. Almost immediately a cry went up throughout the city. *The Leader* summarized the major elements of the ban as follows:

There must be no more 'treats' on 'the house,' and no other inducements to buy can be ordered. Pint and half pint bottles must be thrown out and no liquor bottles can be exposed to view excepting the bar or on the bar sideboard . . . there shall be no 'presents' or 'gifts' in the way of the distribution of bottled liquor or premiums as a reward for past trade or as an inducement for future patronage. . . . The purpose of this regulation is to prevent license holders of the first class from illegally selling liquor not to be drunk on the premises.[5]

The response to the new regulations and the ban on the free lunch was forceful and hostile. Throughout Lawrence, the common man protested the elimination of this sacred institution. Local papers harshly criticized the license commission and grassroots campaigns were begun to eliminate liquor licensing altogether and to recall Mayor Scanlon, who had appointed Chairman Duffy. The "No Lunch, No License" campaign focused the attention of the powerful political and liquor interests on the fall elections. Without the licensing of alcohol, distributors of beer and alcohol would be unable to sell their product. And without licensing fees, which annually pumped about $100,000 into city coffers, local politicians, taxpayers, and other businessmen all would suffer. While Scanlon and Duffy took the brunt of the blame, still others criticized Alderman Cadogan. All that was needed, they insisted, was for his policemen to enforce the existing laws.

Most of the criticism directed at the commission contended that the new rules missed the mark. Rather than attacking the central problem, its shotgun approach intruded into areas that needed no intrusion, such as the free lunch. An open letter printed in the *Evening Tribune* admonished the commission members. "If you were half awake you would hear the roar that is going up from the streets, from the housetops, from the pulpit proclaiming the hotel business in Lawrence. Yet you claim your ignorance of conditions. . . . If you had done your duty you would know all that you seek to know. . . . "[6] Chairman Duffy fired back and blamed the police department, the courts, and especially the *Evening Tribune* in his rebuttal letter published on March 5, 1914.

The Leader would not be outdone in editorial rhetoric. It maintained a nearly constant drumbeat of criticism throughout the winter and spring. One contributing correspondent wrote caustically, "I wonder if that big hearted license board is aware that many a poor devil has existed on hot free lunches given out by charity-inclined rumsellers throughout this period of trade depression, preferring their manhood to accepting the doles of organized charities or of the churches."[7] On February 15, 1914, its lead editorial screamed, "Wake up, License Commissioners! . . . Get down to the real big things. . . . Can it be said fairly that the giving of free lunches by the legalized liquor dealers in the city contaminates the public in any way. Quit trying to bluff the public, at the behest of some radical clergyman . . . Call your police department into action, insist upon the squelching of the "speakeasies," drug stores, dram shops and fake clubs."[8]

The controversy remained hot for quite some time as the Scanlon administration scrambled to end the turmoil. On May 3, 1914, *The Leader* reported, "Crackers, cheese and pickles . . . have brought Lawrence or helped bring it to the verge of a political revolution. The bosses see their plans going awry, their castles tumbling, their dreams of power and pelf fading away like mist before the sun."[9] The politicians started to get the message. By June reports filtered out of the commission that the ban on free lunches might soon be eased.

Mayor Michael Scanlon died suddenly in the summer of 1914, but even in his death there was great controversy. His longtime friend Michael Brogan received a mayoral appointment to the license commission immediately *following* Scanlon's death. For months afterward, growing public outcry could be heard over this appointment, as voters feared more of the same corrupt policies. In December voters narrowly approved the continuation of the licensing of alcohol, but by the smallest margin of victory in twenty years. John Kane was elected the new mayor partially on his promise to clean up the liquor problem and remove several commissioners, especially John Duffy. Once in office, Kane began a public investigation of the license commission and sought the resignation of commissioners Duffy and Woodbury. Interestingly, Michael Brogan stayed on and was appointed chairman in 1916 by the new mayor, John Hurley. A review of news clippings in the years following the free lunch scandal showed little change in city politics regarding the sale and consumption of alcohol.

Peter's poem was written in May of 1914 to lend support to the recall campaign and to call for an end to the ban on free lunches. But he alluded to a specter even more troubling to him than the loss of the free lunch—the city going completely dry if the voters rejected licensing. Eventually, the ban on free lunches was relaxed, but Peter's worst fear came true six years later when national prohibition went into effect.

While tavern life certainly had its influence on daily life for many, one cannot overstate the role that the Catholic Church played in the lives of most Irish immigrants in America. Like most Irish immigrants who came to America after the Famine, Peter was a Catholic and very loyal to his church and parish, St. Patrick's. Given the historic context of the mass migration from

Ireland during the latter half of the nineteenth century, it is easy to understand how poor, frightened, and confused immigrants would readily turn to the force that might diminish their sense of isolation and fear. In cities throughout America, Irish Catholics were drawn into the local parish community by their needs for spirituality and their desire to belong. The church parish was the next best thing to the country villages they had just left. It offered familiarity, stability, security, and spirituality. It also provided a central location where Irish immigrants could share cultural bonds in a world that was openly hostile to both their nationality and their religion. Through church schools, parents could provide their children with religious and secular training that reflected their history, traditions, values, and culture. For these reasons churches were among the first structures to be built in the midst of each Irish settlement.

The earliest histories of Lawrence mention that once the Irish arrived in the new city, they immediately began work on the dam and the factories. They also sought out a location where they could attend Sunday Mass. At first the faithful traveled on foot to Lowell, Massachusetts, for religious services—a journey of about ten miles. By 1846 Mass was being celebrated regularly in Lawrence on the north side of the river. The earliest Catholic Mass celebrated in South Lawrence reportedly took place shortly thereafter at the residence of Michael Murphy near the corner of Newton and Shattuck Streets in Shanty Pond. The first formal Catholic church, the Immaculate Conception, was established in 1846 by Father Ffrench at Chestnut and White Streets. With the explosive influx of Irish into the city, a second Catholic parish, St. Mary's, was established almost immediately thereafter near the corner of Haverhill and Hampshire Streets. Over time, St. Mary's overshadowed the Immaculate Conception church both in size and influence.

Father Ffrench was succeeded at Immaculate Conception in 1851 by Father Taafe, and before long the new pastor realized that a church was needed to tend to the Irish Catholic community growing on the south side of the river: Shanty Pond. In 1868 he purchased land at the present day corner of Salem Street and South Broadway (then called Dover Street and the Turnpike.) At first a mission was started. When Father Orr succeeded Father Taafe, a wooden church was built where the St. Patrick's Rectory is currently located. The first Mass was celebrated in the new church on Christmas Day of 1869, and by the spring of 1872, St. Patrick's mission was designated a separate parish. Father James Murphy was appointed as the resident pastor. As the population around Shanty Pond grew, so did the need for a larger church.

Over the next ten years, parishioners of very meager means made contributions toward the new structure. In 1881, under the leadership of Father McManus, the cornerstone was laid, and within a year Mass was celebrated in the basement chapel. Piecemeal construction continued, and after twelve years of small but generous donations by parishioners, a magnificent, two-story edifice was dedicated in 1894. Each level of the church could hold over 1,000 worshipers and both were regularly filled to capacity. In 1900, Father Gilday became the new pastor at St. Patrick's where he would remain until his death three decades later. He was responsible for bringing the Sisters of Charity to the parish to run the new grammar school in 1906. St. Patrick's High School opened in September of 1925.

In addition to regular religious services held throughout the year, St. Patrick's offered its Irish parishioners a wide range of other spiritual and social offerings. Picnics and bazaars were frequent events as were lawn parties and men's gatherings known as "smoke talks," where entertainment such as musicals, lectures, and boxing matches were held in the school hall. Peter Cassidy pasted newspaper accounts of such gatherings in his scrapbook, especially those in which he performed. "St. Patrick's Holy Name Society held a smoke talk Sunday night at the assembly hall of St. Patrick's School. The feature was a stereoscopic lecture on 'Rome' by Father John J. Gilday. He is very familiar with Rome and its history and proved to be a very pleasing lecturer. . . . Peter Cassidy, 'the poet from across the Spicket' aided in the night's enjoyment by rendering some of his parodies on the 'Swanee River,' about the 'Patch,' and 'Shanty Pond,' and 'The Spicket.' On the whole, a very delightful time was held, and it was hoped that a similar event will be held in the future."[10]

Peter left behind poems about two parish curates who were among his favorites; Father William Carty, who served at St. Patrick's from 1929 to 1932, and Father James Davey, who also arrived in 1929, but was reassigned in 1933. Together they acted as the spiritual advisors to the different religious groups of the parish, such as the Family Sodality, the Holy Name Sodality, St. Patrick's Alumnae, and the St. Vincent De Paul Society. They also served as parish representatives at social committees or events sponsored by the parish. For instance, Fr. Carty was advisor to the St. Patrick's Dramatic Club, which regularly put on amateur productions in the school hall. Together they organized the parish "Field Day and Lawn Party" for the St. Patrick's Charitable Aid Society on July 18, 1932. Thousands turned out to enjoy the festivities. Peter was approaching seventy years old when these young curates came to the parish. He certainly knew them well and must have appreciated the energy they infused into the parish during their brief stays. The local papers published his poems to Father Davey and Father Carty.

Fr. Davey

Peter F. Cassidy, the South Side bard, whose naive, simple, expressive writing over a lengthy span of years has built for him a traditional "nom de plume" of the Shanty Pond Poet, has submitted what he terms a humble reflection of the sentiment of the people of St. Patrick's parish over the departure of the Reverend Father James L. Davey, who has been assigned to work among the faithful in other fields.

> *"Au revoir," Fr. Davey,*
> *May the Good Lord spare thee.*
> *St. Patrick's will miss you*
> *But good friends must part.*
>
> *Prayers for your rise to heav'n*
> *For those of sorrowing heart.*
> *The flock of this parish,*
> *your mem'ry will cherish;*
>
> *Will miss your face,*
> *Benevolence and grace.*
> *Those you've helped in need*
> *Have truly lost a friend.*
>
> *May the prayers of the congregation*
> *Follow you to your new station.*
> *God bless, Fr. Davey,*
> *God bless you![11]*

Father Carty

(St. Patrick's Church)

We'll miss you, Father Carty; it is sad to have you go,
And leave the flock you've shepherded; 'tis sad for you, also.
You'll always in our memory be; we will think of you each day,
And share with you our orisons [sic] when at night we kneel to pray.
You've shared with us our sorrows; you've lived with us our joys;
You watched and prayed, and long hours stayed, with the little girls and boys,
Some you blessed in Holy Baptism; some, their parents you have wed;
You've comforted the sick and dying; said the office o'er the dead.

So for you, dear Father, we shed tears, and heave a heartfelt sigh—
God bless you, Father Carty. Au revoir, but not good-bye.[12]

A long with the parish priest, one of the professions most often associated with the Irish in America was that of policeman. The cop-on-the-beat was one of the earliest and most visible symbols of growing Irish status and power in the late nineteenth century. But the myth about the Irish cop is as deceptive as most stereotypes. While there was certainly truth behind the warm image of the Irish police officer portrayed in films such as *Going My Way*, there was a harsh side as well. Irish policemen had real power over city residents and occasionally overstepped the bounds of their trust. Such transgressions were frequent during Peter's years in Shanty Pond when political patronage was at its peak. The distinctions between right and wrong became clouded as politicians, business interests, and some policemen attempted to re-frame the lines of legal behavior. Not surprisingly, liquor, prostitution, and graft were at the center of such unlawful conduct.

In his song "The Cop on Fixed Post," the Shanty Pond Poet salutes the majority of honest policemen who served on the Lawrence Police Department. Officer William Caffrey was well known throughout the city, serving on the force with distinction for forty-one years. Born in Lawrence on March 24, 1867, Caffrey's education was cut short when he started working as a teamster at an early age. Later, he worked the "front end" of the horse cars that carried passengers throughout the city. He also drove the first electric trolley car from Lawrence to Lowell, having plowed clear the tracks of snow a day earlier.

At the age of eighteen, Caffrey was given a rowing scull by his brother, and he soon took up rowing on the Merrimack River. In 1886 he entered his first race and over the next ten years established himself as one of the premier sculling champions in the country. In 1890, he won the single scull national title in Worcester, Massachusetts, and won it a year later at Washington, D.C. After losing the national championship in 1892, he continued to race for the Lawrence Canoe Club, now located on the south side of the Merrimack River near the mouth of Shanty Pond. He entered his final race during festivities marking the semicentennial of Lawrence on September 17, 1895. Caffrey was arguably the greatest athlete Lawrence ever produced up to that time.

In late June of 1896 Caffrey set aside his love of competitive rowing to accept an appointment to the police department by Mayor George Junkins. During his first years on the force, Bill Caffrey was assigned to an area around Park Street and Broadway in North Lawrence. Not long after, he was assigned to Ward Five, the northwest section of Lawrence, west of Broadway. In 1906 he was transferred to the Essex Street area, the business district, where he served on the early night shift for the next thirty-one years. A lifelong sports enthusiast, he was regularly assigned to duty at sporting events at Riverside Park (later called O'Sullivan Park). For a time, Caffrey walked his beat as a foot patrolman. He later served and commanded a mounted division and played a role in the Textile Strike of 1912. He was also one of the first two officers assigned to traffic posts at the corner of Essex Street and Broadway, the assignment about which Peter wrote his poem in May of 1916.

In the early nineteen hundreds, traveling the streets of Lawrence had become very challenging and dangerous. In addition to pedestrians, the streets were cluttered with electric trolley cars, horse-drawn wagons and carriages, and also motor cars and trucks. Collisions, injuries, traffic jams, and travel-related disputes prompted the city to establish a traffic division to bring order and safety to city streets. As he did with every assignment throughout his career, Officer Caffrey quickly and effectively established order. One firsthand report cited in a local newspaper describes Caffrey's abilities:

"That's no place for a nervous man" observed a citizen the other afternoon as he stood watching the traffic officer at work at the corner of Essex Street and Broadway during a busy ten minutes when he seemed to be overwhelmed with complications arising from a temporary congestion of traffic at the point. "That officer, whoever he is, certainly knows his business," he went on to observe. "I have been watching the way he manages things here, and say, if I had to do that for a half a day I'd be down where I could get fresh vegetables from the county agricultural school. But he doesn't seem to mind it a particle and really looks as if he enjoyed it. But he really has to keep his eyes open and his hands going, I must say."[13]

Caffrey was known and admired by most Lawrencians, especially local businessmen, store owners, and bankers. People felt secure knowing Officer Caffrey was on his beat. Often, during strikes, riots and other times of crisis, city officials would request Bill Caffrey's presence by name, confident that he would promptly restore order. "His robust form has often been seen at the head of special details pressed into service to meet exacting demands. . . . His fearlessness in the line of duty prompted his superiors to place him in command."[14] The youth of Lawrence, however, tended to see Bill Caffrey in a mixed light. For some, he was seen as the one who caught robbers and arrested criminals. For others, he was the guard who made it impossible for them to play hooky or sneak into private gatherings or a local baseball game.

In March of 1937 a mandatory retirement law forced him to end his police career at the age of seventy. Tributes and testimonials recognizing his outstanding service poured in from every quarter as he concluded his forty-one-year police career "without a black mark being entered against his record in the annals of the department."[15] Just nine months later, William Caffrey died on November 22, 1937.[16]

Police officer William Caffrey stands proudly as he nears the end of his career, circa 1935. Courtesy of Thomas Caffrey.

The Cop on Fixed Post

I'm Officer McCaffrey, sometimes the people laugh at me,
When they see me making motions in the middle of the street.
I take care of all the ladies, the carriages and the babies;
I never had an accident to happen on my beat.
I keep everybody moving, for there's always something doing.
I'm on my post of duty be the weather wet or dry,
Shure the crowds they stop and linger, for to see me point my finger,
And to watch me give the signals, for they like to hear me cry.

Chorus:
Just hold there for a moment, till I give you the sign;
Back there to the crossings, till I tell you it is time.
Be careful on the corner; there comes a jitney bus,
And here's a motor cycle, and an ice cart, what is worse;
A dump cart with a heap of bricks, a wagon load of wood,
An auto truck piled up with beer, a grocer's team with food.
Every one has their eye on me till I give them the nod.
'Tis on Broadway I am everyday, since I joined the traffic squad.

The ladies when they come along, I greet them old and young,
They cast such a roguish glance, and I return a smile.
They say "Ain't he a daisy?" Oh! just look at his shape,
If he were only a New York cop he'd surely take the cake.
With my white gloves and cap, I'm the finest on the force,
If the ladies fell in love with me, I can't blame them, of course.
For I always do my duty, to see every one I'll try,
And to guard them all from an accident, you'll always hear me cry.

(Chorus)

————

The first three decades of the twentieth century witnessed some of the most tumultuous years of the organized labor movement in the United States. So frequent were strikes and related work interruptions that the New Deal era also ushered in sweeping federal legislation that helped to level the playing field between labor and management. Labor strife existed across a wide range of job sectors, and it was especially prevalent in the large textile centers of the Northeast, such as Lawrence. The Textile Strike of 1912 was perhaps Lawrence's most famous strike, but it was only one of many serious work stoppages to disrupt the city at this time. One of the longest and most interesting strikes occurred in 1922, the third major textile strike in ten years. While the conduct of strike organizers was self-defeating, the role played by the Irish and their outspoken religious leader, Father O'Reilly, during this and other Lawrence strikes is worthy of attention.

The Strike of 1922 began on Monday, March 27, when several thousand workers stayed away from the textile mills to protest a recently announced 20 percent pay cut. In the days that followed thousands more walked off the job and set up picket lines in front of factories that were still operating. About 18,000 workers were off their jobs by the end of the second week. Several days later, the last of the great mills, the Pacific, was unable to operate with so few workers in attendance and finally had to close its doors. Virtually every major mill in Lawrence had shut down by April. While some workers had walked off the job in protest, many others were fearful of coming to work and crossing the picket lines.

Four unions were involved in the strike: the Woolsorters, the Loomfitters (an affiliate of the American Federation of Textile Operatives), the United Textile Workers of America (UTWA), and One Big Union (OBU). Because their formal membership often reflected only a small portion of the strikers, the unions spent much of their time that spring trying to organize the striking workers. Unfortunately, they were unable to cooperate with each other during the strike. In fact, two of these labor organizations devoted most of their efforts during the strike publicly undermining one another.

Six days into the strike, UTWA President Thomas McMahon announced at a rally that his union would not work with the OBU. Ben Legere, the OBU leader, fired back a bitter public attack against the UTWA that same day. When the OBU tried to organize a one-day sympathy strike of all workers throughout the city, McMahon openly opposed the move, urging sympathizers to donate a day's pay to aid the strikers instead of staying home and losing income altogether. At a rally of OBU supporters in the North Lawrence Common, Legere asked those gathered which union they felt best represented them. Their response was obvious. Legere used it to bolster the claim that his union should represent the strikers. In the weeks that followed, OBU members repeatedly showed up at UTWA rallies to heckle speakers and disrupt proceedings. They filed a law suit to prevent the UTWA from collecting relief funds for their members and even set up picket lines at UTWA headquarters. The schism was huge and in full view of the public and the mill owners. There can be little doubt that this spat prolonged the strike.

As with prior work stoppages, civic leaders and city politicians became involved in the conflict almost as soon as the strike began. A special committee made up of seven clergymen was appointed by Mayor Mahoney to bring the strikers and the mill owners together for a settlement conference. Included on this committee were the pastors from the two large Irish parishes, Father John J. Gilday of St. Patrick's Church and Father James T. O'Reilly of St. Mary's Church. Father O'Reilly, was selected as the chairman of the committee. A decade earlier, his opposition to the violence and to certain leaders associated with the Strike of 1912 played a critical role in the lack of support for the strikers within the Irish community. He was also responsible for organizing the 40,000 person "For God and Country" parade through the city in October of 1912 to counter an earlier march by supporters of the IWW in which a "No God, No Master" banner was paraded up and down city streets.

In 1919, during a protracted winter strike in the mills, Father O'Reilly came under direct assault from the American Branch of the Socialist Party. Angered by the lack of progress in the strike, its leaders passed and published a resolution that read in part, ". . . in every labor trouble that has ever occurred in Lawrence, Father O'Reilly has always opposed the workers and been on the side of capital and has always played the part of the strike breaker."[17] Father O'Reilly responded in the papers with his own letter, exposing his intense mistrust for certain elements leading the unions.

> I reply that the charge against me is in line with their propaganda of falsehood. It is a deliberate lie. I have never taken sides against labor. In the two big strikes of 1893 and 1912 I worked harder in the interests of labor than any man amongst the labor leaders. I would have won the strike for them in 1893 had they followed my advice. In 1912, I labored late and early to gain for labor the concessions it finally received. . . . The question now, quite apparently, is whether a combination of foreign, anti-American, revolutionary forces, camouflaging as friends of labor, conducting a campaign or terrorism, . . . shall succeed in their determination to exploit the city of Lawrence for the abominable forces of radical socialism, Bolshevism, as they tried in the interest of the IWW in 1912.[18]

In 1922 Father Gilday of St. Patrick's Church was a respected opinion maker. Even more significant was Father O'Reilly. In fact, he was one of the two or three most influential men in the entire city. Given Irish dominance of city government, both priests would play a key role in the eventual resolution of this dispute. While Irish Catholics in Lawrence did not follow their pastors' lead on all matters, most in the city understood that opposition from the likes of Father O'Reilly on a given issue was not a positive development. Accordingly, he was frequently courted for his support.

As the strike dragged on through the early summer months, the bold predictions of a quick resolution by strike leader Ben Legere painfully faded. Many disillusioned and impoverished workers were becoming anxious to go back to work, but the majority continued to hold out. Intermittent instances of violence continued, although not on the scale of the Strike of 1912. Mill owners remained firm in their assertion that wages had to be reduced if they were to remain competitive with the textile mills in the south. As tensions mounted, picketing became more aggressive and the courts were called upon to reign in the strikers. One woman who had crossed the picket line found 100 picketers demonstrating outside her home. Other "scabs" were roughed up by gangs of angry strikers. Finally, an injunction was issued restricting the picketing by Ben Legere and the OBU at the Pacific Mills.

Relief efforts that summer continued, but the high number of unemployed outstripped the community's ability to respond. City Almoner, T. M. Riley, reported that suffering was becoming acute in several sections of the city, and many requests for aid from city government were being made by strikers. Regularly, the newspapers would offer accounts of striking workers and their families being evicted from their homes for failure to pay the rent, a sensitive issue in the Irish community. Finally, in mid-July, Father Gilday spoke from the pulpit at St. Patrick's and complained that wages were too low for the textile workers. Shortly thereafter, Father O'Reilly commented on the strike during his Sunday sermon, stating, "It is to the discredit of those who pay 12 percent dividends to say that they cannot afford to pay their workers a living rate of wages." According to the *Lawrence Telegram*, "he declared further that the striking textile workers of Lawrence had determined to remain on strike until given a living wage. His utterances were significant because he is one of two men appointed [to meet with mill owners] in October as to the feasibility of increasing wages at that time."[19]

On August 14, Alderman Edward Callahan called for a mass meeting on the common in hopes of "placing the responsibility for the continuance of the strike." He was frustrated by the lack of progress in the strike and hoped his intervention would force a settlement. Fellow aldermen Michael Scanlon, Peter Carr, and Pat McNulty suggested, instead, that a conference of union leaders first be called, as the "various unions were as far apart in agreement as the employers and the strikers are."[20]

Three days later, the daily newspapers printed a statement by Father O'Reilly that shook the city. The white-haired, seventy-one-year-old priest announced that he had been notified by representatives of the Pacific Mills that they would return the old wage rate on October 1, retroactive to September 5 for those workers who came back to work. He pledged his assurance that this would soon be the formal position of the mill owners, and he strongly urged the strikers to accept the offer. Though public sentiment favored settlement, the UTWA surprised everyone and rejected the offer from the mill owners. Union leaders charged that the offer they received was different from that transmitted by Father O'Reilly. It applied only to certain classes of employees, such as woolsorters and loomfitters, rather than to all striking workers.

Startled by the discrepancy, Father O'Reilly immediately issued a statement on the front page of the city newspapers indicating that the offer received by the workers was "directly at variance" to the assurances conveyed to him earlier by Pacific Mill agent Irving Southworth. He urged calm and patience while he attempted to contact Mr. Southworth, who was "unavoid-ably absent from the city for a few days." Discussions continued behind the scenes and on August 22, the Pacific Mills publicly announced an offer to the unions. This time it exactly matched the offer first outlined by Father O'Reilly one week earlier. With this news the local papers predicted that the strike was "all over but the shouting." All the other mills had moved to the same posi-tion, arguing that wages at the southern mills recently had increased, thereby making it possible for the Lawrence mills to modify their position while staying competitive.

Within days, most of the striking workers had accepted the offer, de-clared victory, and agreed to return to work. The Loomfitters, Mulespinners, and OBU rejected the offer initially. In early September, however, as workers returned to work, Ben Legere angrily declared the strike to have been "broken, and saw nothing else to do but return to work." Most strikers and objective observers felt the strike had been successful. After twenty-three weeks, it was over. One by one the mills returned to full production in the weeks that followed.

Ten years earlier, following Father O'Reilly's lead, Peter Cassidy and most of the Irish community had distanced themselves from the strikers and especially the IWW during the Strike of 1912. In fact, Peter was among a contingent of Irishmen that served as "special" policemen during the strike, buttressing the largely Irish permanent police force employed by the city. At that time he did not write any songs in support of the strikers. The open and public endorsement of the strikers by Father Gilday and Father O'Reilly during the strike of 1922, however, made it easy for Peter and Irish supporters to back the strikers in both words and deeds.

Throughout his life, Peter wrote of the lives of working men and women. Interestingly, he did not dwell so much on their difficult working conditions as he did on the people themselves, on other events that were shaping their lives, or on the politics pertaining to their employment. Though a lifelong laborer accustomed to backbreaking work, and a member of Building Labor-ers Union No. 228, Peter apparently found descriptions of work itself uninter-esting. Instead, he used his poetry and song to advance his traditional themes. In his poem "An Appeal for the Strikers," Peter made only passing mention of the circumstances surrounding the long and bitter strike of 1922. He didn't devote great attention to the plight of the strikers themselves. Instead, he dedicated most of his verse to city policemen, firemen, and school teachers, praising them for their generosity in support of the striking textile workers of the UTWA and the OBU.

An Appeal for the Strikers

In other days I wrote in praise of the Lawrence L.F.D.
And you who read then of what I said, I'm sure you will agree.
The boys are always willing to help those who are in need
They never yet refused to give to any sect or creed.

They're glad to give a helping hand and dig down in their jeans,
Each and every one of them gives according to his means.
They see that no one is in distress, if their cause is right,
That's why the boys of the L.F.D. are helping those on strike.

Our policemen too that wear the blue and patrol the city streets,
Have done their best for those in distress, now living on their beat.
They have gone among the old and young with clothing, shoes and food,
A uniform may look bad, but you'll find their hearts are good.

They always give to charity; they never refuse when appealed,
You'll find they carry sympathy in the heart beneath the shield.
They have shown it in this trouble and are working day and night,
Keeping hunger and starvation from poor families out on strike.

The janitors in the public schools are also doing their part,
With one hundred and fifty dollars they showed they have a heart.
There's more to come, a larger sum, they know that in this fight,
It's money they need to help to feed those people out on strike.

We will soon hear from the teachers, too, when their vacation's o're,
Always in the lead to help those in need, as they ever did before.
We remember them too, when we had the flu, we never can forget,
They will help again, it won't be in vain, to win this strike you bet.

To fight the owners, the strikers say, wouldn't be so very bad,
They say their worst enemy is, what they call the "scab."
When we're out to fight for a living right, they say it's a disgrace,
For anyone, old or young, to go in and take the striker's place.

So let us all give what we can, let it be large or small,
The old saying is that half a loaf is better than none at all.
So we can help those in need, and if we give our little mite,
Then the U.T.W. and the O.B.U. are sure to win their strike.

L ike most immigrant groups, the Irish used the labor movement to advance their economic, social, and political interests. By banding together for a common cause, they were able to offer protection to one another and to improve their condition in life. This same principle applied to the numerous social and fraternal organizations that existed in Lawrence. Early into the twentieth century, the city of Lawrence had a population of about 100,000 people. Many of these participated in some seventy-six different clubs and organizations and over 200 fraternal and charitable societies scattered throughout the city. Almost every nationality and religious creed had a club or society, and while most were started by and for men, many groups also formed a women's auxiliary. All had their own bylaws, governance structures, and membership requirements and many owned their own permanent buildings for meetings and functions. By 1918 at least ninety-six of these organizations were considered secret societies, which represented thirty-seven distinct orders and a wide range of ethnic cultures.[21] The Ancient Order of the Hibernians, AOH, was one of the largest and most influential fraternal organizations in the city with three separate divisions in existence at one time. In addition to governance structures, each of these fraternal societies had its own unique rituals for initiation and ongoing membership, with passwords, symbols, handshakes, oaths, dress, mutual aid functions, and lofty fraternal goals. Each created its own culture around a specific theme. For example, the Masons used symbols and terminology of the stonemason's trade, and the "Redmen" developed rituals loosely based on the traditions of the American Indian.

Peter Cassidy was a member of many fraternal organizations throughout his life. During the 1890s he helped organize Company A of the Hibernian Rifles, along with Timothy Fitzgerald, who would later become a longtime president of the AOH, Division 1. Peter was a member and chief ranger of the Catholic Order of Foresters (COF), Court of St. Patrick #735, an organization for Catholic men that met regularly at Remmes' Hall next to St. Patrick's Church. The COF culture was based on the legend of Robin Hood and admitted Catholic men of "good moral character." Its mission was to provide members of the parish with legal assistance, life insurance and other aid when in need.[22] Another mutual aid society that Peter belonged to was the Fraternal Order of Rangers (FOR), Columbia Lodge #1, that met at Bugbee Hall, 292 Essex Street on the second and fourth Wednesday of each month.[23]

Peter was most actively involved, however, in Lawrence Lodge #440 of the Loyal Order Of Moose (LOOM). He was elected trustee of his lodge, and also its outer guard, a position he held for over two decades. His responsibilities centered on insuring that only members were admitted to the lodge hall. Although the list of officers was heavily weighted with Irish names, the LOOM was open to many nationalities, reflecting the slowly changing view of

The organizers of the Hibernian Rifles strike a formal pose, circa 1896. Left to right, Lieutenant Timothy Fitzgerald, Captain Sullivan, and Peter Cassidy. Courtesy the Cassidy Collection.

ethnic segregation. Most of the Irish politicians in the city were members of the Moose and Elks clubs in addition to their membership in the AOH. Such fraternal groups provided the base for their political support, gave them numerous opportunities to be seen and to speak, and helped keep them in touch with the other prominent men of the city.[24]

In addition to its monthly meetings, Moose Lodge #440 also conducted regular smoke talks for members and guests. Greatly anticipated and always well attended, a typical program looked like the one held on December 5, 1913, at Mule Spinners Hall. Some 500 guests were treated to a rich and diverse evening of entertainment that featured a piano selection by Edward Goddis; a song by Isadore Raymond; an athletic exhibition by "Kid Sullivan" and Tommy Carson; a boxing match between Scotty Grey and Frankie Regan; a reading by Frank Flagg; an address, "The Good of the Order," by Mayor Michael A. Scanlon; a vocal duet by John and William Carey; "fifteen minutes with Irish Comedian Peter Cassidy;" and an address by James M. Cadogan (who was hoping to be elected alderman the following week). Peter served frequently on the planning or social committees for such functions at the Moose and other fraternal organizations. Most often, he would read his poems, sing Irish songs and parodies, or perform a comedy routine for all to enjoy.[25]

In the spring of each year, every Moose Lodge was expected to hold a Sunday memorial service for its departed members. On April 12, 1915, Lodge #440 held its annual service at the Eagles Hall where hundreds of members joined with the relatives and friends of deceased Moose members to pay their respects. The evening was a solemn affair with prayer, music, and speeches. Secretary Trembly solemnly read the names of the departed.[26]

Moose members took their nickname, the PAPs, from their motto "Purity, Aid and Progress." Members had to have *purity* of words, thoughts, and intentions; give *aid* to members and their families through relief and employment; and believe in *progress.* When the Moose Lodge was first formed in 1888, it took the best principles from all other societies to create a new one "that welcomes the enrollment of the laborer, the mechanic, the business man, and the professional man" in a manner that can bring the world nothing but "peace, harmony and brotherly love. All go to make up this great herd . . . One for all, all for one . . . over six hundred thousand members in these United States."[27]

Only Christian men could be lodge members and like most societies of this kind its emphasis was on support for the wives and children of deceased members. Fund-raising activities were ongoing—with regular whist card parties, boxing matches, and yearly fairs open to the public. One of the largest fund-raisers for the PAPs was the Moose Bazaar. The 1914 fair was held at city hall for a full week starting the 5th of May. Peter Cassidy was joined on the organizing committee by Mayor Michael A. Scanlon, Robert Maloney, Peter McGuire, Dictator Bernard O'Donnell, Carl Donavan, Mike Conlon, and several others. Each evening throughout the week, from 7:30 to midnight, thousands of Lawrencians passed through city hall for entertainment and to patronize booths offering teddy bears, moose pillows, ringing watches, a fish pond, embroidered articles, candy, ice cream, and refreshments. Opening night guests saw a minstrel show with performers from Lowell, Boston, Gardner, and Fitchburg. A special contest was also held as young ladies wearing green bows mingled with the crowd ready to award a five dollar gold piece to the first person to approach them and ask, "Are you interested in the Loyal Order of the Moose of Lawrence?"

Daily accounts of the previous night's events were highlighted in the Lawrence newspapers, including this article that reported on the next-to-last night of the fair.

> During the concert program last night, a sensation was caused by the rendition for the first time in public of Peter Cassidy's new song dedicated to the Moose. It was sung by Joe Patterson of Boston, "the boy with the girl's voice," and was most favorably received. Mr. Cassidy is a well-known employee of the street department, a special policeman, a member of Lawrence Lodge 440 L.O.O.M., St. Patrick's Court, C.O.F., and Columbia Lodge 1, F.O.R. He lives in South Lawrence. The usual artists performed throughout the evening, singing some of the

latest successes. Dancing was enjoyed from 10 o'clock to midnight. The chorus from Mr. Cassidy's song will be sung throughout the country at Moose fairs and other festivities of the organization.[28]

The following night at the close of events, it was announced that Michael Coan of 78 Prospect Street won the gold coin, and Peter's twenty-year-old daughter Frances was awarded third prize in the Queen of the Carnival contest.

The Order of the Moose

The poem below by Bro. P. F. Cassidy of Lawrence, Mass., has been set to music, by Brother F. Le Suer and can be had by lodges at 25c the sheet:

To all men we give a greeting
And we're always glad to greet them,
For our aim in life is to help the weak
and aid we ne'er refuse to
The orphans, wives and mothers,
To our sick and desolate brothers,
For we always help each other,
In our order of the Moose.

We've no brothers to distress,
For we always do our best,
When we give to them a helping hand
Their friendship we can't lose.
For our creed is Christianity
And our motto: "Give to charity."
For we stand for love and purity
In our Order of the Moose.

Come, be brothers and join us
Friends in need you'll always find us,
For companionship and good fellowship
None better can you choose.

We'll be always glad to meet you,
And like brothers we will greet you,
With a "How-dy Pap" we'll greet you,
In the Order of the Moose.

Sometime later in 1914, Peter found himself in the position of having a poem written about him when *The Leader* ran the following story. In one of his scrapbooks, Peter indicated that the anonymous author was actually fellow Moose member and friend John Manning. It read:

"The following deserved tribute to our Bard of The Shanty Pond, Mr. Peter F. Cassidy, is from the pen of an anonymous correspondent, who signs himself "Rube." This nom-de-plume is a misnomer as a reading of the verse will suggest."

If I were but a poet, the praises I would sing
Of the man who made the Spicket famous and its name around us ring.
He loves the river Shannon—not for glory understand,
But for the memory that it brings of his old native land.
In song he sang its praises and his lyrics stood the test,
But, friends, I find his latest song to be by far the best.
For the title he has chosen, he offers no excuse,
He calls his latest ballad "The Order of the Moose."
You cannot help but like it, this eternal melody—
'Twas writ to aid our P.A.P. by Peter Cassidy. [29]

During World War I, Peter's support of the war effort on the homefront included sending letters, songs, and poems to the soldiers serving in Battery C, a popular artillery unit made up almost entirely of Lawrence men. Hoping to boost their spirits, he would mail them copies of his work that had been published in the local papers. One poem, "A Letter to Phil Riley," was sent to a favorite neighbor who had lived in Shanty Pond since coming to Lawrence as a child at the turn of the century. In many ways Riley personified the typical resident of Shanty Pond. He was not a great man in terms of his life's accomplishments, nor was he particularly ambitious or influential in the way society often measures successful or powerful individuals. To Peter, however, he was a special friend, a character widely known and very well liked by the Shanty Pond community. Like the Irish cop or the parish priest, Riley was an icon in his own small way and treasured by Peter for who he was. Peter's poem offered readers in Lawrence a warm and affectionate picture of the Phil Riley known to the residents of South Broadway before the war, when this vibrant young man, "Smiling Phil Riley," roamed Shanty Pond.

A Letter to Phil Riley

Phil Riley, Oh, Phil Riley, Come home for just a while,
We miss that red head of yours, likewise your Irish smile.
Things don't quite seem the same, we can't tell night from day,
Everything looks gloomy, Phil, since you left South Broadway.

There's something wrong with all the girls; they all seem quite sad,
Since the day you went away, they said it was too bad.
Not a smile upon their faces, not a jolly word they'll say;
They're thinking of you, Riley, since you left South Broadway.

Everything's so quiet, Phil, around old Tiger Three;
There's no such noise among the boys as what there used to be.
The backroom don't look so bright where the pool you used to play,
Oh, Riley, how we've missed you, since you left South Broadway.

The summer time is coming, Phil; what will we do at all.
We won't have no Irish manager when the "Hurleys" play baseball.
There'll be no one to raise a row, or the umpire lad to flay,
When he gives a bum decision against the boys of South Broadway.

I hear you're quite a cook, Phil; you don't go in the trench,
And that you can parley vous in Irish as in French.
They tell me you'll get married, Phil, to a French ma-ansell so gay,
Phil, if you do, I'm telling you, keep her away from South Broadway.

Give my regards to Johnson, Jack Regan and the rest,
And don't forget Kloby and Luck, I wish them all the best.
When you lads all come back again, for one thing we'll all pray,
That you will bring old Kaiser Bill and show him South Broadway.

When Peter Cassidy wrote "A Letter to Phil Riley" in the spring of 1918, it had been about seven months since several thousand young men had left the city to fight in France. Peter was fifty-eight years old at the time and living in a second-floor apartment at 57 South Broadway amidst a cluster of taverns in Shanty Pond and next door to the Conlin and Ryan funeral parlor. An unskilled patronage laborer much of his life, Peter rarely worked for more than six to eight months a year. The rest of his time he spent fraternizing with his Irish friends in the homes and at the bars and the shops around Shanty Pond. He often frequented the nearby fire station, Engine House #3—Tiger Three. Along with others, Peter spent many a day hanging around Tiger Three with the men on duty—playing cards or pool, smoking cigars, telling jokes, and swapping local gossip. It was along South Broadway, and perhaps at Tiger Three, that Peter first came to know young Phil Riley.

Born on June 22, 1894, in County Cavan, Ireland, Riley and his sisters became orphans shortly after his birth.[30] In the years that followed, relatives made arrangements for them to go to America. As was required of all immigrants, each of the Riley children had to have sponsors who pledged to care and support their charges. Because few families had the ability to provide for more than one additional mouth, Phil and each of his sisters were raised in different homes once they arrived in Lawrence. Though not ideal, it was better than an orphanage.

Like most young men of his time, Riley quit school after the seventh grade and started working as a peddler. By 1910 he was hired to work for an undertaker at Conlin and Ryan's Funeral Home at 59 South Broadway. Over the next six years he boarded at five different locations along South Broadway, traveling the streets of Shanty Pond and passing time with the locals. He later worked as a laborer for the Lawrence Property and Parks Department, and as an iron worker just prior to the war.

As a young man Phil Riley quickly developed quite a favorable reputation among the residents of South Lawrence. He was affectionately known as "Smiling Phil Riley" and was one of the most popular figures to live in Shanty Pond. According to those who knew him, he would "light up any room he walked into," and was friendly to everyone he met. As a parks department employee, Phil would travel throughout the city with his lawn mower and rake, keeping city ballfields ready for play. At every location, he would take the time to shake hands, talk baseball, and always flash his famous smile. Though he earned only about thirty to thirty-five dollars a week, he was generous to a fault. After getting paid on Tuesday evenings, he would cross over the bridge onto South Broadway and pass by the row of taverns where he would be greeted by those less fortunate. Unfailingly, he would offer a good word, a pat on the back, and then reach deep into his pocket to give some of his pay to those in need. A newspaper story said it best: "If you want some experience, just walk down the street with Phil. You will begin to realize that there is hardly a man, woman or child that does not know him, and everywhere he is being greeted with the enthusiasm that is given to presidents."[31]

Phil loved the game of baseball. As a teen he was a pitcher for the Ramblers Athletic Club and a number of other amateur baseball teams. He sometimes played for several different teams at once. With the start of the 1914 season, he began to manage the "J. J. Hurleys," an amateur team in Lawrence made up of young hopefuls in their late teens and early twenties. On most every Saturday starting in April, Phil Riley and "the Hurleys" could be found playing baseball. Home games would bring out the faithful to the field behind the Wetherbee school in the heart of Shanty Pond. In 1915 and 1917, Riley also helped run the successful mayoral campaigns of team sponsor, John J. Hurley, a South Lawrence businessman. As a player, employee, manager, and citizen, Phil Riley gained a reputation for being a good sport, a hard worker, a solid player, and an effective leader. To all who knew him, he was a very special person.

When the United States declared war against Germany on April 6, 1917, Riley responded the very next day to the president's call for volunteers. He was twenty-two years old at the time and like most of his friends from South

Phil Riley, without a cap, and the 1916 Hurley's baseball team. Courtesy of Rosemary O'Neill.

Lawrence he joined Battery C, 102nd Field Artillery. At the end of July, Phil left home with his buddies and headed off to war. Unlike his buddies, however, who were directly engaged in combat, Private Riley served in France as one of the unit's cooks. His daily struggle was with how to provide meals for the hundreds of hungry frontline troops, most of whom were friends from back home. By all accounts he performed well. While overseas, soldiers regularly wrote home sharing brief stories from the trenches, and the old gang back on South Broadway relished hearing the gossip about their boys. Frequently, the local papers would make mention of young Phil Riley and his culinary exploits. It wasn't until the troops from Battery C returned to Lawrence on April 11, 1919, however, that the details of Phil's wartime adventures finally made the local papers.

"Smiling Phil Riley's Reception Committee," read one headline over a picture showing Phil surrounded by a group of smiling veterans back in Lawrence. "Smiling Phil Is Happy to Be Back," read another about Phil's return to South Broadway. "'By golly, it's great to be back in the 'old Patch,'" said 'Smiling' Phil Riley as he peered into the west from in front of Dave Daley's store on South Broadway Friday afternoon." Phil was holding court on his home turf once again and everyone was listening. "As is usually the case when Phil is around, he was in the center of the group, and they drank in every word—yes, every syllable—of his experiences overseas. Wherever Phil is, there is good feeling, . . . [his] smile is infectious. When he gets laughing, the circle he is in. . . does the same thing."[32]

Phil always had the knack of telling a convincing story, but his experiences abroad provided him with the tools to craft gripping tales of his heroism at the front lines. One close friend from Battery C, John "Spec" Donovan, recounted how Phil would linger endlessly over the table at the Red Cross canteen drinking coffee and eating homemade doughnuts, while keeping the wide-eyed hostess enthralled with his adventures from the trenches. Having heard of so many of Phil's trips "over the top," Spec and the rest of the unit began to wonder "whether or not he had gone over sometime when they were not looking." In fact, Spec finally became so tired of hearing him boast to the ladies, that he "clouted Phil across the face, while the canteen worker, who had followed the red haired lad to the door in awe-ful [sic] admiration, saw her hero sprawled in the gutter with one blow." Phil conceded to the reporter that he deserved what he had gotten from Spec.[33]

Though he never married, his blue eyes, flaming red hair, wit and charm made Phil especially popular with women. Upon his return, one newspaper confronted him with the same rumor that Peter Cassidy wrote about in his poem, namely, that Phil had married a "French mademoiselle." If true, many a young woman's heart would have been broken in South Lawrence. Phil laughed the story off and blamed it on friends who had played baseball for the

Tremont Street team in North Lawrence. According to the paper, "With characteristic vehemence, the cherubic Phil denied any such allegation and said 'it's that Billy Menzie and [that] jealous Tremont bunch that's spreading such news about me. Tell the world and 'across the Spicket' that I'm still free but willing to marry some nice Lawrence girl and settle down to peace and quiet forever more.'"[34]

Phil soon reestablished his place in the social circles of Lawrence. On April 30, 1919, the day after his honorable discharge from the army, his picture was the centerpiece of another newspaper story announcing that the "Gaiety Club Will Hold a Party. . . . The Gaiety Club is comprised of all well-known and popular young ladies. . . .'Smiling Phil' Riley of Battery C, who just returned from overseas, is an aid at the Gaiety Club and is working hard among his many friends to make [the party] a big success."[35]

Phil initially survived World War I, but suffered permanent damage from a mustard gas attack while at the front. It wasn't long before he was forced to seek medical help. In May of 1920 he began to schedule regular visits to a local physician, Dr. Levek, complaining of a persistent cough, shortness of breath, "night sweats," and of tiring easily. Over the next three years, his symptoms continued and worsened until late in 1924 when Dr. Levek strongly urged that he enter the hospital. Frightened by this recommendation, Phil Riley stopped visiting the doctor for care.

By January of 1928 his condition had worsened considerably. He had been unable to hold a steady job for some time. Desperate and frightened, he returned to Dr. Levek for help. All of his symptoms had become acute. His cough was incessant and bloody; he was very short of breath; he had lost his appetite and dropped from 145 pounds to 125 pounds in three months. Too sick and scared to resist, he was admitted to the Veterans Hospital in Rutland, Massachusetts, on February 10 for treatment. In their initial assessment, the VA doctors found that Phil had "massive infiltration" of tuberculosis in both lungs and the larynx. Their summary of his long-term prognoses was listed simply as "bad." He had stayed away from care for too long.

Though his condition steadily deteriorated, Phil Riley kept his smile and spirit, and was as popular at the hospital as he was along South Broadway. Sensing the seriousness of his condition, he went AWOL from the hospital in March of 1929 and headed back to visit Shanty Pond one last time. He soon returned to Rutland, and weeks later, on April 24, 1929, he died at the age of thirty-four. A letter sent to his sisters by hospital officials listed everything he had left behind: a carry bag, a silk scarf, a topcoat, one suit, a cup, a unionsuit, four pair of socks, a belt, four dress shirts, and one necktie.

Later that year, on November 11, 1929, Phil Riley was honored by his friends and the Veterans of Foreign Wars when the playground just west of old

Shanty Pond was dedicated to him. On a sunny and balmy Sunday afternoon, several hundred soldiers marched down South Broadway and Salem Street to the ballfield on Everett Street. There they were joined by hundreds of relatives and friends, including Peter, who had come to reminisce and pay tribute to Smiling Phil Riley.

————

Peter lived at a time when great changes were occurring in the lives of women, and he wrote numerous poems about the Irish women in Lawrence. In fact, women are the most frequent subject of his poetry and songs. While most married women stayed home to raise their children, many began to walk a different path, some by choice and some out of economic necessity. Women were working out of the home more than ever before in history. For most, it was not a career but simply a means of paying the rent, supporting the family, and biding time until the right man came along. Having lived in a house with a wife and seven daughters, Peter had ample opportunity to develop an understanding and appreciation for the opposite sex. All of his daughters worked in the mills or factories once they reached their late teens. When married, they all left gladly. Only stepdaughter Margaret remained single throughout of her life.

Unlike most other immigrant groups, Irishwomen came to America in numbers relatively equal to those of Irishmen. Due to changing conditions in Ireland, most were single and unaccompanied by parents or spouses. In post-Famine Ireland there was less opportunity than there ever had been for young women. Parents were able to offer what dowries they could for only one daughter. Land inheritance, albeit limited to begin with, tended to go only to one son instead of being divided among many. Without land, fewer young men could support new brides and families. Without dowries, eligible women could offer men little to help start a home. Jobs were scarce for men and almost nonexistent for women. There was little reason to stay in Ireland.

Once they arrived in America, Irishwomen went to work, usually in the textile mills or as domestic servants for middle- and upper-middle-class Protestants. Relatively speaking, domestic work paid a reasonable wage when one considers that accommodations frequently accompanied employment. It was also "clean" work compared to that in the mills and factories. Immigrant women were more likely than their male counterparts to save money, and they often sent it back to Ireland to relieve suffering or pay steerage for another family member. Though they continued to work in the mills and homes of others, over time, women also branched out into roles as teachers, nuns, secretaries, nurses, and store clerks. Women secured the right to vote in 1920, but did not see an immediate benefit in terms of election to political office in

Lawrence. It would be a year before the first woman was appointed to the police force and three quarters of a century before a woman would sit in the mayor's seat.

Peter frequently wrote songs about women, although he rarely devoted entire poems to well-known or identifiable women. It was still a man's world, and he was a product of his time. He admired a woman's contributions and work ethic, but he was quick to notice her beauty as well. The following sampling of Peter's poems offers a glimpse of his views of Irishwomen and prevailing attitudes about them.

When "My Irish Valentine" was published, Peter was well into his sixties. His verse presents a classic and very nostalgic portrayal of a young Irish colleen who selflessly remains on the farm with her aging parents rather than running off to America like many of her friends. Peter idolized this fictional colleen for her beauty, carriage, and grace. He appeared more impressed, however, by her faithfulness to Ireland and her parents. During the early part of the twentieth century, staying on the family farm actually would have been a significant gesture by a young, attractive, and eligible woman. Land was scarce, work was very hard, and there was little in the way of reimbursement. Most of the eligible men would have long since left for the United States, as had most young women. Peter's colleen would have noticed increasing numbers of aging spinsters in her village or parish. Before long, she too would be old, alone, and poor. While several of Peter's daughters cared for him and Maggie until their deaths, spending one's golden years in a large textile center contrasted starkly with the pastoral scene Peter paints in verse. It was a compelling portrait of a life-style no longer possible in the urban mill towns of the Northeast, but forever present in the minds of countless first generation Irish immigrants.

My Irish Valentine

In the village close to Dingle there lives a pretty colleen:
I have traveled all o'er Ireland but no fairer one I've seen.
She's a real Irish beauty; the equal you can't find
Of this country lass, a colleen Dhas. My Irish Valentine.

She's fairer than the Venus both in carriage and in pose;
Her hair is blonde—she wears it long, has cheeks like a rose.
This country girl has teeth of pearl; her eyes like stars do shine.
You couldn't but love this colleen Oge. My Irish Valentine.

She doesn't use paint or powder, she don't wear flashy clothes,
And she's as sweet as any flower that in a garden grows.
All the while she has a smile, she wears it all the time;
Beauty and grace show in the face of my Irish Valentine.

The farm and cottage both are small where she makes her abode,
It's known as a beauty spot that's along the Dingle road.
Her name I will not tell you now, I may some other time;
Those going to Mass, the home they pass of my Irish Valentine.

The reason she does not marry? Both her parents they are old;
With them she will tarry till God calls them to his fold.
She loves the farm, the cottage where the ivy around entwines,
That's why she said she'll stay unwed, will my Irish Valentine.

In his poem "The Girl at City Hall," Peter took a look at women working in Lawrence rather than Ireland. As Irish politicians took over city hall, Irish women went to work as secretaries and clerks. Written sometime during the Depression, this unnamed secretary apparently caught the eye of many a man standing in the unemployment line down at city hall. Though his subject is not what Peter would call "beautiful," he described her as having splendid carriage, two little dimples, and teeth that were white and even. Above all else, she was charming, graceful and good-natured. Like the Irish colleen, this girl from city hall was the quintessence of womanhood in Peter's eyes. Though he did not mention her name, it is interesting to imagine whether she really existed, or if she was merely another stereotype of his day.

The Girl at City Hall

Let me tell you of a charming girl,
That works in City Hall.
Like all the rest she is neat in dress,
In looks she has the call.
One and all they seem to like her,
And tell you the reason why,
She gives all a pleasant greeting
Whenever she goes by.

She has a splendid carriage,
Her face is that of a saint,
Her cheeks are like the red, red rose
From nature, not from paint.
Her teeth are white and even,
And when you see her smile
She shows two little dimples
That would any heart beguile.

Her black hair looks so splendid
Above her eyes of dark brown,
Her nose is like a Grecian model—
A lovely mouth so round.
I first saw her in the corridor
One day when through she did pass,
When I heard a Scotchman remark:
"There goes a bonny lass."

'Twas my eyes opened wide,
As I saw this girl so fair,
So I walked around, upstairs and down,
I saw none other that could compare.
I watched her while at her machine
Her typing she enjoyed,
I have seen her now, most every day
As I talked with the unemployed.

Many's the time, I've watched her
Through the plate glass in the door
As she steps so light and graceful,
When she walks along the floor.
She seem to be so attractive
That it's often I would stop
And on her gaze, as I a daze,
Till moved on by the cop.

I would not say she is beautiful,
But she has style and poise,
With a voice sweet as an angel's
Her face with good nature shows.
The unemployed in the corridors,
That are always standing around
Always watch the elevator,
To see her going up or down.

It seems they are all in love with her,
If so, you can't them blame,
There are many of you who know this girl;
I will not give her name.
I have told you what I've seen of her,
So I think this is about all,
Take a tip from me, if this girl you'd see,
Go down to the City Hall.

First to the Irish countryside and then to city hall, Peter took another look at a woman's life in Lawrence, this time through the eyes of a "Girl in the Paper Mill." As before, he described her beauty in simple terms as seen through the eyes of a suitor named Pete. The poem draws attention to the relief she shows when she is able to find a man, marry him, and leave the mill. Life in the mills and factories of Lawrence was grueling for men and women. In addition to the rigors of the work itself, they had to endure the heat, dust, and filth that characterized this work environment. Women had to face one other challenge, however. Considerable sexual harassment and abuse occurred in the mills, especially from floor supervisors who would take advantage of young women desperately in need of work. On numerous occasions, *The Leader* would comment on such conditions in the mills. "I wonder if the decent and moral girls are compelled to make room for the casts-offs of the other mills, or are they forced to leave for not catering to the cheap section-hands and male help. I wonder if any decent married or unmarried woman would not rather lose her position and be idle, than lose her morals, her character, and her self respect by following actions of those who let the male help fondle and caress them."[36] For many women, marriage was their means of escape from such working conditions. It was their salvation.

The Girl in the Paper Mill

They say there's a great commotion up on Prospect Hill,
The cause it is a beauty who works in the paper mill.
She surely is good looking, but I have one in my mind.
This girl isn't there and can't compare with the Shanty Valentine.

I know this girl is beautiful, for that I will admit;
She's what Ziegfeld's looking for, an up to date brunette.
She should be in the movies, a talkie or a still
In Hollywood. She never should, work in the paper mill.

I first beheld her beauty; it was at the German ball.
Now she isn't Dutch, don't think such; she's not that kind at all.
She's one of those Irish colleens, who's beauty gives you a thrill—
To help her pa and dear mama, she works in the paper mill.

When I saw her glide around the floor I surely was amazed:
I know she was dumbfounded at the way at her I'd gaze.
She spoke and said, "You'll know me again." Says I, "I certainly will,
But allow me, Miss, I knew you before, you worked in the paper mill."

To a seat she went, quite discontent, I thought I'd take a chance,
To go over to this beauty and ask her to give me a dance.
When I saw those eyes, I was surprised—I surely got a thrill.
In a voice so quiet she said, "You're right, I work in the paper mill."

I said, "Don't be offended," as I whispered in her ear,
"You certainly are beautiful, the best looking girl that's here."
She gave me a stare, I could swear another man 'twould kill.
When he said too bad she ever had, to work in the paper mill.

She said, "My beauty is all my own, so why make such a fuss;
The boys all know I've got a beau—the driver of a bus
On the coast-to-coast, and it's his boast he never had a spill,
Me and him soon will honeymoon, away from the paper mill."

'Twas yesterday I took a stroll and walked up Prospect Street.
A couple was coming toward me, this beauty I did meet.
I said "How do?" She said, "How are you" Introduce me if you will:
She said, "Pete, my husband meet, I'm no more in the paper mill."

A mid-1930s aerial view of Shanty Pond and the Patch. The two-story, white house located near the lower left-hand corner was Peter's home on Everett Street from 1925 to 1938. Courtesy of the Lawrence Public Library.

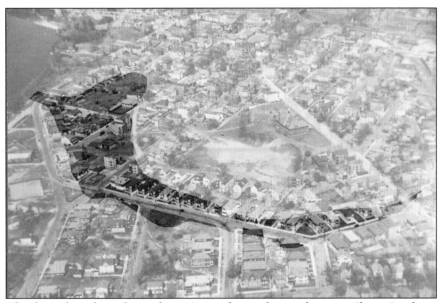

The above photo shows the pond superimposed over what was known as Shanty Pond.

*Maggie Cassidy with two of her grandchildren, Joseph (on left)
and "Buddy" Blanchette. They were the sons of Frances Cassidy
and Edgar Blanchette. Circa 1930*

6

The Irish Go to War

Historically, the Irish have responded vigorously to the call to defend their new land in times of war. Large numbers of Irishmen fought with Washington during the Revolution, and between 150,000 and 200,000 Irish soldiers were engaged during the American Civil War, most of whom fought for the northern cause. During the war with Spain in 1898, the Irish again came forward and served with great distinction. Like those immigrants who came before him, Peter Cassidy was a loyal patriot who had great love for his new homeland. As a young man, he volunteered to serve in Company F of Lawrence's old Ninth Regiment Militia, but never served in the armed forces during wartime. He did, however, play an active role on the homefront during World War I as a volunteer in the Massachusetts State Guard. He contributed further by using his poems and songs to boost morale and encourage patriotic spirit. This was especially true from 1916 to 1919, when the local newspapers offered readers regular accounts of the growing turmoil in Mexico and in Europe.

His song "When We Get to Mexico" probably was written sometime in June of 1916, as men from Lawrence were heading off for an invasion of Mexico along with troops from around the nation. As is typical of Peter's wartime songs, it is full of patriotism, pride, history, and bravado. The long-smoldering hostility between the United States and Mexico flared up as the Mexican civil war spilled over onto U.S. soil. The opposing Mexican leaders, General Victoriano Huerta and Venustiano Carranza, struggled for power with Carranza eventually winning out.

In 1914 Mexican soldiers seized the crew of the U.S.S. Dolphin. President Woodrow Wilson ordered the navy to the port of Vera Cruz where hostilities broke out and 126 Mexican soldiers died. Wilson was widely criticized around the world for overreacting. In 1915 a Mexican rebel named

Pancho Villa revolted against Carranza, and began a series of raids on American citizens and property. In January of 1916 Villa repeatedly led a band of marauders across the Rio Grande into New Mexico and Texas, killing or capturing dozens of American citizens. Wilson sent General John Pershing and 6,000 soldiers some 300 miles into Mexico in search of Villa, dead or alive. War fever surged across the United States. For over two years, the Lawrence newspapers regularly gave the hostilities front-page coverage. The local citizenry was well informed and primed for President Wilson's call for troops in 1916. As was often the case, Peter had something to say about the conflict and, more important, about the willingness of Irish patriots to fight for America.

When We Get to Mexico

The call to arms has sounded, and we answered it like men.
Our ancestor fought in Mexico, and we'll fight there again.
For the starry flag must always fly, in the land of friend or foe,
To protect those stars, the strips and bars, we are off to Mexico.

Chorus:
We are on our way to Mexico,
That's the place we're going to go,
And to the whole world, we can show
That we'll fight for the U.S.A.
We are Yankee soldiers through and through,
And we'll fight for the red, white and blue,
And we'll show Carranza what we can do
When we get to Mexico.

In the war with Spain some years ago, to the front we went
  and fought you know,
And we are always proud to go and fight for Uncle Sam.
We left home and friends when we fought in Spain
And we'll do the same again.
Though we cross the boundless Texas plain
To fight in Mexico.

(Chorus)

On Monday, June 9, 1916, the front page of the *Lawrence Telegram* read, "Local Militia Answers Call of the President." A telephone call shortly after midnight had notified the 125 National Guard members from Lawrence's Battery C, First Battalion, Light Artillery, that they were to report for active duty by 9:00 a.m. At 6:25 a.m., ten strokes sounded on the fire alarm throughout the city, and two other units from Lawrence were also called to report to the armory: Company L of the Ninth Regiment and Company F of the Eighth Regiment. Volunteers signed up at a rapid pace that day to augment the strength of what was a peacetime militia in Massachusetts. Peter Cassidy's future son-in-law, a twenty-year-old named Edgar Blanchette, was among the troops from Battery C called for duty that day. Edgar, or "Scoots" as he was known, had been living in the Patch for about ten years. The Blanchettes were one of many Canadian families that had moved into the Shanty Pond area, a sign of the changing times.

Battery C left Lawrence for Mexico in June of 1916 but returned home in early November of that same year without having seen any combat. In July, 1916, a special commission was set up to resolve the Mexican crisis, and in January 1917, the remaining U.S. troops were ordered back to the United States by Wilson. Poncho Villa remained at large.

The troops had barely arrived home from the Mexican conflict when the United States was finally dragged into the brutal war that had been raging in Europe for almost three years. The day after Congress declared war against the Axis powers on April 6, 1917, the call went out for volunteers. Almost immediately the recruiting station in Lawrence was flooded with young men anxious to "fight the Hun." In the months that followed, the city and the nation focused their energies on preparing to send a fighting force overseas.

In Lawrence, the existing National Guard units were called up to serve as the core of the mobilization effort. These units included infantry Company L of the Eighth Regiment, Company F of the Ninth Regiment, and the light artillery unit, Battery C. Many of Peter Cassidy's younger friends were among the volunteers who left Lawrence that spring and summer. They included numerous South Lawrence men such as Phil Riley, Francis Leahy, Jack Regan, Matt Linehan, Bill Jordan, Ed Coughlin, and about 175 other men from the South Broadway area. In all, some 6,000 Lawrencians served in the armed services during the war. About one third of these reached the front lines and actually participated in the fighting. Nearly 500 Lawrence men served with the famous 26th or "Yankee" Division, which was made up almost entirely of Massachusetts men. It was the first complete American division to land in France.[1]

While Lawrence men were scattered throughout the armed forces, the interests of the local citizenry were focused mainly on the men in the Yankee Division: Companies F and L, and Battery C of the 102nd Field Artillery—all members of the Yankee Division. During the war, not a day would pass without the newspapers running stories on the troops serving with the 26th

Peter Cassidy's future son-in-law, Edgar "Scoots" Blanchette was a member of Battery C. He served in the 1916 Mexican conflict and on the front lines in France, 1917-18. Courtesy the Cassidy Collection.

Division. At first, the papers followed the men's departure from Lawrence to area training camps and then to Montreal or New York where they shipped over to France. On July 26, 1917, Battery C left Lawrence for training in Boxford, Massachusetts. It then headed to Hoboken, New Jersey, where the troops boarded *The Finland* and set sail for France on September 23.

Peter wrote several songs expressing the thoughts of those who witnessed the departure of troops from Lawrence. One was written from the perspective of a mother whose son was marching off to war, and another from a son who tries to calm his mother's worse fears.

I'm Proud, My Boy, You Are a Soldier

A mother, now a widow, watched the soldiers marching by,
The call had come for them to mobilize.
In the ranks was her son, in uniform with gun,
Though she cheered them on the tears had filled her eyes,
How her heart must ache with pain for she sees the sight again
When her husband as a soldier marched away.
He fell fighting the foe in far Santiago—
But she kissed her boy, and motherly did say:

Chorus:
I'm proud to see my boy a soldier,
Though it makes me sad to see you go away.
I'm proud to see a gun upon your shoulder,
Ready to defend the U.S.A.
Your country's calling you, go fight for it. Do!
Show yourself a soldier and a man!
Go face the foe, my lad, if you die fighting like your dad.
I'll be proud to say you died for Uncle Sam.

As the boy and mother bid farewell, two hearts beat as one,
Perhaps that they might never meet again,
For a husband and a father never had returned.
Since he fought in the war with Spain.
Now his son answers the call; perhaps in battle he might fall,
Like his dad did to defend the dear old flag.
But the mother, still she cheered, though for her son she feared,
So she kissed him once again and then she said:

(Chorus)

The Conscription's Farewell

Now the U.S.A. is at war today and my country calls on me
To get ready to go to meet the foe that is far across the sea
My sweetheart true must leave you also my mother dear
Though it breaks my heart that we must part, I'll return again don't fear.

Refrain:
Good-bye sweetheart we must part; farewell, mother, I'm going away,
I'm going to fight for the Stars and Stripes, as a soldier of the U.S.A.
I'm off to war where the cannons roar, with the thousands I'll take a chance.
I'll return again if I'm not slain in the trenches somewhere in France.

2

I will write to you and mother, too, when I get over there
When you write to me my address will deliver in France somewhere
For I'll be fighting among the shells and bombs trying always to advance
I'll pray the Lard to give me life to live to return somewhere from France.

(Refrain)

3
Mother do not mourn for I'll return when this cruel war is o'er
If I'm not maimed or among the slain, I might return before
When on furlough to you I'll go no matter where you'll be
And sweetheart true I'll think of you and I hope you'll pray for me.

(Refrain)

Two weeks after leaving New Jersey, the troops landed in St. Nazaire, France, and began several months of intense training away from the front lines. It wasn't until February 3, 1918, that Battery C fired its first round at the enemy near the city of Soissons on the Chemin-des-Dames front. Sergeant Bernard Lynch's gun crew, which included Cassidy acquaintances Thomas "Kloby" Corcoran and Bill Jordan, reveled in this honor. Although Battery C's role in the fight against Germany lasted less than a year, it was in the thick of most key battles along the front until the end of the war. Kloby Corcoran received notoriety in battle as a volunteer in what became known as the "Sacrifice Battery," a temporary unit led by Sergeant Edward O'Leary of Lawrence. Along with eleven volunteers from the 102nd Field Artillery, Kloby set out on what was considered a suicide mission. Advancing well ahead of the rest of the Allied line, Kloby, O'Leary, and the others were asked to defend a bend in the road leading into the town of Siecheprey. They were to hold it open for passage by a much-needed ammunition train and supply wagons.

Knowing that the Allies' westerly drive was in peril, the volunteers advanced up the road to the infamous "Dead Man's Curve." Their superiors did not expect them to survive even six hours given the intensity of the German artillery, but the men of Battery C successfully held their position and continued to hold its position for three months. Kloby was cited for gallantry and meritorious service. Word of their heroism spread quickly throughout the Yankee Division and at the homefront.

As soon as the men of the 26th arrived in France, the Lawrence papers started to publish letters that had been sent home by the troops. These news stories included photographs, accounts of battles, reports of noncombat "goings-on" and, of course, notices of local casualties. On January 5, 1918, city residents learned of the first local serviceman to die overseas. E. Roy Kenney died of spinal meningitis while serving with Battery C. Another major story occurred when the *Tribune* and *Telegram* announced the death of South Lawrence resident Captain Francis Leahy, one of Peter's friends from the Patch. Although the newspapers offered daily accounts of war casualties, few attracted the attention of the citizenry as did the heroic death of Captain Francis M. Leahy.

It took until August 2, 1918, for the news to reach the Lawrence papers that Captain Leahy had been killed by an exploding shell fragment in France on July 21, 1918, three days after his twenty-eighth birthday. Captain Leahy had been placed in command of the sixty-eight men in Company F of the 101st Infantry just before the 26th Division shipped out for France. He was the first officer from Lawrence to be killed in battle. According to a military dispatch, Leahy was leading his men in Le Fare Woods, outside of Epieds, near Chateau Thierry. As he was leaning against a tree a German artillery shell struck it and cut it in two. A large splinter entered his back and came out his chest, killing him almost immediately. While lying mortally wounded on the ground, Captain Leahy turned his command over to Lieutenant Hanson. His dying words were immortalized throughout Lawrence: "Lieutenant Hanson, the command is forward." With his final breath he whispered, "Good-bye. Take care of the boys." Men from Battery C were nearby when the fatal shell hit its mark. Led by Leahy's friend, Sergeant Joe Mulhare, a number of them lifted the captain's body into an ambulance and brought it to a nearby grave-yard for burial.[2,3]

In the days and weeks following the report of Leahy's death the local newspapers were filled with accounts of the captain's heroism. Numerous poetic tributes were found in the papers, including Peter's memorial work. Almost daily there would be a letter printed from a soldier overseas that recounted the final moments of Leahy's life. Such reports continued through-out the war and for an extended period after the signing of the armistice. The story of Captain Leahy was frequently remembered in speeches, classroom assignments, and at memorial gatherings. After the war and the return of the men from overseas, a Mass and memorial service was held for Captain Leahy at Saint Patrick's Church. On the front steps of the church, the flag that had draped his coffin was presented to the pastor by Alice McParland Leahy, the captain's wife, whom he had married just months before heading off to France.

Lawrencians continued to follow the course of the war throughout 1918. Everyone took great pride in the efforts of the fighting men overseas and eagerly awaited any bit of news that might be printed in the newspapers. The July 24, 1918, *Evening Tribune* printed the "South Broadway Roll of Honor," listing all the troops serving overseas who lived along South Broadway. It took until December 24, 1917, for city residents to learn of Battery C's Thanksgiving dinner menu, but in homes throughout the city readers savored every detail of the published menu, which included turkey, dressing, mashed potatoes, boiled onions, squash, doughnuts, coffee, apple pie, oranges, and nuts. After Thanksgiving dinner, the boys of Battery C performed in a variety show that included Kloby Corcoran reciting the poem "Dangerous Dan

➤✻IN MEMORIAM.✻←

CAPTAIN LEAHY.

" The Command is, 'FORWARD !' Hanson," we
  heard CAPTAIN LEAHY say—
"Good Bye! Take care of the boys! " and from life he
  passed away.
A Shrapnel shell from German foe was cause of Leahy's
  death.
He lived as he died, *a Soldier*—gave command with
  dying breath.

" The command is, 'FORWARD!' Hanson !" the
  last words Leahy said,
As comrades stood around him, and looked on him, now
  dead.
They swore " his death would be avenged,"—on bended
  knees they fell—
"And get the Hun who fired the gun, if they chased him
  into hell."

" See the boys through, Hanson! " was the Captain's
  firm request.
As we knelt beside the silent form, we knew he had
  gone West.
A golden star now takes his place in the home he loved .
  so well,
Next to his country and the flag for which he nobly fell.

Farewell to you, brave Leahy! You were soldier and
  hero too.
You fought and died for freedom's cause, and the flag
  so dear to you—
It will always wave above your grave, though buried
  miles away.
Across the foam, your friends, at home, for you will
  always pray.

                    PETER F. CASSIDY,
                    South Lawrence, Mass.

A copy of Peter Cassidy's poem in memory of the fallen hero, Francis Leahy,
as it apperaed in local newpapers. Courtesy the Cassidy Collection.

McGraw," cook Phil Riley offering an address to the men, and Private Lonergan singing "I Don't Want to Go to War."[4] A January 19, 1918, *Tribune* story reported that Battery C had won high honors in a "firing examination" in France. "Battery C of Lawrence was the best regiment, . . . receiving great praise. . . . Sergeant Weinhold has a wonderful gunner in Corp. Blanchette." The paper also reported "Philip Riley is in good health and helped to get the battery boys their Christmas dinner."[5]

Battery C served with distinction in France and was stationed on the front lines from February through November of 1918 when the armistice was reached. It played an active role in major engagements at Chemin-des-Dames, La Reine and Boucq sectors, Chateau Thierry, St. Mihiel Salient, and Verdun. In December of 1918, Battery C was ordered to pack and prepare to ship home. The order was soon rescinded, and the men didn't return to the States until April of 1919. Throngs of grateful well-wishers greeted the men at New York, then Boston, and finally in the streets of Lawrence, where they arrived at the South Lawrence depot on April 16, 1919. By war's end, the Yankee Division had suffered almost 12,000 total casualties: 1,730 killed; 6,443 wounded; and 3,363 men gassed; including the troops from Battery C. One third of these casualties occurred at Chateau Thierry in July of 1918. Some 200 Lawrence men were killed or mortally wounded in the war, including eight men from Battery C.[6]

———————

Immediately after the United States declared war on Germany in April of 1917, the resources of the country began to be directed toward the war effort. This manifested itself not just in the areas of food, clothing, munitions, and weaponry, but also transportation. With each passing month as mobilization sped up, the nation's railroad and shipping networks made the war effort their top priority. Beginning in the fall of 1917, an anticipated shortage of railcars and steamships for coal transportation started to occur. Up and down the Eastcoast, cities faced a severe shortage of both soft and hard coal. Just as electricity and oil-based products are currently essential to the day-to-day functioning of our society, coal was the key to virtually every aspect of daily life at the beginning of the twentieth century, especially during cold-weather months. Besides being used to power railroad engines, factory machines, and office furnaces, coal was the primary way people heated their homes. Without coal, industrial America and its war machine would grind to a halt. During the winter of 1917-1918, that almost happened.

Early in 1917, well before the coal crisis actually took place, the New England states called a conference to plan for the anticipated shortage. Each state established its own coal committee and appointed a fuel commissioner. These same states also decided to name James J. Storrow director of the entire

New England region. A fuel committee was also established at the federal level under the direction of Dr. Harry A. Garfield, federal fuel administrator.

The coal shortage became prolonged and quite severe in the northeastern states and especially in New England. By January of 1918, a severe winter had set in throughout New England and the coal shortage became acute. A frozen Boston harbor made an already desperate situation worse. Rail traffic was frequently congested as the War Department demanded timely shipments of military supplies and coal to eastern seaports. As a result, coal shipments for the rest of the nation came in second. Matters were further complicated due to a manpower shortage in the coal mines of Pennsylvania. Many miners had gone off to war and production was down. Daily newspapers offered front-page updates on efforts to secure coal by the federal and New England commissioners: "Coal Situation Is Now Acute," "Lines of Men, Women and Children Haunt Coal Yards Pleading For Small Portions [of Coal]," "Supply of Coal Is On the Way East!"

While announcements of hundreds of coal cars headed for New England raised everyone's hopes, few understood that 100,000 tons of coal would heat New England for a mere twelve hours. This notwithstanding, local coal committees attempted to balance the needs of the mills, business establishments, schools, and churches with the needs of individuals desperately trying to keep their homes and families warm. Children and their parents walked the rail lines picking up pieces of coal that had fallen from coal cars. Whenever coal supplies did arrive in the city, the coal committees would supervise the distribution of fifty and one hundred pound bags of coal to residents until supplies ran out. One coal train was left standing for a weekend in the South Lawrence rail yard near St. Patrick's Church. By Monday morning, every car had been picked clean by cold and frightened residents of the Shanty Pond area. Police searched the surrounding homes to reclaim what coal they could find.

Throughout Massachusetts and the rest of the Northeast, fuel committees developed additional strategies to deal with the shortages. Christmas and winter school vacations were each extended by a week. During most of January, February, and into March, Mondays were considered holidays; businesses were ordered closed and workers stayed home. Long and detailed rules were regularly announced that directed fuel consumption restrictions for every segment of the community. On January 17, 1918, New England Commissioner Storrow announced new closing rules.

> The following orders, to take effect at once, shall apply throughout Massachusetts: Office, banking and similar business buildings shall not be heated on Sundays, holidays or on Saturdays

after noon, or on other days after 5:00 p.m., except to prevent freezing. Holders of liquor licenses shall not open their doors for business until 9:00 a.m. . . . Theaters, moving picture houses, bowling alleys, billiard halls, and private dance halls and all places of amusement shall close at 10 p.m. Clubs, club rooms and lodges shall close at 10:00 p.m. Barber shops, bootblacking establishments and cobbler shops are to conform to the rules applicable to retail stores.[7]

On February 12, 1918, the front page of the *Lawrence Telegram* read, "Bad Coal Forces Arlington Mill Weavers Into Idleness." Over 1,000 weavers and spinners were sent home from the Arlington Mill because coal shipments contained a high percentage of non-combustible material. This waste product, known as "screening of culmback" normally is considered unusable in the mining business. But with such demand for coal, unscrupulous owners were mixing in rock, slate, and other waste with good coal as a way to make greater profit. This practice not only hurt large coal users but hit homeowners especially hard. Having spent years down in the Pennsylvania coal mines as a young man, Peter knew the coal business. In his poem, "Keep the Home Fires Burning," he painted a picture of desperate kids bringing home unusable coal. He blamed the coal barons for such an outrage.

Keep the Home Fires Burning

"Keep the home fires burning," The one who wrote that song,
If she were living this winter would know it couldn't be done.
How can we see those embers bright, as we look into the grate,
When it isn't coal we're burning, but only stone and slate.

How many kids we see on the streets each day, pulling and hauling a sled,
Just stop and look, you'll notice the load, just a twenty pound bag.
In it there's fuel, what they bought for coal, but it is sad to relate,
When they get it home, it refuses to burn—it's only stone and slate.

There's a state fuel commish in Boston, we have all read of him
And the coal that is in his cellar—nine tons in the bin,
All sizes, Stove, Chestnut, and Pea, to suit all kinds of grate
For parlor stove, furnace and range, but we burn stone and slate.

I don't wish those coal barons any hard luck, but take this tip from me,
When they depart from this world there's one place they'll never see.
I know they'll never get inside, if Peter is at the gate,
It's down below they will have to go where they burn no stone or slate.

Now don't blame our local dealers, for they must take what comes.
They expect coal when they order it, but they get slates and stones.
It can't be returned to the mines, for who would pay for the freight?
But to keep the home fires burning, it can't be done with stone and slate.

In the winter of 1917, the European war was in its third year, and concerns were growing throughout the United States that American men would soon become directly embroiled in the horror that was playing out in France. Anticipating that National Guard troops would soon be called up by the regular army, Massachusetts' Governor McCall proposed on March 22, 1917, to establish an additional domestic force to "protect the domestic peace and especially bridges, water power, factories, and other structures that might be made the special subject of attack." Fearful of the German Kaiser, the Massachusetts Legislature gave the governor's initiative quick passage during the first week of April as the U.S. Congress formally declared war on Germany. This new domestic militia, known as the State Guard, was to be equipped with uniforms, rifles, cartridge belts, and ammunition. As is often the case with such hastily drawn up plans, however, many details were overlooked. For example, five men initially had to share each rifle, and weapons often were on loan from local rifle and hunting clubs. Criteria for recruitment in the new State Guard were designed so as not to compete with efforts by the National Guard to fill quotas for their local units. Accordingly, volunteers had to be at least thirty-five years of age, or if under thirty-five, married with dependents and physically disqualified from service in the National Guard. State Guard members were to be given the responsibilities and powers of constable, police officer, and watchman.

Men from Lawrence were quick to respond to the call. By May 1, 1917, at least 100 volunteers had signed a petition at the armory to have a State Guard unit from Lawrence.[8] The petition was presented to the city council and forwarded to Governor McCall for approval. Peter was one of those to enlist for a two-year term with the State Guard on July 20, 1917, as 135 companies were being formed throughout the state. He was a member of Company I, the 11th Regiment. In 1898, with seven daughters at home, Peter had been unable to join the fight in Cuba. Having been rejected as an army volunteer in

April of 1917, it was his hope that the State Guard eventually might be called up for service overseas as had the National Guard. He was fifty-six at the time.

During its first year the State Guard was sent to the Halifax Harbor explosion in New Brunswick on December 6 and for two weeks to the East Hampton riots in July of 1918. The regiment was also sent to Boston in early September of 1918 when the police went on strike. Peter, however, spent much of his time working for the government at Portsmouth, New Hampshire. In the fall of 1918 Peter's unit was pressed into duty to help combat a devastating outbreak of influenza that had gripped the nation and the world. This epidemic was especially deadly in large urban areas such as Lawrence where masses of people were huddled together amidst the disease and squalor of tightly-packed, triple decker tenements.

For several weeks in September, Lawrence residents had read of the sickness that had been consuming the residents of Boston. Local papers began an education campaign to encourage city residents to take prudent steps to avoid the illness by following the rule of three C's: clean mouth, clean skin, and clean clothes. Then, the first story was printed in the Lawrence papers about an illness afflicting its own residents. On September 16, 1918, the newspapers reported that Roy Blanchard of 345 Broadway had become seriously ill. Lawrence had its first confirmed case of the Spanish Influenza. The following day, nine more cases were cited and by September 20 the front-page headlines boldly screamed with alarm, "Influenza Epidemic Spreads." Thirty-four new cases now had been reported along with two confirmed deaths. The board of health, headed by Daniel Murphy met regularly to plan its response. The sickness raced through the city, and every action undertaken by the board over the next few weeks always seemed to be too little and too late. On September 27, over one hundred new cases were reported.

The board closed schools and theaters, and threatened to close banks and the bars in hopes of stemming the spread of the disease. As with any disaster of this type, no one can anticipate its duration or the breadth of its destructiveness. Hoping at first to minimize disruption to city routine, the board's sometimes tentative actions were criticized at every turn. Some urged stronger measures while others protested the stringency of its initial restrictions. Not all cooperated. The Catholic churches, for example, disregarded suggestions to limit their Mass schedules. Even a member of the health board, Dr. Sullivan, was openly critical of Chairman Murphy, so much so that Murphy threatened to resign. By Monday, October 14, some 2,852 new cases were reported in Lawrence, and there was little hope that the end of the epidemic was near.

The daily ritual around the city was gruesome. Doctors and attendants would go door to door seeking out the sick, dying, and the dead. Over 4,000 individuals were treated in their homes by 14 nurses and 60 volunteers. At

Peter Cassidy wearing his State Guard uniform, circa 1918. Courtesy the Cassidy Collection.

times, a single nurse was responsible for 140 patients. Many, and perhaps most, simply went untreated. While some wagons worked nonstop hauling away corpses for quick and sometimes anonymous burial, many more served as ambulances bringing the sick to a large tent hospital set up at the top of Tower Hill on Emery Farm. "One ambulance carried a father and mother and eight children, and another father, mother and seven children. Both women died in the ambulance, and there were 15 orphans when the ambulance reached the hospital."[9]

The Tower Hill location provided physicians with the necessary isolation and fresh air needed to fight the airborne contagion. For the next two months doctors, nurses, religious nuns, Red Cross workers, orderlies, and soldiers worked around the clock to tend to thousands of desperately ill people. The more serious cases were brought to Emery Hill, as it was called, where a small city grew in this hay field at the highest point in Lawrence. Row after row of canvas tents and wooden structures were arranged on the sloping terrain according to city wards and precincts, power poles with loosely hanging electric wires crisscrossed the area, and wooden boardwalks were constructed up and down narrow walkways where scores of gauze-masked medical attendants moved constantly from tent to tent.[10]

Although Peter failed in his quest to serve his country in France, he played an important role in fighting the influenza epidemic at home. With the outbreak of the sickness in Lawrence, the local unit of the State Guard was pressed into action throughout the city. When Captain Conners sought volunteers to work as orderlies among the sickest patients up on Emery Hill, Peter was the first to step forward and offer his services. According to a local newspaper, his work "won merited praise." Although the epidemic subsided near the end of October that same year, many patients continued to be treated at the Lawrence General Hospital even after the final tents were emptied on Emery Hill. Peter continued to serve as an orderly until the final influenza cubicle at the Emery location was closed down.

State Guard

I used to be a soldier in the regular army, oh!
When I joined the State Guards, over seas I thought I'd go.
They fit me out with a uniform, a bayonet and a gun,
Then I was sure to go to France to shoot and kill the Hun.

I was disappointed, when on me they turned the trick,
They put me up on Emery Hill with the dying and the sick.
With police drill and guard mount I found it very hard—
The first of June will be here soon and then good bye, State Guard.

When I read the paper, I couldn't well believe,
That I was made a sergeant with the stripes upon my sleeve,
I tried to do the best I could to stand in with the boss;
I am proud of the "V" that is on my sleeve, also the Red +.

I hope I'll n'er see again a sight any worse,
For I tried to please the doctors, the patients and the nurse.
When I went as orderly, working in the dangerous ward,
I had no fear when I volunteered from the ranks of the State Guard.

Some cases were being treated as late as February of 1919. Aware of the continuing need, Peter again offered his assistance to Health Officer Daniel Murphy in January of 1919. In a brief letter, Murphy declined Peter's offer, thanked him for his earlier helped, and added, "I am glad to know you are ready if we should need your help. I take this opportunity of expressing my thanks for the splendid work you did to assist our Department, which was reflected in a great way by the good results obtained by the sick, suffering and dying during a serious situation."[11]

Peter's term with the State Guard expired on August 15, 1919. He framed and displayed his discharge papers, which characterized his contribution in the State Guard as "Excellent service, honest and faithful." Throughout the rest of his life Peter cherished his time in "military" service. He not only saved his State Guard uniform but wore it frequently in his capacity as outer guard for the Moose Lodge and was often photographed wearing it. For this fifty-eight-year-old Irishman, the State Guard was the closest he would ever get to serving his country during wartime. Years later Peter was among the organizers of the Joseph E. Spencer Unit of the State Guard Veterans Association where he served as the historian.

Songs Composed By Peter F Cassidy

1. Young Kloby. N.E. Champion
2. The Table Of Poice
3. Places In. like To See
4. Next Patricks Day
5. Irelands friends
6. My Irish Valentine
7. Lizzie Murphy's Return
8. Over the Top With Pat
9. Sullivan and Killrain
10. Central Fire Station
11. When The Boys Come Home
12. Songs Of long Ago
13. Armorer John R Ryan
14. Old ShawSheen
15. Nora McKenney
16. Shan Von Vogt
17. The Chelsee Fire
18. Keep McCarthy Inn
19. The Big Race
20. Saint Patricks land
21. Here Are Cormac Sing
22. Back There Now
23. Barney come Home
24. The Shanty Valentine
25. For Ould Ireland
26. The Paveing Expert
27. No Egg In The House
28. keep The Fires Burning
29. The Strikers
30. The Paper Mill
31. Island In The Ocean
32. Patricks Day
33. Good Days On The Patch
34. Jock McCurn

Songs Continued

35. Peggie Omoore
36. Salem Fire
37. Sweet Templmore
38. Back There Now
39. My little Colleen
40. Traffic Cop
41. Proud my Boy'a Solider
42. When We Get To Mexco
43. Cornish. Peter Carr
44. State Guard
45. Caplin leahey
46. Make Old Ireland free
47. Order Of the Moose
48. Barney Gcraa
49. Katie McCown
50. Songs I. like To Here
51. My Daughter Has me Craze
52. Andy Callahan
53. Beautyfull. Spicket
54. Champion Jack Johnson
55. Irish Cindrelle
56. McShane from Gortten
57. An Irishmans love
58. Where The Spicket Flows
59. Irish Collens Visit
60. Comming Over
61. Eberhardt
62. Happy Days
63. Father Carthy
64. Rilluys Irish Night
65. letter to Rilley
66. Father Davey
67. Forty Five
68. Some Where

One of Peter Cassidy's hand written list of songs. He took great pride in documenting the over 120 poems and songs that he wrote and had published in local papers.

7

Baseball and Boxing

lthough most Irishmen in Lawrence participated in some kind of sporting activity, there is no record of Peter Cassidy's active involvement in sports. According to most accounts, he was not very athletic in appearance. Those who knew him described him as a short man, about five feet, five inches tall, and a bit on the rotund side—the result of all those nickel beers. Despite this lack of participation, he frequently wrote about sporting personalities in his songs and poems. He regularly frequented athletic events and was especially fond of the people associated with his two favorite sports: baseball and boxing.

Ever since baseball was invented, it has been an integral part of life for the Irish community in Lawrence. The epic poem "Casey at the Bat," was written by Lawrence-born author Ernest L. Thayer in 1888, and Babe Ruth once played baseball in Lawrence during an exhibition game at O'Sullivan Park. During Peter Cassidy's time it was probably the most popular sport around. He loved the game. One of his sons-in-law, Larry Mahoney, played shortstop for the Lawrence pro team during the years leading up to World War I. In the early decades of the twentieth century, the Irish were dominant players on the baseball diamond, both in their numbers and skills. As a team sport, baseball was accessible to many athletes, and it was relatively inexpensive for participants.

Most males played the game at one level or another, and Lawrence had dozens of baseball teams to accommodate those wanting to play. For teenagers and adults there were numerous organized leagues for enthusiasts to join: school, police, amateur, social, twilight, semipro and pro leagues.[1] For the youngsters there were hundreds of pickup games each day in the backyards, streets, and sand lots of the city. The city parks also organized games for the children: baseball for the boys and "kitten ball" for the girls. From spring to fall there was constant talk of baseball and one couldn't help but find a couple of games to watch on any given day. Of course there also were the professional teams of the American and National Leagues playing in Boston: the Red Sox and the Braves.

During Peter's years living in Shanty Pond, Lawrence had its share of big name sports personalities visit the city. Along with "the Babe," Jim Thorpe and Jack Dempsey also came to town. But few garnered the attention or drew crowds quite as large as when Lizzie Murphy first visited Lawrence during the summer of 1922. It is obvious from reading Peter's song about Lizzie that he and Lawrence fell in love with this female baseball wonder, a woman who played ball in a male world.

Women playing baseball was not a novelty, however. Beginning in the late 1860s, Vassar College began to organize female baseball teams and soon other women's colleges followed suit. Not surprisingly, this intrusion into a male sport was unwelcomed many and resisted by some. But the trend slowly expanded over the next several decades. Bloomer Girl teams from several major cities, made up of both male and female players, toured the country from Boston to Texas, playing amateur and semipro clubs. These teams and their games, however, were generally viewed as sideshows that could help improve the gate for the regularly scheduled men's games. In 1922 Lawrence had a number of all-girl teams that played each other or amateur men's teams in the city and from surrounding towns. One such club, the American Eagles, had a lineup that was mostly Irish like many of the all-male teams.[2] Some in Lawrence had their doubts about women playing the sport, but most residents loved their baseball, no matter who was playing. Once Lizzie left town, there were fewer skeptics.

When Lizzie Murphy played baseball, it was no sideshow. She was in the vanguard of a few select women who played on all-male professional teams during the early part of the twentieth century. For a time Lizzie was considered the premier female baseball player in a world dominated by male players. Born in Warren, Rhode Island, around 1894 to a French-Canadian mother and an Irish father, Elizabeth Murphy was the idol of two of the largest immigrant groups found in most urban areas of New England. She first took up baseball by playing catch with her older brother and tagging along when he went to play ball with friends. Once she succeeded in convincing the boys to let her play, it wasn't long before she found herself being among the first players selected in pickup games. She continued to play ball with the boys and before long she would become known as the "Queen of Baseball," the best woman player in the United States.

To Lizzie Murphy

Lizzie Murphy, please come back again, we want to see you play.
'Cause your team it got defeated, Liz, please don't stay away.
The baseball fans are with you Liz; the big ones and the small,
For Lizzie, we're all dizzy since we saw you play baseball.

Everyone's called "Murphy" now—the name it must be good;
'Twas at a corn beef dinner I heard a "Murphy" called a spud.
The women quit the movies, Liz; on each other they now call,
And their only conversation is, "did you see Lizzie play baseball?"

The teachers on vacation, Liz, that teach the golden rule
They're all talking baseball now, and won't go back to school.
The menders and the doffers, Liz, are playing ball at twilight,
For Lizzy, they're dizzy—they forgot they're out on strike.

You'll hear nothing here but "Murphy," Liz, as you walk on the street,
The cops refuse to arrest a drunk, when he's found on their beat
Who says his name is "Murphy," Liz, and at him they will brawl,
"Are you a friend of Liz Murphy, the one who plays baseball?"

There's no female girl like you, Lizzie, that we all must admit,
That can catch and throw the ball, and like you make a hit.
Or, take your place at first base, on them you have the call.
For Lizzie, you're a wonder, the way you play baseball.

So come back to us, Lizzie, come back and play once more,
For we'd like to see you Lizzie, before the season's ore.
So just pay us a visit, Liz, once more before the fall,
For Lizzie, we're all dizzy to see you play baseball.

Lizzie started to play on organized men's teams at the age of fifteen, teams such as the Warren Silk Hats and the Warren Baseball Club. In the decade that followed she honed her skills and started to develop a following throughout the area who came to watch her play. By the end of World War I, Lizzie was ready to step up to the next level. She signed on to play first base with a semipro team from Boston made up of former players from the major leagues: Ed Carr's Boston All Stars. She also played for a similar team called the Providence Independents. Each season these teams would travel throughout the Northeast and eastern Canada to play exhibition games with local amateur and professional teams. As Carr first anticipated, Lizzie proved to be quite a crowd pleaser, and her presence made a big difference at the gate. The five-foot, six-inch Murphy was as good at self-promotion as she was at playing first base. Before, after, and even during games she would greet the crowd, swap stories, shake hands, and sell a ten-cent picture card of herself.[3]

Although she was a unique attraction, Lizzie Murphy was not a token player placed on the team simply because she was a woman. She really could play the game. She possessed great speed and solid hitting abilities, and could play the infield as well as any male player. Soon Lizzie became so respected throughout baseball circles that she was invited to play first base for the American League All-Stars during a charity game against the Boston Red Sox on August 14, 1922. Six years later she was afforded a similar honor when the

Lizzie Murphy. Courtesy of Joseph Sagan

National League All-Stars asked her to join them in play against the Boston Braves. This type of notoriety, combined with seventeen years of playing over one hundred exhibition games each season, made Lizzie Murphy a very popular baseball commodity.

On June 20, 1922, the afternoon newspapers in Lawrence made brief announcements of Lizzie's first visit to the city with her team, the Providence Independents. "With the visitors [team] will be Lizzie Murphy, a girl, who is reported to play the sack as well as any man. She has been making a big hit wherever she has performed."[4] The game would be played that night at the North Lawrence Playstead, the ballfield across the Spicket River. Her arrival in town brought with it a tremendous sense of ethnic pride among the Irish in general and the Murphy clan in particular. But the response from all baseball fans in Lawrence was astonishing. A huge crowd of spectators, far larger than normal, filled the stands on that warm summer evening, bedecked in short sleeve-shirts and straw hats to enjoy the sight of this red-headed Irish wonder.

It is clear that Peter and the Irish in Lawrence were thrilled by her presence and proud of her achievements. According to newspaper accounts "There were more than 9,000 fans and fanettes there to see the fun. The fans gave Lizzie a great hand when she first came to bat in the third inning. She can play ball in her own right, too. She hits the ball well and can field with the best of them."[5] The box score listed "Miss Murphy" as getting one hit that night as the visiting Independents defeated the home team, 3 to 2. The *Evening Tribune* commented, "Hats off to Miss Murphy. She was the object of 10,000 wondering eyes . . . last night, yet she fielded at the initial sack as well as the best of the fielding first basemen. . . . Disregarding the fact that she is a woman, it might well be said that her performance was scintillating, but when you stop to consider that she is a woman then her play was nothing short of remarkable. The women folk attended the game in large numbers and they had numerous chances to cheer their idol. . . ."[6] Everyone wanted to be like her. In the weeks and months following her appearance, brothers could be heard calling their ball-playing sisters "Lizzie."

Just two weeks later, Billie McDonough, the owner/manager of a local professional team, proudly announced to the papers that Lizzie and her team would return to Lawrence to play his Lawrence Independents. Everyone knew that the caliber of play would be better this time as pro player was pitted against pro player. On Sunday afternoon, July 9, 1922, the two teams met as fans lined the field at the South Lawrence Common. Despite an ongoing textile strike, game attendance approached that of two weeks earlier. Even the poorest strikers came to see Lizzie play ball. The fans were treated to a spectacular game as the Providence club held the lead going into the top of the sixth inning. But three Providence errors, including one by Lizzie herself, gave the Lawrence team the lead and eventually the victory, 4 to 2. Despite her error and only one hit, Lizzie was as popular as ever. "Lizzie was the magnet that she was on her first visit here a few weeks ago. And she played a fine game at first base. . . ."[7] It was during the weeks following this game that Peter Cassidy, fearful that the defeat might keep her away, wrote his poem pleading, "come back to us, Lizzie, just come back and play once more" because "Lizzie, we're all dizzy to see you play baseball." She did return to play later that season.[8]

In the decade following World War I, the man most responsible for advancing boxing and professional baseball in Lawrence was William "Billie" McDonough, the "Boy Baseball Millionaire." Peter Cassidy thought a lot of McDonough, whose father ran the saloon next to Peter's apartment before the war. In his eyes, Billie had everything going for him. He was Irish, Catholic, served with Battery C, and lived in South Lawrence after returning from the war. McDonough was a shining star that passed quickly through Lawrence, however. Though well-known before the war, his association with boxing favorite Kloby Corcoran and his pro baseball team, the Lawrence Independents, made him a household name throughout the city during the twenties. Peter's poem is a testament to this fact.

To Wm. E. McDonough
The Boy Baseball Millionaire

North Lawrence may be proud of her new high school,
Likewise the renovated city hall,
Her Playstead, the Common and the new swimming pool;
Sure, she is welcome to them all.
She can take the city offices, the aldermen and the mayor,
But the old South Side you can bet takes more pride yet
In her "Boy Baseball Millionaire."

In years he's young, for sport a lot he's done
To buck up the national game,
As once 'twas played by the New England league
When the local club won fame.
Of his wins and loses he never speaks, no money does he spare;
We should him support, this one good sport,
Our "Boy Baseball Millionaire."

To give us a good ball club this boy has done his best,
And to make a better one he'll try.
Players he's brought from east, north, south and west—
He's got the best that money e'er could buy.
Clubs black and white, to play at twilight, so the worker fans could share,
Enjoy the fun, see games lost and won
With "The Boy Baseball Millionaire."

He has shown us what it is to be a sport,
Though "Billy's" only yet a boy.
Though thousands of fans who saw the Independents play

These games, they surely did enjoy.
This season's near its close; next year we hope he's there,
For there's no doubt, he is one good scout.
This "Boy Baseball Millionaire."

In the years following the World War, McDonough kept his hand in boxing, but spent most of his time and talents on baseball. In 1921 he joined with two local ball players, Harry Donovan and Francis Kennedy, to form the Lawrence Independents, a pro baseball team that played clubs throughout New England and beyond.[9] The Independents were not affiliated with any league during the 1921 and 1922 seasons, but entered the Boston Twilight League in 1923. The team was made up mostly of Irish players, but McDonough was more interested in good players than Irish ones. As a pro team, the Independents played over 100 games a season, with O'Sullivan Park being their home field.

Unlike many of his fellow owner/managers, Billie was an innovator who possessed a daring spirit and keen marketing ability. He jumped at the chance to have Lizzie Murphy and her baseball team play in Lawrence, a wise move that drew huge crowds to the gate. McDonough also was willing to pay the high salaries necessary to bring good ballplayers to the city. One of his most famous coups was signing Jim Thorpe to a $3,500 baseball contract to play right field during the 1924 season. Although most advisors predicted financial catastrophe, Billie proved everyone wrong. Thorpe presence on the field was a huge drawing card and the team had a solid season, winning the league championship for the first half of the year.

The New England League was reorganized in 1926. Billie kept a team in Lawrence until 1928, when financial difficulties forced him to move the team to Attleboro, Massachusetts. One year later, he was forced to take his team to Haverhill, then to Fitchburg, and later to Gloucester in search of better attendance. During these years, McDonough struggled to keep his franchise financially afloat. The team's salaries often outstretched the income he was able to generate at the gate, but he never complained or blamed his players.

While he pursued his baseball dreams, he still kept his hand in the boxing game. In classic McDonough style he was able to bring world heavyweight champion Jack Dempsey to Lawrence on August 14, 1922, for a four-round exhibition bout with local boxer Kloby Corcoran. In the days leading up to the match, the local papers began to hype Tiger Jack Dempsey's boxing prowess and his appeal to the "fairer sex." The bout was scheduled to go on at 3:00 Saturday afternoon at O'Sullivan Park with a baseball game between the Independents and St. Joseph's of Lynn to follow. Ticket prices in Lawrence were $1, $1.50, and $2 with the war tax added. Billie paid Dempsey $3,500 to attend, and he incurred additional expenses amounting to another $1,000 getting ready for the bout. The papers took note. "Manager McDonough has 'taken a long chance' in bringing Jack Dempsey . . . to this city and boxing fans should appreciate this fact and turn out en masse to give the champion a big greeting."[10] On the big day, the champ came, Kloby came, and so did the rain. McDonough lost his shirt. Just 1,550 boxing fans attended, and many of them had been given complimentary tickets. Besides the weather, August was the final month of a seven-month-long textile strike. For those out of work, a dollar was a lot of money. The Independents played their game in spite of the rain, and beat visiting St. Joseph's behind strong pitching by Johnny Newell.

The pressures from team ownership finally caught up with young Billie McDonough during the winter of 1929-30. He became quite ill and his condition grew worse until April of 1930 when he underwent surgery for stomach ulcers. Complications arose from the operation and he died in Lawrence on Wednesday, April 30, 1930. He was just thirty-one years old at the time. The sporting world was saddened by the death of the Boy Million-aire, and tributes filled the newspapers in the days and weeks that followed.[11]

William "Billie" McDonough. Circa 1927.
Courtesy Immigrant City Archives

While most stereotypes often have little bearing on reality, the association of the Irish with fighting may well be one that was on target. The Irish immigrants' quest for acceptance in their new land was always a struggle, but especially so after the flood of Irish Catholics poured into the United States during the decades following the Great Famine. Despite their willingness to work tirelessly for meager wages, they continued to face countless hurdles in their quest for the American dream. Their first big chance to reshape public attitudes came as the nation witnessed their heroic contribution during the Civil War. Large numbers of Irishmen volunteered to help preserve the union, and they quickly earned the reputation of being fearless fighters. Commenting on the nature of the Union Army early in the war, Confederate Colonel Edward Porter Alexander said, "His cavalry is numerous but can't ride and his infantry, except the Irish, can't fight."[12]

Unfortunately, the Irish reputation for fighting did not focus so much on their courage and tenacity on the battlefield, as on the derogatory stereotype of the drunken brawler. In many instances, the reputation was well deserved. With their arrival in the nation's urban centers came a social catastrophe that has always accompanied such gatherings of impoverished humanity. Poverty, hunger, and illiteracy, breed prostitution, drunkenness, family turmoil and, too often, physical violence. Seeking a release from the pressures of poverty, many Irishmen turned to alcohol and street fighting. Nativist factions quickly branded all Irish as brawling drunkards, and soon it became almost synonymous with the Irish. A look at the court dockets and lists of those arrested and incarcerated in major cities in the Northeast from about 1850 to 1880 would likely turn up a large majority of Irish names. This is certainly the case in Lawrence. Quite often, their crime was public drunkenness and fighting.

While the frequency may have declined during the early decades of the twentieth century, the Irish still took pride in their ability to do battle. *The Leader* recounted a brief story that typified such cocky Irish bravado. In response to a German immigrant's public boast in an Essex Street pub that he was looking to fight an Irishman, the following bit of guidance was offered by a businessman sitting a few stools down from him at the bar. "I'm of Irish descent and but for the notoriety of it, I'd accommodate you. Now you say you'd like particularly to fight an Irishman? I'll tell you how to do it. You go up to Davy Doyle's house on Elm Street, or Maurice Ryan's on the same street, . . . just open the door and say what you said here now, and see what'll happen."[13]

Although fighting became a social release for some Irish immigrants, it also became a vehicle for social advancement. Sports have always offered those on the lowest rungs of the social ladder a means to reposition themselves. It is true today and was as true over one hundred years ago. Boxing was one of the two major sports dominated by the Irish for almost three quarters of a century. While prizefighting reinforced the nativist stereotype about the Irish, it proved to be an effective vehicle for individuals to climb out of poverty and a major ego boost to the collective Irish psyche. In the 1880s the bare-knuckled fighter John L. Sullivan captured the attention of a young Peter Cassidy as he worked in the coal mines of Pennsylvania.

John L. Sullivan was born in Roxbury, Massachusetts, in 1858 and by 1877 he started to build a local reputation as a tough amateur boxer. At the age of nineteen, while attending a prizefight in Boston, he accepted a challenge to enter the ring and take on an established fighter. Sullivan made short work of his opponent and then turned to the crowd and shouted, "My name is John L. Sullivan and I can lick any man in the world." Known as the "Boston Strong Boy," he then toured the New England area, devastating his opponents with his famous right-hand punch. With each fight his reputation grew, as did the newspaper coverage and the size of fight purses. While fighters like Sullivan became wealthy, many a common Irishman brought a little more money home, or to the tavern, as a result of a well placed bet on the likes of Sullivan.

Prizefighting in those days was a very physical, very bloody confrontation by bare-knuckled combatants. Besides punching, the rules allowed kicking and wrestling, and each round lasted until one fighter was knocked down or fell to the floor. The match itself continued for as long as it took for only one man to remain standing. Prizefighting was also illegal in most states. Many events were broken up by the police and on occasion Sullivan and others spent a few nights in jail and paid hefty post-fight fines.

Following his Boston debut, Sullivan toured the eastern half of the country offering fifty dollars to any man who could stay in the ring with him. He averaged three or four fights per month and sometimes three exhibition bouts a night. Rarely did he have to pay out any money. His big break came on February 7, 1882, when he fought and beat the heavyweight champion, Paddy Ryan. After this fight he traveled from coast to coast, taking on all comers and entertaining crowds with his relentless fighting style, great strength, and brash Irish cockiness. From late 1883 to early 1884, he was reported to have knocked out twenty-nine men.

On July 8, 1889, at the age of thirty-one, Sullivan faced Baltimore's Jake Kilrain for the heavyweight championship of America. By this time in his career, Sullivan was a very rich man with a huge and loyal Irish following. His fights were the stuff men talked about while digging canals, laying tracks, working in the textile mills, or laboring at the bottom of coal mines. He was a genuine Irish hero to most Irishmen. Local newspapers throughout the country covered this bruising, bare-knuckled fight with Jake Kilrain, which lasted an unbelievable seventy-five rounds and took well over two hours to complete. In the days and weeks that followed, the fight was the talk of the country and the world. It would prove to be the last of the great bare-knuck-led fights.

One can almost imagine the lively discussion that went on in the dark-ened mine shafts of Pennsylvania as Peter Cassidy relived the big fight with fellow miners, some of whom had traveled to Richburg, Mississippi, to witness the bout in person. He was so inspired by the newspaper accounts and tales offered by his co-workers that he was moved to write his first poem. According to an account provided by a Lawrence newspaper almost forty years after the fight, "Peter discovered his gift many years ago at the bottom of a coal mine in Pennsylvania. How rare to find gold in such a place. Fellow workers had been discussing a championship prize fight they had witnessed. The steady stream of vivid description excited Peter's sensitive brain. He didn't know exactly what was the matter . . . until rhymes started flooding his mind. With the stub of a pencil, Peter wrote his first poem. It was about the fight."[15]

Sullivan and Kilrain

You lovers of the manly art listen and draw nigh,
I'll tell you of a fight took place on the 8th day of July.
Between John L. Sullivan of Boston, from that city of great fame,
At Richburg, Mississippi, where he defeated Jake Kilrain.

Chorus:
Then here is long life to Sullivan, and long may he remain,
That champion of champions which title he nobly gained.
He never was defeated and he always toed the scratch,
They have searched this world wide over and they never found his match.

Thousands assembled on the grounds to witness the affray,
The greatest stake ever fought for was on that eventful day.
To fight for twenty thousand dollars on Mississippi's shore,
Between Sullivan of Boston and Kilrain of Baltimore.

As both men appeared in the ring bets there then were made,
Odds were pinned on Sullivan, but Kilrain's men seemed afraid.
As time was called both men came up smiling to the scratch,
And to see these gladiators, you would say they were well matched.

Time was called that morning a few minutes after ten,
And in speedy action these men they did begin.
In the first round Sullivan was thrown down, it seemed to cause him pain,
As the cheers went up all around the ring from the friends of Jake Kilrain.

As Sullivan came up for the second round to win he meant to try,
He says unto his seconds: "I'll win this fight or die."
His friends knew he was determined then, and loud for bets did call,
When both men clinched Kilrain went down and Sullivan won the fall.

The third round called, both men came up a smile upon their face,
And up to the scratch they went and each man took his place.
Kilrain rushed in and made a clinch and as both men broke apart,
Sullivan hit, with his left hand, Kilrain beneath the heart.

From the third round on to the seventy-fourth, Kilrain he was knocked down,
Sullivan proved he was the best man in nearly every round.
The championship he won that day upon the Mississippi shore,
He won his battle nobly and beat Kilrain of Baltimore.

(Chorus)

After the fight with Kilrain, Sullivan soon switched over to Queensberry rules to avoid the legal troubles that had plagued him for fighting without gloves. Finally, the out-of-shape fighter met his match when he was beaten in a championship bout by a young and dashing upstart, "Gentleman Jim" Corbett, on September 7, 1892. Sullivan's habit of heavy drinking and carousing was said to have played a role in his defeat—that along with Corbett's speed and finesse. Four years later, John L. Sullivan retired from the ring, renounced his drunken ways, and became a leading advocate for the growing temperance movement in America, something that no doubt tarnished his image with many Irishmen, including Peter Cassidy.

Peter wrote at least two versions of the Sullivan and Kilrain song. The first and earlier version was published in Lawrence sometime before the war. The other was written sometime in 1937 shortly after Jake Kilrain's death. In this latter version, the chorus read:

With bowed down head for those men now dead, let us say a little prayer.
That John L. and Jake do well with angels bright up there.
They never flinched when time was called on the heavenly roll,
So good Christians pray and these words say, "Lord have mercy on their souls."

The song has some controversy surrounding it. Apparently a friend from Lawrence, or former friend, named J. J. Sullivan had taken some undeserved credit in a Lawrence paper for the earlier publication of the song about the Sullivan and Kilrain fight. In a handwritten note scratched at the bottom of the page where he pasted the text of the published song, Peter angrily asserted his claim to the crafting of the lyrics, with the exception of "the last line of the first verse." He defiantly closed with, "Every song that is in this book belongs to me and no one can dispute the same. Peter F. Cassidy."

Peter Cassidy's handwritten note in defense of his authorship of the Sullivan and Kilrain song, circa 1937. Courtesy the Cassidy Collection.

Thomas "Kloby" Corcoran was perhaps the best known and most popular boxer ever to fight in Lawrence during the city's first 100 years. While Peter had always enjoyed boxing, he was especially proud of Kloby who, like Billie McDonough, was an Irish Catholic and a veteran from Battery C. [15] In 1904, at the age of sixteen, Kloby won his first fight against a boxer named "Kid Pink." Over a five-year period, he amassed a remarkable record in the ring and became the favorite of sports fans in Lawrence. In 1909, he left the professional fight game with only an occasional appearance in exhibition matches. When the war broke out, the twenty-eight-year-old Corcoran joined with hundreds of other men from Lawrence in responding to the call for volunteers in 1917 to fight overseas. He served with honor and distinction on the front lines with Battery C, 102nd Field Artillery, 26th Division. It was after the fighting in France had stopped in November of 1918, however, that Kloby's fame began to reach new heights with McDonough's help.

After the signing of the armistice, the troops were anxious to board transport ships for the journey home. They soon learned, however, that it would take five or six more months before they would be able to ship home. The top military brass knew they quickly would have a morale problem with so many troops sitting around with nothing to do. The men were expected to participate in daily military drills during the morning, and authorities organized football, basketball, soccer, and baseball events in the afternoon. The competition among military units was keen.

Slowly, Kloby and the rest of Battery C began to move westward toward the Atlantic coast, crowded onto the same railroad horse cars that had brought them to the front a year earlier. When the troops arrived at Pouilly, France, Captain Howe of Battery C began making arrangements for a fight between a boxer named Mulvey from Battery F and "Young Kloby," as he was known during his early days in the ring. Because the fight wasn't to take place until after the new year, it gave the men something to anticipate.

The Lawrence men had arrived at Mayet in the Le Mans area by late January, 1919. In the middle of the town square, a huge platform was erected and soon weekly boxing matches began to occur. Battery C had the reputation of having many talented boxers. They had good men ready to fight in all weight classes, but Kloby was the boxer everyone counted on to win. In the long-awaited bout against Mulvey of Battery F, the men from Battery C bet their entire payroll of 65,000 francs on their battery mate. Kloby didn't let them down. On several occasions they doubled their pay in a similar fashion. His only loss unfortunately occurred in the highly contested championship bout.

By the third week of April 1919 the men from Battery C arrived home and ready to get back to the lives they had before the war. News had already spread throughout Lawrence about Kloby's boxing exploits in France. Thanks to two lengthy letters from Billie McDonough that were published in the local papers, sports fans in Lawrence were thrilled to learn that Kloby soon would attempt a boxing comeback upon his return from overseas. Though Billy McDonough had been his manager in France, Billy Bell would handle those duties for Kloby in Lawrence.

On May 30, 1919, Kloby began his quest and won his first local fight by knocking out a boxer from Lowell, Massachusetts, named Finney Boyle in just one round. Two weeks later, on June 16, Kloby knocked out Charlie Parker in three rounds. On June 23, the Lawrence boxer stopped Johnny Donovan by a knockout in the eighth round. His first real challenge came on June 30 against Harry Carlson, who took Kloby the full twelve rounds before losing by decision. One month later, he again knocked out Johnny Donovan of Boston, this time in three rounds. The stage was now set for the New England welterweight title match against Eddie Shevlin, the reigning New England champ and a U.S. Navy man from Roxbury.

Throughout the summer, Lawrence residents closely followed Kloby's comeback. Fight fever had taken hold of the city. Residents were thrilled with the thought that the championship battle between Kloby and Shevlin would take place at O'Sullivan Park on Saturday afternoon, August 23. During the weeks leading up to the bout, newspapers from throughout the region ran frequent stories about Shevlin and the underdog, Kloby Corcoran. Shevlin was a skilled boxer who had fought in Lawrence before in 1911. He was known as a fast, hard-hitting, and clever fighter who had a fight record of seventy wins against only three defeats. The Boston papers warned local fight fans that unlike Kloby's other opponents, Shevlin would take the fight to Kloby. Now almost thirty-one years old, Kloby still had a reputation as a three- to four-round boxer by the out-of-town fight establishment. They also felt he was too old to match up against the twenty-six-year-old Shevlin. It would be Kloby's sixty-third fight, and up to this point, the 142-pound boxer had lost only four decisions.

As the fight day arrived, the bout between Kloby and Shevlin was the talk of Lawrence, Boston, and all of New England. Over ten thousand fans crowded into O'Sullivan Park, which was located on the north shore of the Merrimack River. Much of the city's Irish population was in the stands. At least two thousand Shevlin supporters from Boston came with their money in hopes of turning a profit that day. The main attraction started shortly before noon, after the crowd had been treated to three preliminary bouts. Kloby led in the first and second rounds, but Shevlin took over the fight and went ahead in rounds three through seven. The final minute of the seventh round saw a turnaround as Kloby landed two solid blows to Shevlin's chest that knocked the wind out of him. In the eighth, Kloby continued on the offensive, striking spectacular blows at a torrid pace. As soon as the bell rang for round nine, Kloby jumped from his seat, ran up to Shevlin, and hit him with a left and then a right uppercut that knocked the champ to the ground for the ten count. It was over.

The Lawrence crowd screamed with joyous surprise as Shevlin stumbled back to his corner after the fight was called. Shevlin fans sat stunned as their man slumped down upon his stool. Kloby had successfully completed his comeback with six straight victories in less than three months. He was the New England welterweight champ. Seven weeks later, on October 12, Kloby

Corcoran put his title on the line at Braves Field in Boston against a Revere fighter named Nate Siegel. This time Kloby was favored to win, but the 15,000 fans who attended saw Siegel take the title. Kloby's professional career clearly was coming to a close. He had one more major fight in which he knocked out a Boston fighter named K. O. Muggsy in the winter of 1920. Over the next few years, Kloby fought several more times, but never reached the heights he achieved in 1919. He formally retired from the ring in December of 1922 and became a realtor.

The Champion of the Yankee D
Battles Won and Lost by Kloby

You can talk about your heroes that fought on land and sea,
Lawrence feels proud of her boys that fought with the Yankee D.
Who volunteered and crossed the seas, to fight the German Hun,
We can't forget those heroes for the fighting that they done.
They showed those Germans fighting that they never saw before
With shot and shell they thought that hell had opened wide her door.
When they saw those Yankees before them they did flee
In quick retreat afraid to meet the boys of the Yankee D.

There are heroes that are past and gone, whose praise you might sing,
That fought in wars and battles, also in prize ring.
Our hero I will mention he has fought in ring and trench;
He fought for the world's democracy alongside the French.
For eighteen months he fought the hun on a foreign shore.
When he got back to God's own land, he starts to fight once more.
Though he brought no "croix de guerre" or medals back with V.C.
Still he came back a hero, and champion of the Yankee D.

I would like to name our hero's fights, if only I had the space.
Among the prize ring heroes, Kloby's name will have a place.
The greatest battle he ever fought is now in history,
When he fought in France and took a chance with Lawrence's Battery C.
Straight away without delay, once more on Yankee soil,
Not afraid, a match he made for to fight Phinny Boyle.
The fight took place, he set the pace 'twas short you will agree.
Less than a round Boyle was downed by the champion of Yankee D.

He next fought Charlie Parker in three rounds he was done,
In eight rounds he knocked out and down Johnny Donovan.
Twelve rounds he fought Carson, the decision he did get.
Again gave Donovan a beating that he will never forget.
He fought and beat Ed Shevlin, he was the Navy's pride.
In the eighth round a clip, he gave that ship, and sank him broadside.
From New York, Fitzsimmons was brought, he'd a fighting pedigree.
A defeat to duck, a low blow struck, the champion of Yankee D.

In Cuddy's tent twelve rounds he went with Dundee the "Scotch Wop,"
Up and Down each other did pound and punches they did swap.
I heard fans say, the fight that day, was the best they ever did see.
'Twas the first defeat our hero did meet as Champion of Yankee D.
An Italian from Boston, with an Irish name of Doyle
Wanted to be the champion and our hero's record spoil.
The fight took place and Kloby won, so said the referee.
Another victory for our hero, the champion of the Yankee D.

His next fight was with Muggsy, poor Muggsy done his best,
He fought two rounds, he went down, knocked out like the rest.
A decision he lost to Frankie Britt the New Bedford Portegee.
Though he lost the title of welterweight he's still the champion of the Yankee D.

In the years that followed, Kloby participated in a number of exhibition bouts in Lawrence, but stayed away from any serious boxing activity. Nonetheless, he always remained a hero in the eyes of the Irish in Lawrence—as a boxer and a soldier, and for the time he saved an elderly woman who had fallen in front of a baggage truck at a train station. During his comeback, Kloby was reported to have earned upwards of one hundred thousand dollars. He was known to all as a warm, gentle, and lovable man, loyal to his friends. On November 15, 1968, six days after celebrating his eightieth birthday, Thomas "Kloby" Corcoran died.[16]

Battery C members just back from the war – Smiling Phil Riley and boxer Thomas "Kloby" Corcoran, April 1919. Courtesy of the Ed and Jen Retelle family.

8

The Struggle for Irish Freedom

From 1914 to 1918, the world's attention remained focused on defeating the German Kaiser and the Axis powers in Europe. The campaign for a free Irish republic was at best a distant concern to the international community. This remained true even after the failed Easter Rising in Dublin on April 16, 1916, when the Irish Republican Brotherhood (IRB) and the Irish Volunteers instigated another in a long line of bloody revolts designed to end more than seven centuries of Britich rule. Patrick Pearse stood on the steps of Dublin's General Post Office on Easter Monday, 1916, and read the "Proclamation of the Provisional Government of Ireland." Joined by over 1,000 men and about 90 women, he led the ill-fated uprising, which had very little popular support at the time. One week later, after over 1,300 hundred people had been killed or wounded, Pearse and his followers surrendered to over 4,500 British troops. The subsequent execution of fifteen IRB ringleaders, including Pearse, made instant martyrs of the rebels, and Irish public opinion soon switched to the cause of the new Irish Republic and Sinn Fein, the party leading the fight for Irish freedom.

With the end of World War I in November of 1918, the cause of Irish freedom was thrust back onto the agenda of the victorious world powers. Throughout the war, England continued to face occasional hostility from Irish forces committed to an independent and sovereign Irish Republic, but once peace was restored in Europe, the pressure for change dramatically increased. In the two and a half years that followed the failed Rising, the sentiment of most of the Irish people had solidified around the idea of an independent Irish Republic. By the end of 1918, Sinn Fein had won seventy-three seats in the British House of Commons. When Parliament met in January 1919, the Sinn Fein members refused to take their seats. Instead, twenty-six representatives met on January 21 and declared themselves the first Irish Parliament, or Dail, of the independent Irish Republic.

At this same time, the Allied powers were beginning to meet for the postwar peace talks in Versailles, France. Article X of the draft treaty called for all allied nations to "preserve the existing territorial boundaries of the member nations. . . ." thus keeping Ireland as a formal and subservient part of the British Empire. Eamon de Valera, head of Sinn Fein and president of the Dail, went to France to argue the republic's case. His plan was to elicit the support of U.S. President Woodrow Wilson, who publicly had been espousing his famous Fourteen Points for lasting peace. De Valera and his supporters felt the treaty talks would be a perfect opportunity to gain international support for their cause. They were wrong.

The British government was successfully applying great pressure upon its Allied partners to avoid the Irish question. Key aspects of Wilson's plan were to be applied only to territories that had been under German oppression. All other territorial matters pertaining to the Allied powers were viewed as domestic matters, outside the bounds of treaty discussions. It was clear that the talks at Versailles didn't offer de Valera much hope. Undeterred, and still insisting on self rule, he proposed that the Irish Republic sit as a full and equal member of the League of Nations. Once again, however, the Sinn Fein leader realized that the League Covenant was nothing more than a document designed to perpetuate the status quo for the Allies.

Throughout the spring of 1919, the Dail set about the task of forming a government. More officials were named and an administrative structure was put in place. The task was greatly frustrated because so many members of the Dail were in British jails. The Dail's effort to set up a government without adequate financial resources proved equally as challenging. The new government needed money, lots of it, and soon. De Valera sent an envoy to the United States to secure external loans for the republic, but he met with little success. By May, de Valera realized that Ireland had no chance of gaining any recognition or relief at Versailles, so the Dail gave formal notice to Lord Clemenceau, president of the peace conference, that England had no right to sign a treaty on behalf of Ireland. Shortly thereafter, de Valera decided that his only recourse was to make an appeal directly to the American people.

In the United States much of the Irish community was actively involved in the self-rule campaign. Most offered words of support and financial contributions, while others advanced stronger political endeavors. This was especially true in Lawrence where public rallies and fund-raising efforts in support of Ireland had been held for every Irish cause since the city's founding. Since 1912 local papers had provided the Irish community with regular and detailed coverage of the events unfolding in their homeland: the Home Rule talks just prior to the war, the 1916 Easter Rising, and de Valera's efforts on behalf of the Dail. On Thursday, December 12, 1918, several thousand Irish men, women, and children packed Lawrence City Hall for a rally urging President Wilson to use the peace process to end British rule in Ireland.

This was one of the largest indoor gatherings in the history of Lawrence for the Irish cause. After opening remarks by Father James T. O'Reilly of St. Mary's Church, the main speaker, Charles E. Fay of Boston, offered a thorough rationale in support of the resolution to be brought before the gathering that night. By unanimous vote those present passed the resolution, which read in part, "Whereas, Ireland has been prevented from the enjoyment of the exercise of this principle [self-determination] for centuries and is still prevented therefrom by military force; now therefore, be it resolved, that we, as American citizens, respectfully petition his excellency, the President of the United States, to employ the influence of our government to that end that . . . the principle of self-determination shall be so applied that Ireland may stand upon a equal condition and receive the same consideration as Poland, Serbia, Belgium, and all other nations of the world. . . ."[1] De Valera's message had already found fertile ground in Lawrence.

In February of 1919 the Irish Race Convention was held in Philadelphia, and the plight of the Irish Republic was addressed. This large convention helped to reinvigorate American support for Ireland. The Irish Victory Fund was started to raise money for the newly formed Irish government. In Lawrence, the drumbeat for funds and for a free Irish Republic continued at a heightened pace. The McBride Branch of Friends of Irish Freedom met at Hibernian Hall on April 24, 1919. In addition to discussion about the local Victory Fund drive, President James O'Neil announced that eighty membership applications had been accepted as they moved toward their goal of a thousand new members. As was always the case at such meetings, the Irish faithful were given more instruction about the rightness of their cause. "Attorney John Haverty spoke on Ireland's part in the Great War. He told of the work done by the Irish race to aid the United States in making its history and the number who laid down their lives for their adopted country." Daniel W. McCarthy spoke on the likely perils of the League of Nations, and John J. Donovan delivered an address on "Ireland Claims for Freedom."[2]

The Irish community in America immediately embraced the fund-raising initiative. In Lawrence alone, tens of thousands of dollars were raised through raffles and donations. One would be hard-pressed to find an Irish man or woman in the city who had not contributed something to the cause. As of Saturday, June 28, 1919, just over $19,000 had been donated in Lawrence, and the drive was being extended another week in hopes of reaching the $20,000 mark. Local papers regularly printed a list of recent benefactors along with the amount of their contributions. The large and small donors were given equal credit for their generosity: "Dr. T. J. Daly, $25; Michael J. Driscoll, $2;

Catherine Breen, $1; Nellie O'Connor, $1; Mary Sullivan, $2; Jeremiah Donoghue, $20; The Augustinian Fathers of St. Mary's, $100; John W. Duffy, $5; John Delaney, $1; Robert Gordon; $25; and William Carroll, $25."[3]

The campaign received a boost when Sinn Fein President Eamon de Valera arrived in the United States in late June of 1919. He immediately set about meeting with government officials, bankers, and Irish sympathizers. His goals were threefold. First, he hoped to get the government of the United States to recognize formally the new Irish Republic. Second, he sought to float an external loan to support his government. Finally, he hoped to get support from the American people to force Wilson to disregard Article X of the Treaty Covenant and to assert Ireland's right to be free of British rule. Over the weekend of June 28-29, 1919, de Valera arrived to a hero's welcome in Boston. According to *The Pilot*, "Boston was stirred to its very depths on the occasion of the visit of the Honorable Eamon de Valera, President of the Irish Republic. Never in the history of this nation was there a more enthusiastic outpouring of freemen to wish success to their oppressed brothers across the seas. Never before was there such a vivid demonstration of sympathy for the cause of any people as was witnessed at Fenway Park on Sunday."[4]

A newspaper report from Peter Cassidy's scrapbook described an incident that occurred when de Valera spoke at Fenway Park that Sunday afternoon.

> . . . de Valera, the Irish statesman, came to Boston and was given a reception of immense proportions. The affair had taken place at a baseball park. Peter [Cassidy] had written a ballad in honor of the famous visitor and had copies made. He also had composed some music to fit the words. During a lull in the program, Peter went onto the field and sang his ballad. The spectators were delighted. Within a few minutes Peter had sold practically every copy that he had. Peter repeated his performance when de Valera spoke in another Massachusetts city. Once again his magic was effective and more copies of the ballad were sold.[5]

Early in the evening on Monday, June 30, 1919, while on his way to Manchester, New Hampshire, Eamon de Valera made a brief stop in Lawrence at the Irish fund-raising headquarters located at 408 Essex Street. His appearance carried on a long tradition. Lawrence had frequently played host to important Irish leaders including temperance leader Father Theobald Mathew, Fenian founder John O'Mahoney, John Boyle O'Reilly, and Michael Davitt and Charles Stewart Parnell of the Land League. After being introduced by Mayor John J. Hurley and given the keys to the city, de Valera pleaded his case before a large and enthusiastic crowd that had gathered hastily. His message was clear, "Ireland's cause is a simple one. Ireland deserves her freedom and demands it."[6]

Several weeks earlier, on June 16, 1919, the Lawrence City Council had voted to recognize formally the Republic of Ireland, thus becoming the first governmental body in the United States to do so. The council's resolution stated that "We declare ourselves unreservedly in favor of the independence of the Republic of Ireland and demand that our government recognize the Irish Republic." The resolution was signed by the entire council: Mayor Hurley and Aldermen Peter Carr, Robert Maloney, John Finnegan, and John Flannagan. In his June 30 speech, de Valera thanked the city of Lawrence for its support of the republic and for the council's earlier vote, saying, ". . . soon other cities throughout the United States would follow Lawrence's lead and take similar action until the United States government would recognize the Republic. . . . When this happened Ireland as a nation would be a reality."[7] One week later the Irish Victory Fund in Lawrence had topped $22,000 with over $9,000 coming from Ward Six, the Shanty Pond area.

Peter Cassidy's song, "Table of Peace," was written in the spring or early summer of 1919 in honor of Eamon de Valera. Anticipating his visit to Boston, Peter had copies of the song printed as a Sinn Fein handbill with the heading "For Friends of Irish Freedom." In the song Peter spoke of the war's end and peace talks, hoping to encourage public sympathy and support for Ireland's participation at Versailles. He invoked the names of several Irish heroes, including veterans from Lawrence and Massachusetts, who had served their country overseas. Early in the war, the British government had made promises to the Irish that their loyalty in wartime would result in more favorable policies after Germany's defeat. Most doubted the sincerity of the British government, and when it tried to conscript Irishmen to fight, de Valera and Sinn Fein played a key role in organizing the opposition. Many Irish volunteered nonetheless. Peter's song called for accountability by the British. It was time for the government to live up to its prewar promise.

In January of 1920 a new ten-million-dollar drive was announced in the United States to fund loans to the Irish Republic. Fund-raising drives had continued almost nonstop in the United States over the previous two years. At every Irish tavern and social event, the hat would be passed and many a man would forego a nickel beer to make a contribution. In Lawrence alone, tens of thousands of dollars were quickly raised through raffles and the sale of Irish Savings Bonds, ranging in price from ten dollars on up. T. P. Donoghue and C. J. Corcoran were appointed to head up the 1920 campaign. Individuals could make "certificate contributions" over a ninety-day period and would then hold a non-interest bearing certificate until one year after Ireland was recognized internationally as a Republic. Thereafter, these certificates could be exchanged for bonds earning 5 percent interest. These, in turn, could be

FOR FRIENDS OF IRISH FREEDOM !!

Sinn Fein   Sinn Fein

TABLE OF PEACE;
OR
MAKE OLD IRELAND FREE

By PETER F. CASSIDY

57 South Broadway, Lawrence, Mass.   (Copyright Applied For)

Tune: "The Journey Man"

I.

The cruel war is over—we've returned to peace once more;
Irishmen performed their part, as they have done before.
For fighting done and victories won, in justice we demand
At the table of peace to have a place for dear old Ireland.

II.

We'd like to know the reason, and also know the cause,
Why Ireland should be humbled by England's cruel laws.
It's time her yoke should now be broke and chains come off her hand
And make a place at the table of peace for dear old Ireland.

III.

Erin always had her heroes, like Kelley, Burke and Shea;
O'Ryan broke the German line with Logan and Gilday.
The words of Captain Leahy, killed leading his command,
Should have a place at the table of peace for dear old Ireland.

IV.

The fight at Chateau Thiery, that battle of great fame,
On the roll of honor you'll find many an Irish name
Who fought and bled—some now are dead and lie in No Man's Land
Their lives they gave that others might live, to free old Ireland.

V.

Don't blame Irishmen because they love the land St. Patrick blest,
We want to see Ireland once more a nation 'mong the rest.
We are ready to go and meet the foe and fight for liberty;
So give us a place at the table of peace and make Old Ireland Free.

Sinn Fein   Sinn Fein

This "Sinn Fein" handbill prepared by Peter Cassidy and distributed on the occasion of Eamon DeValera's visit to Massachusetts in the summer of 1919. Courtesy the Cassidy Collection.

redeemed one year after issuance. By March 17, 1920, the Irish community in Lawrence had sent $36,000 to Ireland, reportedly the highest per capita contribution level of any city in the United States.

De Valera returned to Ireland in December of 1920. Eighteen months earlier, on June 28, 1919, the terms of the Versailles Treaty had been reached with no accommodation made for Ireland. Neither Woodrow Wilson nor the United States Congress undertook formal action to recognize the new Republic of Ireland. That same year, during the national election for the presidency, many Irish Americans abandoned Wilson and the Democratic party for their lack of support for Ireland's participation at Versailles. While unsuccessful in his efforts to move the United States government, de Valera had succeeded in further galvanizing the support of the Irish community in America and raising considerable sums of money at a critical time. Within a few years, during the height of the Anglo-Irish War, a much broader cross section of the American people would bring pressure to bear on the British government to end its occupation of Ireland.

Peter's song "Ireland's Heroes" was written to commemorate the pivotal breakthrough in Ireland's seven-hundred-year struggle to break the chains of British rule. Written during the last week of June 1921, it marked the occasion of British Premier Lloyd George's invitation to Dail President Eamon de Valera to come to London for immediate truce talks and long-term discussions aimed at settling the "Irish Problem." In the months immediately following the Declaration of the Irish Republic by the Dail in January of 1919, the British government responded to this growing crisis as it had on numerous occasions since the Normans first invaded Ireland in 1170—with massive and often brutal force. Tens of thousands of British troops poured into Ireland in support of the local government police force, the Royal Irish Constabulary (RIC). These troops included a ruthless band of marauders called the Black and Tans, who proceeded to terrorize the population. Thousands of innocents were injured or murdered, women were raped, and villages were burned.

Unlike in the past, however, the response of the Irish people was different. Instead of breaking their spirit, the many atrocities only strengthened the will of the people. Twentieth-century communications made the world a smaller place, and word of British atrocities began to spread among nations. International criticism eventually played a role in forcing the British to seek a peaceful resolution to the Irish problem.

Even more instrumental in stopping the British assault on the Irish, however, was a remarkably brutal guerrilla war waged against the British by Michael Collins and his small band of young assassins. President of the Irish Republican Brotherhood's Supreme Council, Collins was also the finance minister of the newly declared Irish Republic and de facto head of the Irish Republican Army (IRA). He used a select group of young men from the newly formed IRA to bring a relentless and similarly ruthless, quick-strike terror campaign to the RIC, British troops, and the hated Black and Tans. This Anglo-Irish War began in January of 1919 and lasted until July of 1921 when the King of England and Lloyd George called for a truce and invited Sinn Fein to peace talks. A formal truce was signed on July 11, 1921. De Valera chose not to attend the subsequent talks but instead sent Collins and Arthur Griffith to lead a delegation to London that fall.

"Ireland's Heroes" pays tribute to Patrick Pearse, one of the leaders of the 1916 Rising, and three Sinn Fein hunger strikers who died resisting British oppression in 1920. The first of these was Michael Fitzgerald, a member of the Irish Volunteers. He died in Cork Jail on October 17, 1920, after going sixty-eight days without food. The second, Joseph Murphy, was also a member of the Volunteers, and died in Cork Jail on October 25, 1920. The most famous of the three was Terence MacSwiney, the Lord Mayor of Cork and a prominent Sinn Fein and Irish Republican Army leader. MacSwiney had been repeatedly arrested, deported, and incarcerated by the British since 1916. Finally, after a seventy-four-day hunger strike, he died at Brixton Jail in London on October 25, 1920. The Lord Mayor reportedly rebuffed repeated pleas to end his hunger strike, saying that if he were to give up the fight, he would "give away Irish Liberty" and he would "rather die than do that." MacSwiney became the focal point of an international outcry, especially in America. Lawrence newspapers shouted the headline, "Terence MacSwiney Dies," and provided extended coverage of his life and eventual death.[8]

In the weeks leading up to MacSwiney's death, regular news accounts provided updates on his condition and additional details about the brutality of the Black and Tans. On any given day, Lawrencians would read a story of Sinn Fein members being killed, arrested, or executed. On another, they would read of the assassination of members of the RIC or the Black and Tans for murdering innocent villagers. While a pattern of more sympathetic reporting had already begun prior to MacSwiney's hunger strike, the frequency of coverage about the Anglo-Irish War unquestionably increased as a result of his sacrifice.

Several days after MacSwiney's death, representatives from St. Patrick's and St. Mary's Churches met with leaders from all the Irish societies in Lawrence to plan a massive parade in honor of MacSwiney, Murphy, and Fitzgerald. On Sunday afternoon, October 31, 1920, an estimated four thousand mourners wearing black arm bands silently marched through the streets of Lawrence to the sound of muffled drums. The procession stopped at the common across from city hall where prayers were offered and speeches made. Similar demonstrations took place in Boston, New York, and other cities with large Irish populations.

In September of 1921, the Irish Dail sent its delegation to London to begin settlement talks with Lloyd George. By December of that same year, a

FOR FRIENDS OF IRISH FREEDOM

Sinn Fein   Sinn Fein

"IRELAND'S HEROES"

MacSWINEY   MURPHY   FITZGERALD

By PETER F. CASSIDY.

Lawrence,   -   -   -   -   Mass.

Tune: "Roving Irishman."

I.

Every nation in this world has heroes that come and go,
You'll find heroes every day in the land where the Shamrocks grow.
England today admits and says she could ne'er make the Irish
     yield.
For centuries she's tried them, she's crucified with hunger, lead
     and steel.

II.

Where can you find such heroes as Pearce and his brave band,
Who in Easter week nineteen sixteen made such a gallant stand,
When they seized Dublin Castle, the Sinn Fein flag unfurled,
And proclaimed Ireland a republic to the nations of the world.

III.

A hero was Lord MacSwiney, who in prison starved to death;
For Ireland's cause defied British laws. He said with his dying
     breath:
I'm only one of Erin's sons; thousands will follow me.
We'll ne'er give in till this fight we win, and make old Ireland free.

IV.

Ireland always had heroes and she has heroes today.
England may kill and murder them, in spirit they will always stay
On that Irish sod that's blessed by God, that island in the sea,
Will always have her heroes until old Ireland is free.

V.

Those heroes that lie in Cork jail behind dreary prison wall
With hunger are dying for Ireland's sake, soon will be beyond
     recall.
MacSwiney, Murphy and Fitzgerald have answered to death's toll.
Good people pray, and these words say, Lord have mercy on their
     souls.

VI.

The time is coming, "Lloyd George," you'll have to pay for your
     'dirty work.
The crimes you've done in Ireland ne'er was equaled by the Turk.
You've raped and racked, burnt and sacked, with your hellish black
     and tan
(England), Ireland loves your people, but your Government be
     damned!

Sinn Fein   ◆   Sinn Fein

Written and distributed in 1922, this handbill, like Table of Peace, *was sold by Peter Cassidy to raise money for the Irish Victory fund and, no doubt, to help support himself. Courtesy the Cassidy Collection.*

draft treaty was initialed by the two delegations and brought back to the Dail and Parliament for ratification. The proposal failed to provide for Ireland's unification or its full and complete separation from the British Empire. Instead, it institutionalized the earlier partitioning of Ireland into north and south, and it failed to give Ireland full independent status. De Valera and Michael Collins, brothers in battle against the British, now found themselves on opposite sides of the ratification debate. On January 6, 1922, after a strenuous and divisive month-long debate, the Dail ratified the treaty: sixty-four in favor and fifty-seven against. De Valera and his supporters walked out in protest.

Tensions mounted between the opposing factions throughout the winter. The anti-treaty forces, now referred to as the Irregulars or Republicans, began acts of civil disobedience such as occupying in Dublin from April through June of 1922. Catholics in Ulster, seeking unification with the south, began to riot against the Orange government as Collins secretly provided them with arms. All of this caused the British government to threaten direct involvement against Catholics in the north and the Republicans occupying the Four Courts in the south if the Free State provisional government failed to intervene. In late June, despite making great efforts to avoid war with his friends, Collins finally was forced to lead the provisional army against de Valera's Irregulars at the Four Courts. Civil war had begun.

The next ten months saw many bloody confrontations as hundreds were killed in skirmishes, assassinated, or executed. So deep was the split, so bitter the feelings that Collins and de Valera reluctantly oversaw the deaths of dozens of loyal friends who had helped them win the Anglo-Irish War just one year earlier. By May of 1923 it was over, but not before Ireland saw many of its beloved leaders die, including Cathal Brugha, Rory O'Connor, Liam Mellows, and Erskine Childers on the Republican side, and Michael Collins on the Free State side. Even after de Valera called for a cease-fire, intermittent incidents of terror continued for some time.

In his poem "To Ireland's Friends" Peter Cassidy pleaded with his fellow Irish men and women in Lawrence to stay united in their quest for a free Ireland. Written during the winter or spring of 1922, his words reflect the concern of republican supporters in the United States and Ireland that the controversy over the treaty not result in a fragmenting of the once unified forces. Peter knew full well how many times over the course of Ireland's history internal divisions had undermined efforts to overthrow British rule. Just as the debate in Ireland became intense over the terms of the recent treaty, so too did its provisions spark debate in Lawrence. Up until now the various Irish societies had a clear and focused goal. The split between Collins and de Valera, however, caused stress and division among American supporters. The Lawrence Chapter of the American Association for the Recognition of the

Irish Republic, AARIR, now found itself in the midst of a potentially devastating internal debate. For Peter, only a unified position would bring about an end to British rule and establish an independent Irish republic.

To Ireland's Friends

All friends of Irish liberty, of color, race and creed,
When you read these lines that's here in rhyme, I hope you will give heed.
Let's stick together and have no split, united we should be,
The day is drawing on, it won't be long, when old Ireland will be free.

For years we know the sufferings of poor old Granuale,
And we know the best friend she ever had is the good old Clan-na-gael.
The friends of Irish freedom, too, gave their money and sympathy,
The A.A.R.I.R., both near and far, want old Ireland to be free.

Don't have England give us the laugh, and say we can't unite.
As we fought for other nations, now for Ireland let us fight.
So our rising generations, England's slaves will never be,
They will love the cause that drove British laws from that island in the sea.

Think of the boys that's over there fighting for their lives,
God bless their Irish mothers and those heroes' wives.
Their sisters and their daughters, too, every Irish colleen,
Their hearts and souls are in the fold, to free that Isle of Green.

I ask again all Ireland's friends, of color, creed and race,
Together join us in one combine, and have Ireland take her place,
Among the nations of the earth, where Erin ought to be,
So let us stick, and have no split, and make old Ireland free.

In the years that followed the 1916 Easter Rising, Peter's songs and poems took on an increasingly nationalist tone. Each year in honor of St. Patrick's Day, he would publish a song that would inevitably focus on one theme: a free and independent Irish Republic. Indeed, this cause continued to be the centerpiece of St. Patrick's Day celebrations in Lawrence during the early decades of the twentieth century. With the founding of Sinn Fein in 1905, the rise of the Home Rule movement from 1912 to 1914, and the frequent

Victory Fund campaigns, Irish Americans had a heightened sensitivity about the growing republican movement. The Easter Rising, the Anglo-Irish War, and the Irish Civil War intensified those passions and made this period one of tremendous nationalism throughout the Irish community in Lawrence. Not surprisingly, it reached its peak each year in mid-March. Overthrowing British oppression had taken a back seat to the far loftier goal of supporting the new Irish state. Parades were no longer in vogue. They were also costly. And merely demonstrating one's "Irishness" would no longer suffice. Aggressive fund-raising campaigns in support of the republic now accompanied this day of Irish remembrance and celebration. Though different from the St. Patrick's Day celebrations that he first encountered in the 1870s, Peter was very much a part of the new rituals, faithfully publishing his nationalist songs in honor of "Patrick's Day."

Patrick's Day in Ireland

Since the Saxon has departed from Erin's holy shore,
We often pray night and day they'll return never more.
From the Dublin slips they sailed in ships, across the channel far away;
So there is quiet and peace in Ireland now on Saint Patrick's day.
The Saxon flag came down in Dublin town where martyrs met their death,
Each one cried "God Save Ireland," with their dying breath;
They fought and bled, those now dead, are smoldering in the clay.
While we celebrate in Ireland on this Saint Patrick's Day.

Irish hearts do long for freedom. It will come yet, never fear.
It was Ireland's faith she got Free State so freedom's drawing near.
The north and south, there's no doubt, will together join someday;
And we will rejoice all over Ireland on some Saint Patrick's day.
No more by the bayonet Ireland is kept down,
It's no crime to pluck the Shamrock from Ireland's holy ground,
The Croppy Boy and Pat Malloy, every band can play,
And we can sing the "Wearing of the Green" on Saint Patrick's Day.

Now it would be grand if all Ireland only would unite.
Throw aside their bigotry and stand up for Erin's rights,
Help make Ireland a free nation as she was once before
When Brave Red Hugh and Brian Boru drove invaders from our shore.
Why not fly old Erin's flag from the spires of Belfast town

All be one together, the Far Ups and Far Downs,
And we will all sing, God save Ireland, and for freedom pray,
It's an Irishman's wish we will all see the next Saint Patrick's Day.

The emphasis of the celebration for the early part of the twentieth century focused on smaller gatherings held by the church schools, taverns, and the fraternal and benefit organizations. Irish history, ethnic pride, the Irish Republic, and fund-raising were at the heart of the day's events. Because so many Irish children attended parochial rather than public schools, they were now fully involved in the planned activities. The 1912 celebration at St. Patrick's School found fifty children joining with adults in an Irish Night performing skits, dramatic readings in English and Gaelic, songs, and dance before a capacity audience. Each child wore a white outfit trimmed with green. That same year, over 400 children from St. Mary's School, along with many adults, put on two grand performances much like their Irish counterparts from South Lawrence.

Three different divisions of the Hibernians in Lawrence held their own festivities that year. Division 1 met at the Spanish American Veterans' Hall, and members from Division 15 gathered in Lexington Hall. Members from Division 8 met at Hibernian Hall at the corner of White and Oak Street, the very heart of the Plains. The committee in charge of that year's festivities included future alderman Peter Carr, who was soon to launch his bid for the Statehouse, and Pat McNulty, who would serve as commissioner of engineering during the twenties. A sample of the evening's program included the following: Welcome by acting chairman Dr. M. F. Sullivan; recitation, Frank Carey; song, Robert Clifford; address, Father James T. O'Reilly; song, Nora Murphy; xylophone solo, Rose Wheatley; address, Mayor Michael A. Scanlon; Irish jig and reel, Michael Reardon; address, Katherine A. O'Keefe Mahoney, and a song by Lou Carrol.[9] Mayor Scanlon and Father O'Reilly also gave addresses at the Division 1 celebration that same night.

An account of the 1915 Patrick's Day festivities at St. Patrick's Parish read as follows: "St. Patrick's night was appropriately observed at St. Patrick's School hall last night with a real old fashioned Irish night. Vocal selections, readings, sketches and dances, all of a character to bring back tender memories of the mother land and to inspire youth with the patriotism that still lies dormant in every true Irish heart, were included in the elaborate and well presented concert program."[10]

Throughout the city, fraternal organizations held their own gatherings in halls decorated with green banners, shamrocks, sprigs of green, and Irish and American flags. That same year, Peter Cassidy spent St. Patrick's night at the Moose Lodge for a St. Patrick's whist party and dance. Peter served on the evening's organizing committee with several other lodge members including John E. Lowe, Timothy Shine, J. F. Manning, Arthur Pollard, and future alderman John W. McCarthy. Many of the societies held similar events. At each gathering one would find Irish poetry readings, songs and dance, food and beverage, lofty addresses on Irish history, impassioned speeches railing against England or longing for the Old Sod, somber toasts to Robert Emmett or Wolfe Tone, and lots and lots of green.

One traditional gathering spot for the Irish on St. Patrick's Day was the front window at McGrath's Department Store at 302-312 Essex Street. The *Evening Tribune* offered a front-page account of McGrath's "Irish window" in 1914, listing a small sample of "relics, souvenirs and mementoes of dear old Ireland" that were on display. Included were an oil painting of St. Patrick, a gold bracelet made in Dublin, Hibernian pictures, a seventy-five-year-old blackthorn stick, a picture of Robert Emmett, a pot of real shamrocks in Irish soil, rifles, a bayonet found after the battle of Vinegar Hill, an old Irish skillet and teapot, Irish lace and handkerchiefs, a 125 year-old Irish noggin, an oil painting of Captain Deacy, an Irish flag, and a shillelagh.

Not all of Peter's St. Patrick's Day poems reflected a forceful nationalistic tone. He frequently wrote in a more nostalgic voice that touched on one of the other dominant themes of Irish writers and musicians: the Irish diaspora. Irish immigrants historically viewed themselves as the victims of a forced exile from their homeland, who were caught in a dilemma of longing to return to Erin's shores while not wanting to leave the relatively prosperous life they had found in America. It was a subject about which Peter frequently wrote, and one that always touched the Irish community in Lawrence. As a contemporary critic wrote, "Homesickness has visited the heart of many an Irishman after hearing one of Peter Cassidy's songs of the Old Sod."[11] In his 1922 poem "Barney Agraa, Come Home" he blended two traditional longings of the Irish: the cry for a free Ireland with the call from a mother for her son to come home.

Barney Agraa, Come Home

Barney agraa, your old mammy wants you to come back home,
It's now a year since you left here, and sailed over the foam.
I thought I'd soon be with you, son, in the land across the sea,
My mind I've changed, here I'll remain, till I see old Ireland free.

You've heard my son, what England's done, Ireland she did vacate.
Liberated all Irish prisoners, and made Erin a Free State.
It looks like freedom's dawning on this Island in the sea.
My own gossoon, it's coming soon when Ireland will be free.

The British troops are going back to their dear old London town,
From the staff on Dublin's Castle the English flag's hauled down.
It's a Sinn Fein flag that's flying now, where the Union used to be,
So Barney, dear, come home here, we will soon have Ireland free.

There's a sight in Dublin, boy, that makes Irish hearts feel gay,
Those Black and Tans are now like lambs as they go to the quay.
No marching line, no flags flying, no playing of the band.
That's how Ireland's foe is forced to go, away from Ireland.

Barney o'chone, here alone for you I'll watch and pray.
That the good ship will bring you back home for St. Patrick's Day.
Some day you may go back again, to the land across the sea,
But you'll stay agraa, with your old mamma, till you see old Ireland free.

The first home owned by the Cassidy family in America was located at 53 Everett Street, just west of Shanty Pond. The South Side Grove is seen in the background. Courtesy the Cassidy Collection.

9

Politics and Patronage

I n May of 1921 Peter turned sixty years old and was still living in the second-floor apartment at 57 South Broadway with Maggie. He occasionally performed seasonal work as a common laborer, and he remained active in numerous fraternal and church organizations. All of his daughters had left the house except for the youngest, Frances, who was twenty-eight years old and working in a shoe factory. On June 22, however, she married Edgar "Scoots" Blanchette, Peter's first non-Irish son-in-law. Too poor to get their own apartment, Frances and Edgar moved in with Peter and Maggie. As a veteran of Battery C and a local bartender, Scoots and Peter became fast friends and readily adjusted to shared accommodations. Having Frances living with her mother made it easier for Peter to maintain his daily travels about the city. Having a grandson one year later made the arrangement even more enjoyable.

Several years later, Peter's daughter Tess and her husband also moved into the apartment. By the winter of 1925, the Cassidy home became even more crowded. Besides his wife, his two daughters and their husbands, now two young grandsons, Joseph and Buddy Blanchette, also called 57 South Broadway home. At this point, stepdaughter Margaret Coughlin decided to provide a better home for her parents as they moved into their final years. Never having married, she had saved enough money from her job as a domestic to build a two-story house on Everett Street in South Lawrence, just west of Shanty Pond in an area known as the Grove. Frances and Edgar Blanchette also moved to Everett Street. Though Peter now had to walk three blocks to the taverns and church on South Broadway, he kept up his daily routine and rarely went without a nickel beer and a smoke of his favorite cigar, Kelly Kids.

Peter continued to write and publish pointed commentary in poetry and song. Politics and patronage were still central themes. With the end of World

War I, thousands of veterans were looking for work and ready to support those who would oblige them. The Roaring Twenties were just beginning. Women got the vote, the nation's economy was on the upturn, and Calvin Coolidge was elected president. City government continued to grow larger, both in terms of employees and its budget. The new commission form of government was about ten years old, and the Irish held a comfortable stranglehold on major elected offices. The Irish politician was alive and well.

Patronage in Lawrence also had reached its peak. It was still the heart of economic and political advancement within the city, especially now, during the height of the Irish ascendancy. The mother's milk of politics, patronage was reaching new heights in its scope and openness. With hundreds of employees in their charge, all with family and friends, elected officials skillfully and sometimes aggressively used the power of their office to maintain their political base and thus their post. With a large veteran population in search of jobs, that task became more complex. The job market was oversupplied. Hard choices had to be made—political ones. Tensions mounted as too many men chased after available city jobs and veterans demanded special treatment. Peter's song about the "Newly Elected Aldermen" provided a transparent look at a time when patronage faced new challenges, but continued to be the essential craft of skilled and sometimes brazen practitioners.

The Newly Elected Aldermen
Callahan and Scanlon

You see before you now two men that's been elected;
When we ran for office that's what we expected.
We are proud to say that we we'e selected
As your two newly elected aldermen. (Break)

We ask our friends upon us for to call;
Sure you'll find us down at city hall;
You'll be welcomed any time at all
By the two newly elected aldermen. (Irish Jig)

To put our friends to work, it is our desire,
But the veterans say, that them we cannot fire;
They will stay on the job, till with old age they'll retire,
They tell the newly elected aldermen. (Break)

Soldiers that volunteered, and the soldiers in the draft,
Sailors that were on the seas, sailed ships fore and aft.
If you tell them they're fired, they just give the laugh,
To the newly elected alderman. (Irish Reel)

Callahan: "I'm sorry for Dan, for he filled the situation,
I was like a man I asked him for his resignation."
He said "My boy let's have an explanation"—
He told your newly elected alderman. (Break)

Scanlon: "Why I should keep vets to work? I really can't see,
When there's nothing for us to do now on the P.P.
To keep down expenses, its a good way you'll agree,
With your newly elected alderman." (Soft Shoe)

Both: We want to thank our friends for the way they stood behind us.
If there's anything you want, you'll know where to find us.
If we've forgot anything we promised, you want to remind us.
Your newly elected aldermen. (Break)

Call down and see us on a meeting night,
If anything goes wrong, you bet we'll make it right.
You can make up your mind, we won't be bluffed by White—
Your two newly elected aldermen. (Shimmy)

Peter wrote this song in mid-January of 1921, a week or so after the swearing-in ceremony for the two newly elected aldermen: Edward C. Callahan, the director of the public health and charities department, and Michael F. Scanlon, the director of the public property and parks department. Both men had previous political experience, but were serving their first terms in office under the commission form of government. Whether a small department such as property and parks or a large one like health and charities, all city departments shared one thing in common, their reliance on patronage. It served as the source of their employment pool and an enforcement mechanism for local politics. It would be hard to identify an elected official in Lawrence during this time who did not reward political friends and punish political enemies. Though everyone complained, everyone engaged in the same practices. How maddening it must have been to deal with the constant change in employment rolls of city government. The week before the election there was one list of men, and a few weeks later the list was very different.

Peter and his friends knew the rules well. It was the key to their life whether under the old city government or the new. The rules were simple. If your candidate won, you would likely get work over the next two years; a day here, a week there, and sometimes a month or more depending on whom you knew. To be sure, many job assignments were charity appointments to aid a family in need, such as the widow whose unemployed sons could bring much needed income into the home if only they had a job. On the other hand, if your candidate lost, you would likely be looking for work before too long. This was especially true for the higher-ranking positions that usually saw quick and wholesale terminations once the new alderman came into office. Each alderman needed loyal and trustworthy managers and supervisors. It was very common for these higher-profile casualties of an election year house-cleaning to return two years later to oppose the commissioner who put them out on the street.

The fall election of 1920 saw contests for the health and charities, and the property and parks seats on the city council. It marked the first year women were allowed to vote. The health and charities position was vacant because the incumbent, Robert S. Maloney, recently had been elected to the state legislature. Edward Callahan and William H. D. Vose vied for this large department. Michael Scanlon was seeking to defeat incumbent Alderman John A. Flanagan as director of property and parks. This election was calmer than most. There were no major controversies. The standard matters of lower costs and greater department efficiencies were debated, along with how the newly elected alderman would handle the distribution of work in his department. Mike Scanlon pledged to eliminate unnecessary expenses, cut waste, and substitute efficient men for inefficient men. Both Scanlon and his opponent expressed concern about holding the line on costs because wages were governed by union pay scales.

On December 14, 1920, Mike Scanlon and Ed Callahan defeated their opponents; Callahan by 825 votes and Scanlon by 1,576 votes. The following day local newspapers reported the thoughts and plans of the newly-elected aldermen. According to the *Lawrence Telegram*, "At the present time Mr. Callahan has not the slightest intention of any changes in the department. The new alderman is free to act as he sees fit. He has made no promises . . . not even to a laborer. Whether or not there will be any change in the administrative officers in his department, he has not yet decided. 'I intend,' said Callahan, 'to carefully study the department before making any changes.'" Like Callahan, Mike Scanlon indicated the need to "make a thorough survey of the ground" before formally announcing any changes in the employment rolls. "Of course there are some men who have worked with me whom I intend to reward, but I am going to look the ground over carefully before I make any changes."[1]

Two weeks later, on January 3, 1921, the careful study had apparently been completed by both men. On Mike Scanlon's first day on the job he ordered a shutdown of his department for several days, saving the city $1,620. At the same time, he announced his first key-position changes: John H. Reynolds would be the new foreman of the carpenters; Albert Noble was the foreman of painters; Bartholomew Young was named the department plumber; and Ed Flynn was appointed as superintendent for the suppression of gypsy moths, a position paying $2,000 a year. Scanlon also sought out the names of those workers who were protected from dismissal by civil service. On January 6, he endeared himself to the average workingman by proposing that the city council immediately start a public works program to put the unemployed to work. Scanlon maintained ambivalent feelings about the value of such charity programs, however, which he felt "pauperized the recipients." Ed Callahan had likewise felt the urgent need to provide work as he had been "deeply touched by the plea yesterday of at least 500 men seeking work."[2]

A serious controversy arose shortly after the election that dogged Scanlon for the next two years. Despite his order to shut down the department, fourteen veterans reported for work and later contested the loss of pay. They had worked throughout the morning on January 3 before the noon shutdown had occurred. After handing in their time cards to the department clerk, however, they were denied pay. According to Alderman Scanlon, he had not directed them to report to work in the first place. This spat soon proved to be about more than a few hours' pay, however. Veterans throughout the city became upset that they were being treated unfairly. Some felt that according to the Veterans Preference Act they were entitled to preference in job placement ahead of other men who had not fought in the war, almost equating their status to those in civil service positions.

Scanlon harkened back to his campaign promise to run a cost-efficient department where "inefficient" employees would be let go, and he challenged the expectations of veterans in job assignments. Stating that he was not unfriendly to veterans and that he still had many on the payroll, Scanlon asserted his right to direct his department. In a public statement he declared, "As a citizen, I have seen them [certain veterans] loitering and loafing, and I cannot get results from them. I want to start with a clean slate [and hire men] in whom I have confidence. . . . Why, if these men can retain their positions, within five years veterans will hold all the jobs in Massachusetts." Then he added, "There are some men in the department who were drafted into the army who were never within 500 miles of battle."[3] Within a few weeks, he discharged twelve veterans.

This power struggle grew rapidly, and before long the American Legion

Post in Lawrence had mounted a vigorous campaign against Alderman Scanlon. The veterans hired an attorney, and fired off a letter demanding an apology to all veterans and the reinstatement of those recently laid off. The Legion also threatened a recall drive. Scanlon astutely reassessed the situation and at a highly charged meeting on January 25, 1921, he offered a terse apology to the veterans who filled city hall, and agreed to rehire the dismissed veterans. The incident was not forgotten, though, as Scanlon's political opponents rubbed his nose in the controversy during the election campaign in November of 1922.

Ed Callahan began to flex his political muscle as quickly as Mike Scanlon. On Tuesday, January 4, 1920, Callahan announced a "belt-tightening move" and sought the resignation of longtime political foe, Superintendent of Sanitation Daniel Murphy, who also served as the head of the board of health for several years. As with the veterans controversy, things did not go smoothly. Murphy submitted his resignation from the health board but asked reconsideration by Callahan for the sanitation position. Callahan would have none of it, and Murphy took him to court.

Callahan's replacement was Dr. William Sullivan, also a fellow member of the board of health, and a critic of Murphy during and after the influenza outbreak of 1918. On January 5 the *Evening Tribune* headlines reported with some editorial slant, the "Official Axe Is Swung On Health Department Help," "Operations Were Resumed Wednesday and 50 of the Old Employees Dropped," "Callahan Rewards Supporter With Place At Health Department Stables—Frank McManus Goes After 29 Years of Service." The story continued, "Alderman Edward C. Callahan swung the axe when the Health Department resumed operations . . . and the heads of 50 employees dropped by the wayside; those who were left out in the cold being supplanted by a like number of new men who were on the right side of the fence at the recent election."[4] The paper went on to print the names of all the new men, most of whom were Irish. Several weeks later, Callahan closed the city store as a cost-cutting move. This resulted in the dismissal of several more men who were ex-veterans.

As mentioned earlier, those who were laid off after the election usually set about getting their friends elected two years later, or running for office themselves. Sometimes, however, more immediate responses took place. In early March, Alderman Callahan was walking through an alley near Oak Street on his way to work when he was approached by a recently laid-off laborer from the sanitation department, John Robertson. Two weeks earlier, Robertson had been pushed out of his job when pressure had been brought to bear to hire Robertson's nephew. Not wanting to retain two people from the same family, Callahan let the older Robertson go. After being denied a chance to return to work, Robertson attacked Callahan, striking him several times about the head before several men came to the alderman's aid. Later that same day, Callahan announced that he would not press charges against Robertson because his assailant was under the influence of "moonshine" at the time and did not fully realize what he was doing. He also stated that he would give Robertson a job with the department immediately. "I am charitable," said Callahan, "The good Lord said, 'Forgive them for they know not what they do.'"[5]

So started the first months on the job for the newly elected aldermen. Peter's song voiced his apparent support for both Scanlon and Callahan. Although Peter certainly felt a loyalty to the veterans, he appeared to be more in tune with the rules of the patronage game: to the victors go the spoils. Both Scanlon and Callahan hired many veterans while in office, but they were veterans of their own choosing, not their predecessors. Peter also mentioned Mayor Billy White near the end of the poem. No friend of Mayor White, Peter alluded to the mayor's early efforts in January to intimidate the new aldermen into establishing spending practices and priorities that were in line with his own. White's strategy proved unsuccessful and his approach provocative. He would be a one-termer in office. Finally, in his song Peter included mention of various dance steps at the end of each verse: the Irish jig, the Irish reel, the soft shoe, etc. A curious addition, he may have engaged in the dance steps at various points while performing his song. Given his reputation as an entertainer, this is probably the best explanation.

It is worth noting that during the first decades of the commission form of government, the names of the same two dozen men come up over and over again. Often, they switched roles within city government, usually serving multiple terms in office. These men were the heart of the Irish ascendancy in Lawrence. In November of 1922 it was Callahan's and Scanlon's turns to seek reelection, each aspiring to multiple terms. Not surprisingly, Ed Callahan was opposed by Daniel Murphy, William Vose, and a host of other contenders. Mike Scanlon likewise faced a broad slate of candidates, including the man he had defeated two years earlier, John A. Flanagan.

During the primaries and the days leading up to the December 12 election, Callahan suffered accusations from his many opponents. Among other things, he was charged with offering sweetheart deals to friends, buying inferior trucks, dismissing an ex-veteran, overpurchasing milk for the city hospital, and allowing the patients at the tuberculosis home to go without care for days. Besides issuing strong denials and a defense of his record, Alderman Callahan promised voters a new incinerator, a new municipal hospital, and a new trunk sewer line for the residents of South Lawrence. He also reminded organized labor of his support during the Strike of 1922, and the 780 baskets of food that had been distributed to strikers and their families by his department. Alderman Callahan focused most of his campaign on the need for improving the city hospital and poor home by building a joint facility at a different location. This would not come to pass for many years, however. According to the newspapers, Callahan had been poorly served by his advisors while in office and they predicted he would have difficulty being reelected.

Mike Scanlon had a more successful term in office than had Callahan, and his campaign was not as fiercely fought. Nonetheless, he repeatedly faced references to the veterans' controversy early in his term. To make matters worse, one of his primary opponents was William Donohue, a veteran who had lost a limb during the war. Scanlon was also criticized for his role in having the city purchase the Fr. Mathew Temperance Society property. As that organization's former president, the sale begged for charges of conflict of interest. Scanlon fought the accusations and charged his main opponent, Flanagan, with allowing city property to fall into disrepair, failing to live within his budget when he was in office, and, interestingly, spending "10 cents on public property and 90 cents on patronage." Flanagan supported more funding for the schools and the construction of a new city hall, which would begin one year later. On election day, Mike Scanlon lost to John Flanagan by a mere 174 votes. Ed Callahan was soundly defeated by William Vose, 11,867 to 7,026 votes. Callahan and Scanlon came into office together, and they left together; both were one-termers.[6,7]

Another skilled practitioner of the patronage system in Lawrence was Peter's friend Pat McNulty, who also sat on the all-Irish city council with Ed Callahan, Mike Scanlon, and Peter Carr. Not surprisingly, a look through the list of city employees continued to reveal many Irishmen on the payroll, and McNulty hoped to keep it that way. Playing on themes from the trenches of World War I, Peter's poem "Over The Top with Pat" was written just prior to the aldermanic elections in December of 1923. He tried to rally supporters to do the hard campaign work necessary to insure victory for his friend. Two years earlier, in December 1921, the forty-eight-year-old McNulty had won a hard-fought election for the director of engineering seat by defeating the three-term incumbent, Alderman John F. Finnegan. Pat McNulty now controlled one of the larger city departments, and he would carry on that tradition. He was outspoken, flamboyant, knowledgable, and quite popular— a perfect match for the job. McNulty also possessed what was possibly the most important qualification for the director's post: thick skin. During the winter of 1922-23, when complaints mounted about his department's failure to clear the snow promptly from the city's streets, McNulty's arrogant response was, "God put it there, let God take it way."[8]

Over the Top with Pat

Mac, we're glad to see you're well coming on election time,
We'd like to see you once more on the firing line;
You have got good officers and men let me tell you that
They all do swear they will be there to go over the top with Pat.

The big battle is drawing nigh, the caucus will come first,
The enemy you beat two years ago, this year you'll beat him worse;
Like your last campaign it will be clean, throw no mud or spat,
We'll put on a spurt and get to work to go over the top with Pat.

Don't forget the ladies, Pat, they're with you one and all,
They are holding rallies in their homes, rallies in the halls.
You hear nothing but McNulty, the way that they do chat,
Sweethearts and wives will give their lives to go over the top with Pat.

When the ballots they are counted and the battle is all o'er,
Headlines on the papers will read, "McNulty, two years more."
The big and small, short and tall, lean ones and the fat
Will be the crowd that will feel proud to go over the top with Pat.

The second stanza of the poem indicates Peter's desire that the reelection campaign be free of mudslinging, just like the previous election when McNulty defeated Finnegan. A close study of the campaign indicates, however, that it didn't quite work out that way. In fact, the previous election wasn't a model of political etiquette, either. In the weeks leading up to the election of 1923, the issues were vigorously debated. Next to the mayoral race, the fight for director of engineering was the hottest of the remaining contests. During the two weeks before the December election, John Finnegan mounted an aggressive campaign to retake the seat he had lost two years earlier. He and McNulty frequently traded political jabs as they stumped for votes. At every opportunity, Finnegan would attack McNulty, centering his attacks on issues of department priorities, waste, political patronage, and, not surprisingly, snow removal.

McNulty didn't hesitate to fire back at his opponent. When Finnegan attacked McNulty's decision to finish the Shanty Pond Sewer extension, McNulty charged that Finnegan lacked the courage to tackle the sewer project during his tenure in office. Finnegan focused on McNulty's snow-removal policies during the previous winter and linked them to political ambition and

Alderman Pat McNulty, circa 1922.
Courtesy Immigrant City Archives.

payback. Frequently, after a number of the large snowstorms, McNulty had his crews clear snow from Essex Street, Lawrence's main business thorough-fare, but not the many adjoining side streets. Finnegan charged that McNulty was saving money in his budget so he could hire men onto patronage jobs just before the election. He protested that hundreds of extra employees had been hired during the fall for the building and street departments.

McNulty responded, stating that Lawrence had received more snow during the most recent winter than it had during the entire six years Finnegan was in office. He also attacked Finnegan's ability to manage his department's budget while an alderman. McNulty never shied away from the issue of giving men work. In fact, he was proud of it. In May of 1922, when McNulty proposed that the city council allocate money to further develop the Shanty Pond Sewer, he partially justified his expensive proposal by stating that it put many men back to work. The council agreed. When subjected to the same attack during the 1925 campaign, McNulty said, "I have been accused of putting boys to work during the bad times and I have done so. But the boys I put to work were the sons of widows who needed their support and as long as I am in office, I will be glad to give work to the sons of widows."[9] All politi-cians, including John Finnegan, took care of their friends and supporters, often with part-time work throughout the year, or by helping a constituent who had a personal problem.

On the second Tuesday in December, 1923, one day after receiving the endorsement of the *Evening Tribune*, Pat McNulty won reelection as director of engineering, defeating John Finnegan 12,631 to 9,777 votes. In January 1924 he was elected president of the city council by his peers. Two years later, Alderman McNulty faced a new challenger, a successful business man from South Lawrence, John W. McCarthy. Not surprisingly, all the same issues came to the fore once again, including snow removal. This time, some of the local newspapers chimed in on the issue well before the campaign even started. An *Evening Tribune* editorial scolded McNulty for his practices: "Under Alderman McNulty . . . the shoveling of snow out of the gutters has become more or less a lost art. . . . snow storms seem to be a sort of nemesis for him."[10] In December of 1925, Pat McNulty turned aside the challenger thanks to a strong bloc of support, including the Shanty Pond Poet.

As happens with most political incumbents, time in office generates increasing numbers of political enemies. Pat's final term was marked by a great deal of controversy and criticism. As a result, the December 1927 election saw a rematch between McNulty and his opponent from two years earlier, John W. McCarthy. For several weeks leading up to the election, McCarthy pounded at the incumbent accusing him of waste, overspending, cronyism, and hiring men around election time to "buy" their votes. McNulty fired back by calling McCarthy the "spite candidate," who was looking out only for himself and who was making more promises than he could ever hope to fulfill. McNulty claimed that he "knew of eight men who have been promised the engineer position at the pumping station by [McCarthy]."[11] Both candidates played to their regional bases of support. McCarthy openly courted his friends and neighbors in South Lawrence, telling them, "If I am elected, there are many streets in this district sadly neglected that I will take care of."[12] For his part, Pat McNulty warned, "You people in North Lawrence better look out. If a South Lawrence man is elected you will be [out of luck] because he will never be able to fulfill all his South Lawrence promises."[13] This time, McCarthy won the battle of campaign promises, defeating Pat McNulty by almost 2,500 votes. He took his seat in January of 1928.[14]

John W. McCarthy was a favorite political acquaintance of Peter Cassidy. It had been just two years since the brutal campaign that resulted in McCarthy finally beating McNulty for the director of engineering seat on the council. McCarthy's 2,500 vote margin of victory was due in large part to support from his Irish neighbors in the Shanty Pond district, Ward Six. It was so strong that he took all of its eight precincts by margins approaching two-to-one. The political cycle was about to repeat itself, however. The fall of 1929 meant that it was now John McCarthy's turn to defend his seat. Not surprisingly, McCarthy found himself the victim of many of the same charges that he had hurled at Pat McNulty just two years earlier.

The timing of the poem "Keep McCarthy In" coincided with the final days of a difficult campaign between John McCarthy and his challenger, Robert F. Hancock. Published on Sunday, December 8, 1929, the poem made reference to the "slanders, mud and dirt" that characterized the campaign. So badly did Peter want McCarthy to win his reelection bid in December of 1929 that he wrote and published three poems about his friend during the brief election period. Right from the start, McCarthy was attacked by a handful of primary candidates in November, with Hancock being the most organized, vocal, and well funded. After placing second in the primary results, Hancock set his sights on the December elections and continued his daily barrage of allegations against McCarthy. As a former technical education student at Wentworth Institute, Hancock questioned McCarthy's engineering skills, knowing full well that his educational and technical background was limited. Calling McCarthy the "egotistical candidate," he repeatedly accused the incumbent of courting his political friends and paying too much for road-building materials, especially on the recent Den Rock road project. In addition, he chastised McCarthy on the size and power of his political machine, alleging numerous instances of political favors for loyal supporters.

Some local newspapers, especially the *Lawrence Sunday News*, pounded McCarthy as well. The *News* repeatedly printed scathing, full-page attacks on the incumbent, publicly accusing him of graft, removing veterans from the work rolls, and shaking down helpless employees for campaign contributions. "Well McCarthy . . . hang your head in shame. Why did you vote to remove the war service clerk? Why did you remove Frank Fox, a world war veteran who was gassed and awarded a medal for bravery . . . What did you do to Eddie O'Leary, the hero of Dead Man's Curve? . . . What did you do to 'Spec' Donovan? . . . Shame McCarthy!"[15]

In spite of these charges, John McCarthy was considered by many in Lawrence to be an honest, hard-working, and self-made man. When he left school at the age of fourteen, he went to work for the Lawrence Rubber Company for three dollars a week. Later, he was employed at a shoe store, which he soon came to manage. Wanting more for himself, he struck out on his own, purchased a wagon and started selling shoes on the streets of South Lawrence. At the age of twenty-two, he purchased a larger covered wagon for forty-five dollars and a horse for thirty-five dollars, and expanded his shoe business. Confident of his condition in life at this time, he once said "Everything looked so good to me that I did not even carry an umbrella when it was raining."[16,17]

In 1912, McCarthy began one of his most productive business endeavors—a public garage that was so successful it doubled in size within three years. Working twelve-hour days, seven days a week, McCarthy's newest enterprise soon grew into a garage and truck sales business on South Broadway. He constructed a second building at 218 South Broadway that was the start of a new auto district in the city. Later he purchased an even larger tract of land near the railroad tracks on South Broadway where he built several more buildings. John McCarthy was very successful and well respected by his friends and neighbors in South Lawrence. If he hoped to hold off the challenge of Robert Hancock, he would need all of that support from Shanty Pond and help from Peter as well.

Keep McCarthy In

The caucuses are over now; we know McCarthy won.
The people appreciate all the good work he has done.
The fight isn't over yet, soon the last clash will begin,
So get out your votes election day and keep McCarthy in.

There never was an alderman that did such work before,
He rounded so many corners with sixty streets or more.
Four thousand jobs he gave out too, a regiment of men,
They all will vote election day to keep McCarthy in.

You could find McCarthy on the job; he was never known to shirk.
Every man he'd meet with a smile who was seeking him for work.
If he couldn't place you right away he would tell you "Call again."
And then you'd bet a job you'd get. So keep McCarthy in.

Let them throw their slanders; let them cast their mud and dirt,
With the people of the present day such tactics do not work.
You cannot keep a good man down, that's why they'll stick by him.
So cast your vote election day and keep McCarthy in.

Chorus:
Let the slogan be McCarthy; make it very long and loud.
Talk McCarthy to your neighbor, talk McCarthy to the crowd.
Talk on the street to those you meet, the tall, fat, short or slim,
Then you'll have the votes on election days to keep McCarthy in.

Needless to say, Hancock focused his attention on McCarthy's less flattering traits. On the day before the election, he purchased large ads in the local papers that listed almost three dozen allegations about Alderman McCarthy. Entitled "The Final Sum-up of Truth," Hancock publicly pledged to donate a hundred dollars to both the Lawrence City Mission and to Catholic Charities if McCarthy would respond "honestly" to his accusations and allow the district attorney to review the matter. Excerpts from this final salvo read as follows:

> How many private driveways . . . have you built since you took office? Why wasn't the oil contract . . . and copper pipe contract given to the lowest bidder? Have you not now the greatest political machine in the city? Why should you take double the amounts of money to build your streets? Is it a fact that you added one hundred men to the street department force [last] Saturday, and now have four hundred employed with little or no real work to do? Are they to be discharged on Wednesday [the day following the election]?[18]

McCarthy did his best to respond to Hancock's charges in the final days of the campaign. He accused his opponent of being unfair and misrepresenting the facts and figures about the road projects. He denied accusations that he forced department employees to contribute money to his campaign or to take campaign cards for display purposes. And he strongly rejected Hancock's claim that he had "thumbed his nose at him in Lexington Hall in the presence of 400 people." Fortunately for McCarthy, time ran out for Hancock and the election was held on Tuesday, December 10, 1929. As before, the support from Shanty Pond and the rest of South Lawrence was very strong, and McCarthy handily beat his opponent 14,432 to 10,292 votes.

Like virtually all successful politicians during this era—Carr, Finnegan, Maloney, McNulty, Scanlon, and the rest—John McCarthy had a large and politically savvy bloc of loyalists behind him. It was the exception for campaign rhetoric not to include charges that an incumbent was improperly using patronage jobs to buy votes, or that a candidate had behind him a large, ruthless political machine that extracted financial support from employees. In this respect, John McCarthy was very much like his political peers. He did, infact, have one of the largest and best organized blocs behind him, and he treated his supporters well. Annually in the fall, he would sponsor the John McCarthy Outing for engineering department employees, their families, and friends. Several thousand supporters would attend and spend the day eating, drinking, playing games, competing in sporting contests, and winning gifts and prizes. The outings provided supporters with an opportunity to demonstrate their loyalty to the alderman and for him to court favor with his constituents.

Although all politicians played the patronage game to some extent, McCarthy paid a higher price for playing than most. During May and June of 1931, an election year, serious allegations of wrongdoing were made against McCarthy that crippled him politically. When the election season formally began that fall, the incumbent spent his days on the witness stand instead of on the stump seeking reelection. For eight days in October, testimony was given in court against McCarthy and two friends who worked as department supervisors and campaign organizers: John F. Sullivan and Joseph M. Rinehart. The trial exposed to public view the inner workings of the patronage system in Lawrence. Each week the front page of the local papers would print verbatum accounts of courtroom testimony, detailing the political intrigues being played out behind the election scenes. With each new commissioner would come a multitude of jobs for campaign supporters, while those loyal to the ousted candidate would face certain layoffs. For Peter and thousands like him, such patronage jobs and the manner in which they were doled out were commonplace. As his poems suggested, this was just the way things were done.

That same fall, on consecutive Sundays in late September, a total of 7,000 friends and supporters once again attended John McCarthy's outings. On September 27, the eve of his upcoming trial, he spoke to a crowd of 5,000 people and thanked them for their loyal support. "It is very encouraging for a man to know he has so many friends who have confidence and faith in him despite the efforts of his enemies to discredit his public acts in trying to do his duty to the best of his ability and with the best interests of the people at heart. I feel this vast gathering is the best possible answer to my criticizers because it shows you have confidence in me and are satisfied that I have done my best to conduct the Engineering Department under my control honestly and faith-fully."[19] Peter wrote of this gathering as well.

McCarthy's Outing

Was you at McCarthy's outing, now let me tell you boy,
That sure was some outing every one there did enjoy;
Plenty of eating and drinking, 'twas of the Volstead kind,
There was nothing such, as a drink of hooch, no man had a sign.
Some came on bicycles, in autos; and others came by air;
They came in trucks and bus, made no fuss, just wanted to be there;
Some came in hacks, and on horse-back, also the one horse-shay,
To shake the hand, tell the Alderman, they'd be with him Election Day.

The morning was murky, but the day turned out fine,
Everyone that came to the outing, was there for a good time.
To hear the cheers from that crowd when McCarthy took that stand,
You could hear the sound for miles around, joined by the Legion band.
Though the day came clear, they had no fear of sunshine or rain,
For such a throng of five thousand strong will ne'er be seen again.
John felt proud to see the crowd, he knew it was the sort,
That one could declare, all was there was a McCarthy vote.

At McCarthy's trial testimony focused on a fund-raising scheme before and during the election of 1929, and offered telling insight on how politics in Lawrence worked. Sullivan and Rinehart helped organize a social club for workers of the engineering department: the "S and W Club." Witnesses at the trial stated that department supervisors Sullivan and Rinehart would approach club members, most of whom had received jobs from McCarthy, with requests for contributions to help pay for past and present campaign expenses. Members were reminded of all the good things the incumbent had done for them and the city. Sullivan would add, "I am working like the rest of you and only get $33 a week. Now do you fellows think it is fair for one man [McCarthy] to have to bear the expense himself?" Rinehart would insist "We are going to ask for a lump sum, but some of the members of the department have been loafing for a long while so we will make weekly assessments [usually $10 a week for five weeks]. We don't want any of you fellows bellyaching."[20] The money was used to meet campaign expenses including the popular McCarthy outing. Although McCarthy's attorney attempted to defend his client by pointing to the long-established campaign practices of other politicians, the judge objected stating that McCarthy's conduct was on trial, not politics in Lawrence.

In spite of his popularity, less than one month later, McCarthy was convicted of accepting a bonus and soliciting and accepting political contributions. Sullivan and Rinehart were found guilty of similar crimes. The *Lawrence Sunday News* was elated. "Like butter and cheese, city jobs have been put on the blocks . . . with the highest bidder standing the best chance to land the berth. Folk who have sought to get friends city jobs have had to see the bagmen, . . . Grafting in the city of Lawrence has to stop."[21]

All three men appealed their convictions to the Essex County Superior Criminal Court, but the lower court decision was upheld on February 11, 1933. Judge Fosdick directed John McCarthy to begin serving a one-year jail term immediately and to pay a $500 fine. Sullivan and Rinehart were each given three-month sentences. John McCarthy and his contemporary officeholders now realized that the rules of the political game in Lawrence were changing.

With McCarthy embroiled in his courtroom ordeal in the fall of 1931, his old nemesis Robert F. Hancock defeated Joseph A. Jordan for the director of engineering post. Jordan was a McCarthy loyalist who openly voiced proud support for his friend during the campaign. By the summer of 1933, McCarthy secured an early release from jail. With encouragement from his many loyal supporters, he again ran for the director of engineering position that fall against John T. Kilcourse. During the pre-election debates, McCarthy was defiant when his past troubles came up, stating that he could look every citizen in the eye because "I did everything in my power to give Lawrence an honest, honorable administration. Some people thought I would stay down and crushed. They didn't approve of McCarthy and his methods. I was your true director of engineering. I was not controlled by contractors, nor was I a mechanical toy in the city council." He added that if he had tried to please everybody, "he would not have had to go through the experience he did."[22]

For his part, John Kilcourse ran a highroad campaign, making only broad allusions to McCarthy's past. His final campaign ads righteously read, "Being by nature a kindly, bighearted man, John T. Kilcourse draws a veil of charity over the complete record of his opponent."[23]

On election day, 1933, John McCarthy's attempt at a comeback was turned aside by the voters. Kilcourse defeated him 17,662 to 11,084 votes. Four years later, McCarthy was narrowly defeated in the 1937 primaries by Daniel Ferris and John T. Kilcourse. In 1941, however, he succeeded in making his comeback by defeating incumbent Dan Ferris for the engineering seat by almost a two-to-one margin. He remained in office until he retired from politics in 1949 and even served as president of the city council for several years. John McCarthy was not the first elected official in Lawrence to suffer legal consequences for his political ambitions, nor would he be the last. For a time, his troubles did have a chilling effect on his political peers. The convergence of power and money that has always accompanied politics resulted in an eventual return to business as usual. Though the names and tactics had changed, political payback remained.[24]

Peter Cassidy proudly holds his infant grandson, Buddy Blanchette outside his new home on Everett Street. Fall 1925. Courtesy the Cassidy Collection.

10

The Wets vs. the Drys

The stereotype of the drunken, red-nosed Irishman has been around for over a century. To some degree, this image can be attributed to the vicious, nativist campaign waged against Irish Catholics during the latter half of the nineteenth century. It also has its roots in certain cultural traditions originating in Ireland, and may be a by-product of strict religious teachings on moral issues. As with most stereotypes, there is also a bit of truth bound up within the myth. Much of Peter Cassidy's social life was spent in local saloons. There were hundreds of them scattered throughout Lawrence. Peter and his cohorts certainly enjoyed drinking beer, whiskey, and a host of other libations while sharing good times together. Understandably, they became alarmed as the temperance movement continued to gather support among the voters. The controversy surrounding the free lunch in 1914 paled in comparison to subsequent proposals calling for a ban on the production and sale of alcoholic beverages. It was a specter that caused Peter considerable distress.

The temperance movement began in Lawrence almost as soon as the first stone slabs were laid for the great dam across the Merrimack River. The city's Irish community and the Catholic Church were at the center of the move- ment right up to and through Prohibition. In September of 1849, Father Theobald Mathew, the famous leader of the temperance movement in Ireland, came to Lawrence to speak. In the years that followed, the Irish had their own chapter of the Fr. Mathew Temperance Society. Year after year the citizens of Lawrence would wrestle with the problems related to the use of alcohol. From 1852 to 1870, the city was considered "dry," but the sale of beer and wine was permitted from 1870 to 1875. Thereafter, either the citizenry or the board of aldermen would vote annually on the "license option." With two exceptions, 1887 and 1892, they always voted favorably.

Throughout the rest of the nineteenth century, the nation struggled with the question of alcohol consumption. Numerous organizations sprang up with the shared goal of eliminating the production, sale, and consumption of alcohol through local and state legislation. They included the Prohibition Party in 1869, the Woman's Christian Temperance Union in 1873, the Anti-Saloon League in 1893, the Lincoln-Lee Legion in 1903, and the Scientific Temperance Federation in 1906. Their strongly held views were a direct reaction to the negative social consequences that accompanied alcohol use: drunkenness, absenteeism, violence, crime, poverty, and a host of other antisocial, anti-family behaviors. Here again, Lawrence fit the mold. During the latter half of the nineteenth century, the city's Irish population frequently made up the highest percentage of individuals appearing in police court. As frequently, the crimes involved were related to alcohol consumption.

Father O'Reilly was the leading Catholic clergyman in support of the temperance movement. In fact, he is most responsible for the few occasions when the license option resulted in "no" votes. An eloquent speaker, he effectively framed the arguments against the consumption of alcohol in the minds of many of the faithful. "The popular custom of drinking in social life, the prevailing sentiment that associates intoxicating drink with all forms of relaxation and pleasure must be met by the heroic virtue of total abstinence. . . . [T]he good things of life can best be enjoyed in the full use of the faculties of the soul. . . . [H]e who purchases pleasure at the loss of his senses and in the delirium of intoxication is his own greatest enemy."[1] At a meeting of the Fr. Mathew Temperance Society on December 5, 1897, Father O'Reilly summarized the sentiments of the temperance movement and urged political action at the ballot box. "This question is a purely moral one. We all recognize the degrading influence of intemperance. Every man, woman, and child knows that it is the great evil that is eating at the foundations of public liberty. . . . The law gives us a weapon."[2]

In many respects, the temperance movement was a battle between rural and urban America. It was a drawn-out contest between the "wets" in large northeastern cities and the "drys" just about everywhere else. In the decade leading up to World War I, the movement became more noticeably focused on complete national prohibition. It was clear the drys were winning the day. The old battle cry of "The Saloon Must Go" was replaced by a call for a complete ban on the production, distribution, sale, and consumption of alcoholic beverages. State governments across the country had imposed prohibition statutes in all but a handful of states, including New York, Massachusetts, and New Jersey. With America's entry into the war, the prohibition forces made their final successful push. In December of 1917, Congress passed legislation calling for an amendment outlawing alcoholic beverages. Within just thirteen months, on January 16, 1919, the necessary thirty-six states had voted their concurrence. One year to the date, on January 16, 1920, Prohibition went into effect.

The Volstead Act was the enabling legislation behind the Eighteenth Amendment, which made it illegal to produce, sell, and consume alcoholic beverages. As with much of the nation, enforcing Prohibition in Lawrence proved to be a significant challenge for law enforcement officials. While Lawrence had struggled throughout its history with the social ills related to alcohol sales and consumption, the Volstead Act greatly magnified these problems. On the eve of the ban, parties and mock funerals were held at establishments throughout the city. The day after the ban, Lawrence police began to arrest those in violation of the new law. The *Lawrence Telegram* promptly published the new rules on the front page for all to see. "From now on, Don't drink liquor in public or take it there, Don't transport liquor. . . or carry it on your person, Don't make home beverages containing one half of one percent of liquor or more. Don't tell anyone where or how to get a drink . . . ." After listing fourteen of such admonitions, the paper finally cautioned, "If you DO, in any case, the government'll get you."[3] While many heeded the warning, many did not.

Prohibition went into effect within a year of the return of millions of soldiers from France. While most of these young men were already accustomed to the saloon life-style before the war, many months in France had given them a more worldly view of the good life. Hence, the famous World War I song, "How You Gonna Keep 'em Down on the Farm after They've Seen Par-eee." It should also be noted that Prohibition was voted in by Congress and the states while millions of men were overseas. To come home to such a restrictive new social order was too difficult for many to bear. In urban areas such as Lawrence, disregard for the law was rampant.

Throughout the following decade, the daily newspapers offered nonstop accounts of police raids, court appearances, fines, and jail terms. Yet, there was no letup in the production, distribution, use, and abuse of this illegal substance. With the passing of each month the number of violations of the Volstead Act increased. The members of the local liquor squad from the police department were kept very busy confiscating a host of alcoholic concoctions that flooded the city: "moonshine," "jakey," hard cider, "raw alkie," paint thinner, whiskey, Jamaican Ginger, wood alcohol, and one-ounce bottles of split alcohol known as "smiles." Store proprietors and local entrepreneurs were hauled into court and fined for violating the law. By October of 1920, the local judge became frustrated by repeat offenders and began issuing jail sentences. "The first jail sentence imposed by Judge Mahoney in a liquor case was ordered this morning in the case of Louis Beaumier, proprietor of a "near beer" shop at 426 Broadway, who was sentenced to three months in the house of correction on his second appearance."[4]

Though fines and jail time were consistently handed out by the courts, the number of violations steadily increased. By the end of Prohibition's first year, the number of arrests related to liquor law violations in Lawrence had risen from 9 cases in 1919 to 171 in 1920.[5] In the years that followed, the city's 126 police officers would have their hands full. Judge J. J. Mahoney called for mandatory jail sentences for those caught selling moonshine. It was becoming clear that the public was not abiding by the new law of the land. In fact, many were contemptuous of it. More troubling for some was the reality that the theory behind Prohibition was flawed. Proponents argued that once the saloons had been shut down and the sale of alcohol made illegal, the absence of intoxicating beverages would discourage use by the public at large, and especially by the younger generation. They were wrong.

Judge Mahoney continued to lament the flaws of Prohibition. "It was thought that our young men would not care to drink after the Volstead Act went into effect, but what do we find? We find them going in search of the stuff when before prohibition they never touched it . . . [and] we find many young men under age drinking the stuff. . . . There's a spirit of unrest among the fellows who sell these liquors. They see other fellows going up to Canada and transporting the stuff to the city and making from $1,000 to $1,500 on a cargo and wonder why they can't do it. Then they try it and here's the result."[6]

An entire culture evolved around the procurement of "hootch." Alcoholic beverages were concocted throughout Lawrence and surrounding towns, and shipped in from as far away as Canada. The Lawrence police spent much of their time on stakeouts, peeping into windows and digging up basement stashes of moonshine. Very often dealers would employ youths in their distribution schemes, hoping to deflect their own guilt. In one such case, John J. Sipsey and sixteen-year-old James Carroll were charged with illegally keeping and selling alcohol at Sipsey's "near beer" shop at 389 Chestnut Street. Only young Carroll was present when police raided the establishment. Standing before the judge, Sipsey said the liquor was left in his shop several days earlier by an unknown man, and it was to be picked up by the former owner, Thomas McGuire. Carroll asserted he was only "minding" the place and did not know that the large can in the basement marked "Mobil Oil" was full of moonshine. Swift justice was handed down as Sipsey was fined $100, and the charges against Carroll were dismissed.[7]

By 1925 the local papers gave almost constant attention to infractions of the Volstead Act. "Again today, for the fifth day this week, liquor law violators held first place in the district court docket, eight appearing this morning."[8] On this now typical day, Morris Rosenthal of 79 Lowell Street came to court to take the blame for his wife's illegal sale of liquor. Theodore Greenwood, Ernest Sicard, Peter Barilo, and Patrick Cunningham were brought before the judge on charges of "illegal keeping," and several other men were charged for drunkenness. Members of the liquor squad patrolled the city, day and night, looking for liquor law violations. Later that same year, the newspaper reported the arrest of Philip Bouchard of 199 Lowell Street. Police patiently watched their suspect through a basement window as he filled bottles with alcohol ". . . [W]hen he came to the top of the cellar stairway they accosted him. 'What 'cha got there?' they asked. 'Cough medicine,' answered Mr. Bouchard. 'Cough up!' the minions commanded, and they caught him 'cold.'"[9]

Early in 1925, the *Evening Tribune* ran a story about a policeman who had drowned in the north canal. Earlier that same evening he had been seen drinking heavily while on duty at the winter carnival. In the days that followed, editorials and official pronouncements condemned any further instances of drunkenness by police while on duty. That same winter carnival offered even more examples of how prevalent the illegal liquor trade was in the city. "Hip-pocket bootleggers are plying their nefarious trade at the winter carnival grounds. . . . The youth of the city who journey to the toboggan chute and ski slides to participate in winter sport activities are being tempted by the demon rum in flasks being concealed in the hip pockets of the 'dollar chasers.'. . . Some dealers sell only by the drink, carrying with them a whiskey glass, while others carry a sufficiently large stock to enable them to deal with half pints and pints. . . . However it is sold, the hip-pocket bootleggers are doing a 'land office' business at the winter carnival grounds."[10]

Not surprisingly, the moonshine problem brought charges of corruption against politicians, bar owners, brewmasters and members of the police force. As the fall of 1925 approached, there was great displeasure among the voters with the performance of the incumbent director of public safety, Henry W. Marshall. Conditions had become so bad that eight candidates entered the primary election for Marshal's seat. His tenure was the subject of wide-ranging attacks by his opponents, each of whom publicly assaulted his record of the previous two years. Alderman Marshall's reorganization of the police department drew fire, along with the alleged lack of parking, the need for more police call boxes, the cost of running the department, and the menace of the dance halls scattered around the city. He was vilified most often, however, for failing to live up to his earlier campaign promise to rid the city of "deadly moonshine" and the crime and corruption associated with it. In addition to their attacks on Marshall, most of his opponents also made their own promises to the electorate. These included a more cost-efficient department, an end to corruption and favoritism, public swimming pools and even a rather unique plan by candidate Dennis Carey to provide city residents with cool drinking water in the summer by putting ice in the city's 41,000,000 gallon reservoir on Tower Hill.

Patrick "Patsy" O'Connor, was also a candidate in the primary election for director of public safety. O'Connor didn't fit the mold of most Irish politicians in Lawrence. On the surface he may have looked like all the others, but his campaign style in the fall of 1925 set him apart.[11] As soon as O'Connor landed in Lawrence from Ireland, he had set about making his way in his new homeland, first working as a dyer in the mills until 1902 and then as an office clerk. In 1907 he started his own business, a saloon at 106 Lawrence Street. When Prohibition went into effect in January of 1920, Patsy and his saloon fell upon hard times. He went to work as a shoe dealer and later moved into the real estate business where he was quite successful. In 1925 Patsy O'Connor decided to try his hand at politics.

Like his competitors, O'Connor felt "the Lawrence Police Department [was] without a head," and he, too, expressed the need to rid the city of the corruption related to the moonshine business. He pledged to "do what is possible . . . to aid in the betterment of the comforts of the people . . . " and promised that "all appointments . . . will be made on the basis of Character, Merit and Legal rating."[12] In an unusual move, he even made his first appointment prior to being elected. Three days before the primary, he announced that if elected he would appoint Sergeant James P. Gallagher, a policeman of high repute, as city marshal in charge of the police force. O'Connor hoped this declaration would signal to the voters and to bootleggers that he was serious about cleaning up the city. One handbill shouted in bold typeface, "The battle for a clean city has been won by one stroke of publicity . . . [this appointment] has been received by lovers of our city, our homes and our families with words of praise, and a shock has been given to the opposition."[13]

The focus of O'Connor's campaign, however, was on the issue of his own positive character traits rather than the typical approach of attacking his opponents. His handbills and advertisements were full of slogans such as "A Man of Few Words, But He Means What He Says," or his favorite, "A Clean Man Means a Clean City." He pledged honest enforcement of the law and protection for the home and family life. Beyond this, he had few specifics and kept to the high road. Night after night, Patsy rather bravely would tell his audiences, "I am not going to say yet what I intend to do, or not do, if I get elected. . . . I would rather wait until I get into office and then show the voters of the city just what I mean by my slogan." He would often challenge voters to rally behind him, saying, "[This] fight is the fight of the mothers and fathers of Lawrence—with the children at stake." One of his better tag lines was particularly poignant as he urged citizens to vote for him "if you want to protect your sisters."[14]

O'Connor had strong ties in the Irish community in Lawrence and was well liked. Unfortunately, his deep roots in the Irish and fraternal community failed to pay dividends in the election. Peter Cassidy could not have been impressed by the former saloon operator's pledge to rid the city of moonshine.

Thus, he crafted a satiric portrait of an all-Irish work force under O'Connor's watch. More significantly, Patsy was unable to overcome the strong popularity of another Irish candidate for the same office, Peter Carr, who hoped to return to office after a failed try for the mayor's seat. In the primary held on November 18, 1925, Carr received 11,271 votes, Charles Woodcock 2,442, and Patsy O'Connor 2,087 votes. Patsy was never elected to public office.[15]

When Patsy's Alderman

They call him Pat O'Connor of the great O'Connor Clan,
He's now a politician and he's to run for alderman.
Pat says if he's elected the first thing he will do,
He'll get rid of all the moonshiners and give us some good home brew.

We all remember Patsy before the Volstead Act did pass,
When Pat gave big scooners, sixteen ounces to the glass.
'Twas then the beer was good and clear—it cost a nickel then;
But now the ounces are down to six, the prices UP to ten.

He will have the police in uniform the finest ever seen,
White pants and stripes of yellow, coats and caps of green.
Each cop will carry a shilallah, that famous Irish stick,
And every man that's on the force will have to be a "Mick."

When they turn out for escort duty every cop must be a "Tad,"
And wear a bunch of shamrocks to make the eyes be glad;
They will have to march like soldiers in military style,
And Pat himself out in front with that good old Irish smile.

Every man pulled in will get the best; that's what Pat has said!
A bathing tub in every cell, a mattress, spring and bed.
And for Sunday dinner he will give them Irish stew;
For lunch a corn beef sandwich with a bucket of home brew.

Ivy will grow around the station so the red bricks won't be seen,
The blue lights up in front will change and up will go the green,
Every cop must talk the gaelic if he wants to hold his job;
It's hod carriers for the liquor squad—not a soldier or a gob.

Each traffic cop won't have to stand, he'll have a chair for a seat,
And umbrellas also when it rains, Brussels carpet at his feet.
He'll have no whistle to blow at night, they'll use colored lights instead,
Red and white for left and right, green to go ahead.

Pat will be delighted when the counting it is done,
For he knows that his opponents will be sorry that they run.
And Pat will surely bless the day when for office great he ran,
To his friends cross the sea, his address will be: "Pat O'Connor, Alderman."

After his failed attempt at politics, O'Connor tried to operate a confectionery shop for a few years but was unable to earn a living. Finally, with the end of Prohibition, he got back into the beer and ale business and opened a beer garden known as "The Place," in the heart of the theater district in North Lawrence. One newspaper story reported it to be "bright in front and an attractive appearance inside. It is spotlessly clean. There are varied German dishes and sandwiches of all kinds on the menu. Real beer served with a foamy collor *[sic]* and savoring a yeasty tang, chilled in a most appetizing style is found in 'The Place.'"[16] Patsy had finally returned to that which he did best.[17]

One of the better known hot spots for illegal revelry in the greater Lawrence area during Prohibition was Pleasant Valley. Partially located in a small, northeastern section of Lawrence, Pleasant Valley was found mainly within the boundaries of neighboring Methuen. This area along the road to Haverhill was considered rural by the standards of the day and outside the almost constant scrutiny of the police that was found in the heart of the city. Interested parties could easily find a steady diet of booze and female entertainment in the roadhouses in Pleasant Valley, "far from the maddening crowds." As one newspaper put it, these roadhouses were the seedy havens for those "who are wont to assemble alongside the flickering lights in the houses where bitter wine and smelly sandwiches are dispensed from menus which were trysts for flies last summer."[18] Visitors knew they were more likely to be left alone given its quiet, out-of-the-way location, but most everyone knew what was taking place. "Nude girls dance and wine flows freely in [the] Pleasant Valley district of Methuen where bacchanalian orgies, rivaling those of the Roman Baths, nightly hold sway in the sequestered shanties converted into roadhouses. Behind drawn curtains, girls . . . [with] shapely curves that are seductive, cut up high-jinks *[sic]* till the wee small hours of the morrow."[19]

Pleasant Valley

(As seen by the Shanty Pond Poet)

Most poets say the brightest place
Is the land that gave them birth,
But they tell me Pleasant Valley
Is the brightest place on earth.
There is moonshine there all the time
That's what I hear them say;
That down on Pleasant Valley
There is moonshine night and day.

There is moonshine on the river bank,
There is moonshine in the brook,
There is moonshine underneath the trees,
In every shady nook.
There is moonshine in the dewy fields
and in the new-mown hay;
Oh, down in Pleasant Valley
There is moonshine night and day.

There's a girl in Pleasant Valley,
For short I'll call her "Lil,"
Though she's a moonshiner's daughter
I love her father's still.
I court her nights, we need no lights,
Electricity, gas or flash,
We have moonshine every minute
While her father's making mash.

There is moonshine in the parlor,
There's moonshine in ev'ry room—
Behind the delf that's on the shelf,
Beneath the mop and broom.
There's moonshine 'neath the kitchen sink
Where the little mice oft play;
Yes, down in Pleasant Valley
There is moonshine night and day.

There's moonshine on the roadside
And underneath the trees,
Its fragrance permeates the air,
Haunts every passing breeze.
Each tomato vine exhales moonshine,
Even the eggs the chickens lay—
For down in Pleasant valley
There is moonshine night and day.

Peter was approaching seventy years old when he wrote his poem about the happenings in Pleasant Valley. Although he wrote it in the first person, it is unlikely that he was out cavorting with the moonshiner's daughter Lil. Aside from his age, his wife and seven daughters would have extracted a heavy price for such a dalliance. Nevertheless, he did capture the feel of this area where the moonshine freely flowed. The goings-on in Pleasant Valley reflected the utter failure of Prohibition eleven years after its implementation. With the election of Franklin Roosevelt in November of 1932, legislation was passed repealing the Eighteenth Amendment. The spring of 1933 saw a loosening on the sale of certain malt beverages, and on December 5, 1933, the constitutionally required approval by three fourths of the states had been achieved. Although national Prohibition was over, many states retained local bans on saloons, while others remained dry altogether. In Lawrence, however, two hundred applications were received for liquor licenses even before Prohibition formally ended. City Council members anxiously anticipated an additional $100,000 in license fees annually coming into the city's coffers. Officials planned to issue eighty-five licenses, about one for every thousand residents, if authorization was given by the voters at the ballot election on December 12, 1933. Not surprisingly, it was.

Like most Irishmen in Lawrence, Peter was not wanting for libation throughout the Prohibition years. Although the local pastors from the Catholic churches repeatedly spoke against the evils of alcohol, and the Fr. Mathew Temperance Society remained a strong presence in the city, few Irishmen went without their favorite beverage. Many found their way into court on charges of producing, keeping, or selling moonshine. Peter and his friends knew where to procure alcohol and how to produce it. One of his earlier scrapbooks includes a faded and well-worn page that listed recipes for homemade whiskey, rum, and brandy.

Irishwomen also came to enjoy the good life during the so-called Roaring Twenties. Women had recently secured the right to vote and were more fully engaged than ever in the high-flying social life found in large cities such as

Lawrence. In the following poem, also written during Prohibition, the Shanty Pond Poet provided a glimpse into the nightlife of a young and rather rambunctious Irishwoman as she traveled the darkened streets of Lawrence and broke her mother's heart. With one exception, all of Peter's daughters were married by 1922, and family accounts of each make it unlikely that Peter had any of the Cassidy women in mind when he wrote this poem.

My Daughter Has Me Most Crazy

I am an old woman, I'm four score and five,
I take in washing for a living I strive.
Sometimes I don't know if I'm dead or alive,
For my daughter she has me most crazy.

You'll find her at picnics, dances and balls,
Shindigs and raffles at Shannagan's hall.
What to do with her I can't tell at all,
For my daughter she has me most crazy.

She went down to Valley Street last Saturday night,
And wid Biddie Mulvaney got into a fight.
When they tried to make peace they couldn't help her quite,
For my daughter she has me most crazy.

She hit Casey a blow. Laid him out on the floor.
Then smashed on his head with a big cuspidor.
For the police, they commenced for to roar.
For my daughter she has me most crazy.

She comes home in the morning at thirteen o'clock
It's hard on the door she begins for to knock.
She wakes all the neighbors that lives on the block.
For my daughter she has me most crazy.

Then along come the cops, and brought the patrol,
And they took away the whole bunch, body and soul.
Poor Mary they put her down in the black hole.
For my daughter she has me most crazy.

In the morning the judge said, "You've been here before!"
And like a trooper she then cursed and swore.
The judge said "Two years? I'll change it to four."
For my daughter she has me most crazy.

Between good and bad she took her choice.
She never would take her mother's advice.
She's now on the Island, living on bread and ice.
For my daughter she has me most crazy.

The great social experiment proved to be a costly failure. There were few winners. The police and the courts were consumed with their attempts to enforce an unenforceable law. Hundreds of citizens were jailed or fined. With the closing of saloons and restaurant bars, city government struggled to find ways of making up over $100,000 in lost revenues from liquor licenses. Liquor businesses were forced to shut down, further denying the city much-needed tax income. Despite the lack of legal distribution sites, however, anyone who chose to drink was able to drink. Only those involved in the illegal production, trafficking, and sale of alcohol prospered during Prohibition.

Sitting proudly on the front stairs of the new Cassidy home, circa 1925, three of Peter Cassidy's daughters offer their warm, but reserved smiles. On the lower step is Frances Cassidy Blanchette, to her left is Tess Cassidy Mahoney, and on the top step is Peter's stepdaughter Margaret Coughlin, who paid for the house. Courtesy the Cassidy Collection.

11

The World Closes In

Anyone who lived through the Great Depression brings a perspective to life that escapes those of us born in the latter half of the twentieth century. What began with the stock market crash on Black Tuesday, October 29, 1929, spiraled into more than a decade of enormous pain and hardship for most Americans. Herbert Hoover, president at the time of "the Crash," watched and waited for recovery to take its own course. With each passing month, the situation worsened as the stock market continued its slide until reaching the bottom midway through 1932. Bellwether stocks were at lows that could never have been imagined. The AT&T stock price dropped from 310 $^1/_4$ in 1929 to a low of 69 $^3/_4$ and General Electric fell from 403 to 8 $^1/_2$. As the economic foundation of the nation eroded, so did every other aspect of society. The unemployment rate averaged 25 percent nationwide and was even higher in certain parts of the country. In addition, tens of millions were without food and shelter. Soup kitchens and charity lines sprang up and remained a part of the nation's landscape for the better part of a decade.

Lawrence, Massachusetts, suffered through just like every other city. No segment of the local economy escaped the effects of this downturn. Traveling through the city, one would see unemployment lines and people waiting for handouts of food and clothing. City services were stretched beyond capacity. Due to such high unemployment, tax revenues were way off and municipal budgets were dramatically cut. During the winter months, people would scavenge for coal or wood to heat their homes. In fact, it was during this period that what remained of the stately pines just west of old Shanty Pond were cut down and burned.

In several poems, Peter vented the frustration he and others felt during the early years of the Depression. "Not An Egg in the House" was written during the spring of 1931 or 1932. He dismissed the political finger-pointing that attributed the prolonged economic downturn to the Smoot-Hawley Tariff passed by Congress. As he so often did, he painted a simple yet poignant picture of the pain so many like him were experiencing. He also identified what he believed to be the real cause of the continuing hardship: Prohibition. At this time, many throughout the nation argued that continuation of the Volstead Act was costing the economy millions of jobs and tens of million of dollars in lost revenue. Whether these economic theories were true or not, the Volstead Act did meet its demise.

Not an Egg in the House

Let us join and sing alleluia, Christ he has arisen;
Peace on earth to men of good will; angels rejoice in heaven.
In many a home this blessed morn the church bells people rouse,
To give thanks to their Creator—and not an egg in the house.

It's sure been tough this winter, but what did good weather bring?
They said there would be plenty of work with the coming of the gentle spring.
Not a job has man got yet, and he feels just like a louse,
To get up on Easter Morning—and not an egg in the house.

It's first blamed on the tariff, then blamed on the South;
But governments are sure to blame for every hungry mouth;
Sure the times will be better when the Volstead Act gets doused,
Then we'll get up on Easter morning with ham and eggs in the house.

The Depression must have evoked many difficult memories for Peter. His parents had been forced to emigrate from Ireland eighty years earlier in order to secure food and shelter. Though born a dozen years after the Famine, Peter's early childhood was full of the stories of the starvation and hardship suffered by his relatives in the old country. Most historians argue that far fewer Irish men and women would have died had British landlords and Parliament acted earlier and with greater commitment as the potato blight first took hold. This historical perspective was not lost on Peter as he watched President Hoover's ineffective response during the early years of the Depression. Hoover felt that a *laissez-faire* approach to the economic crisis would best serve the country. He was proven wrong.

Hoover's miscalculation led to Franklin Delano Roosevelt's election on November 8, 1932. During his first "100 Days" in office, Roosevelt pushed dozens of reform programs through Congress in an effort to jump-start the nation's economy and ease the burden of the common man and woman. Among the most famous and effective of these programs were the National Recovery Administration, the Emergency Relief Act, the Public Works Administration, and the Civilian Conservation Corps. His strategy was successful and millions were put back to work. Although the economy never fully recovered until the outbreak of World War II, most Americans felt a difference as a result of the president's efforts. More importantly, they felt someone cared. To an Irish immigrant, FDR must have seemed a man of truly heroic proportions.

Like millions of Americans, Peter and Maggie were frightened by the hardship that swept the nation. They were also thankful, however, when Roosevelt pushed through his agenda to provide relief, even though it did little to help them directly. In his poem of thanks, Peter innocently expressed the genuine love he felt for FDR, the man who fed and housed so many Americans during this time of crisis, the man who gave them hope. While Roosevelt's efforts eventually made national recovery possible, Peter and many like him continued to live under considerable hardship throughout the decade.

Roosevelt

The balls and dances are now over,
His fifty-second birthday has passed.
It will linger long in our memory —
In history 'twill always last.

No man was ever so honored,
Or may never again:
As a nation we loved our Presidents;
We must show honor to this man.

He returned men to their labor
And given to the poor, relief
With pork and eggs, beans and bread,
Potatoes and corned beef.

He has given to the poor tons of coal
To keep their children warm;
He has also helped the farmer
To pay the mortgage on his farm.

Thousands now are working
That would have no work today,
Only for the fight he thought was right
When he started the NRA.

And those who once only worshipped gold,
Now recognize the cent.
All hail to our chief commander,
Franklin D. Roosevelt, President!

FDR was born on January 30, 1882. He turned fifty-two in 1934, and Peter sent him a birthday poem in early February. Peter would turn seventy-one in two months. He preserved the brief response he received on White House stationery and framed it for all to see. The local papers also published the note from Roosevelt's secretary. It read: "My dear Mr. Cassidy: The President has received your note of February sixth and has asked me to thank you most heartily for your kind thought in sending your poem to him. Very sincerely yours, Louis McHowe."

Although Peter did his best to remain active during his later years, his health took a turn for the worse. As a seventy-three-year-old man, he already had lived a full and active life in spite of his eating habits and his penchant for nickel beers and cheap cigars. Sometime during 1933 or 1934, he suffered a heart attack severe enough to require care at the City Hospital and Municipal Home, sometimes called "the poor farm." Peter was out of commission for several months, and his friends throughout the city worried about his health. *The Leader* offered a reassuring update of Peter's status to its readers.

> Peter Cassidy, song writer, *The Leader's* 'Shanty Pond' poet laureate and contributor in prose and verse for more than twenty years in these columns is ill and in bed under a doctor's orders for a period of at least a month. His brethren at the Moose report Peter to be cheerful as usual under the infliction, *(sic)* while 'Red' Donoghue, . . . declares that everything will be done that is possible to restore Peter, hale and well to the society of his friends. Peter is a great old scout and the hope is everywhere expressed for his recovery. He simply cannot be spared.[1]

In the following poem, "The Municipal Home," Peter takes the reader on a tour of the Muncipal Home in Lawrence. As was often the case with the Shanty Pond Poet, his poem served a twofold purpose. On its face it paid tribute to the wonderful nursing staff at the hospital and home, all of whom Peter appeared to have been quite fond of, and whose habits and traits obviously impressed him. He found the living arrangements to be more than satisfactory—especially the quality and abundance of food.[2]

On February 20, 1849, the City of Lawrence first opened its alms house to provide shelter and assistance to the poor residents of the city. This wood frame structure was located at 121 Marston Street on the "mud flats" of North Lawrence. Near the end of the century, the city's indigent sick were also housed at what had come to be known as the Municipal Hospital and Home. (Also called the City Hospital, the City Home, and a host of variations.) Normally, the hospital could accommodate about seven people while the home housed many more for a variety of purposes. Several rooms were padded for residents who were experiencing "the horrors," and other rooms were used for the poor or homeless, as recovery rooms from the hospital, and resident quarters for certain staff members and even some city officials. During the early part of the twentieth century, the poor farm became a bone of contention during many political campaigns for the aldermanic position of director of health and charities.

The second objective of the poem was political. Written during the fall of 1934 in advance of the primary elections in November, its final lines mention the fine changes made by "John Joe." John Joseph Ford was the incumbent director of public health and charities, who was locked in a difficult reelection bid against a large number of contenders, including David J. Burke, Sr., the man he had ousted two years earlier. For decades the poor farm had been a hot political topic that shed light on the attitudes of the Irish community and the city as a whole about caring for the needy. By the late 1920s, a proposal was advanced to build a new municipal hospital that would serve not just the poor but all the city's sick at one location, regardless of social strata. Many area physicians were troubled by the decrepit and unsanitary conditions of the seventy-five-year-old wooden buildings that had the maternity ward located in the attic. By the end of the decade the city hospital and home served about 250 residents.[3]

The Municipal Home

The old farm is a grand place, 'twas once thought a disgrace
For those aged men and women to go there,
A great change has come o'er, folks don't think that any more.
There's no City Home has its equal anywhere.
Those evil thoughts are gone, you can find there old and young,
Along the fields and river banks together they roam;

They sit on the grass, thinking of days that have passed
With a blessing for the Municipal Home.

They get good board and bed, no longer dread
The name of being a pauper, which never should be so;
In this city they have always lived, and their taxes they've always paid
And have settled for what they're getting long ago.
All the feeds are good, just the way they always should,
In the fish or meat one never finds a bone;
Everything's served clean, its large frankfurters and beans
Every weekend at the Municipal Home.

Doctors and nurses there, give their patients the best of care,
Always on the watch to see what they can do;
For those that are sick or sore, none can do any more
Doing the best to help the patients pull through.
Everyone is used alike, taken care of day or night,
When they're called upon, there is no favor shown;
One may be as poor as Job, or rich as a duke or lord,
There's no difference in the Municipal Home.

Every patient there is fond of that tall good-looking blond,
She's head nurse and takes charge every day;
She may win no beauty prize, but those sympathetic eyes
Win the hearts of those that are sick and have to lay
In bed , none can tell how long, maybe till they go beyond,
When God calls them to come before His throne;
Then with dying breath, Miss McCarthy they will bless,
And all the nurses at the Municipal Home.

Each evening Mrs. Ahern comes on and takes her turn,
To the others, she gives orders for the night;
It certainly does seem strange, how quick comes a change,
There is not a move, just everything goes quiet.
As she passes along the ward, one never hears a word;
The airplanes passing o'er head refuse to drone,
She sure is one good kid, I can't forget what she did
When I was in the Municipal Home.

Lovely Miss Bronson, she keeps the sick from being lonesome,
Face all smiles, a good word, with a cheery "How-de-do;"
Each morning its her hobby, coming through the sick ward lobby
Stopping at each sick patients's bed, saying "How are you?"
Miss Neversky, since her birth, has been an angel on earth,
Though others are in heaven, she is here alone;
They must have left her behind, because she is so kind
To those patients in the Municipal Home.

Miss Frederick and Miss Kobos, I swear by hokes pokeses,
As nurses they are wonders, none better could be found;
For bandaging and dressing, they have their patients' blessings,
They handle each one gently, so easy and so kind;
And genial Miss Wood, she's as stout as she is good,
Always showing her good nature, for her humor she is known.
Seems her work is never done, always on the run
Giving aid to those who need it, in the Municipal Home.

John Joe has made a wonderful change, everything for the best;
Dempsey could live on the food he gives those poor folks, his guests;
Dessert with dinner every day, Sundays, veal and lamb,
Tuesdays too, a big beef stew; Fridays they have clams,
Every day enough to eat, one day fish, all others meat,
Choice of coffee, tea or milk, and cream without a cone;
Those doctors one can't forget them; nurses, too, God bless them,
It's the prayer from every patient in the Municipal Home.

Although the average citywide daily attendance was only 113 persons, proponents of the new hospital continued to press for a modern facility at a different location to serve the dependent and chronically sick. The opposition contended that no real need existed and that the cost would strain municipal coffers. According to one newspaper, there was also "an undercurrent of Protestant against Catholic attitude" at the heart of the controversy. "How strong this is may be gathered from the declaration of certain Catholic people of Greater Lawrence who say there is no place they can go for hospital treatment and feel right about it, other than the hospital attached to the poor farm."[4] Year after year, a ballot measure was put before the voters that called for the construction of a modern hospital, and each year it failed. The debate dragged on.

As the city faced the ravages of the Depression during the thirties, it became harder and harder to provide for the needs of an ever-increasing needy population. In December of 1932 Dave Burke was the incumbent alderman who was completing his first term as the director of health and charities. For most of his life he lived at 141 Marston Street directly across from the Municipal Home. In 1927 he was elected to the school committee in Lawrence, but he failed in his first attempt for the health and charities seat in 1929 when he was beaten by John F. Finnegan. Two years later, however, he was able to secure the post by defeating John S. Maloney, 14,447 votes to 11,559.[5]

By all accounts, Burke's first two years as director of health and charities were very successful, especially in light of the serious funding cutbacks associated with the early years of the Depression. In fact, most people thought quite well of him. In the weeks leading to the December 13, 1932, election, the *Lawrence Telegram*, the *Evening Tribune*, and the *Sunday News* constantly sang his praises. Newspapers headlines and articles called for his re-election: "From Every Angle . . . Dave Burke Merits Re-election"; "Dave Burke has done more to help the poor of Lawrence than any man who previously held the office"; and "If for no other reason than the fact that . . . he has physically renovated into convenient and livable quarters the City Hospital and the City Home, and surrounded it with an atmosphere of tenderness and kindness and care—yes, human sympathy."[6]

His opponent was John Joseph Ford, a fifty-year-old resident of South Lawrence. In 1909 and 1910 Ford served on the old common council and board of aldermen as a representative from Ward Three. In 1916 he received an appointment as acting stable foreman for the street department from Alderman John F. Finnegan. Six year later, in 1925, he was appointed to a position in the health department by Robert S. Maloney. When Burke defeated Maloney for director of health and charities post in December of 1930, however, Ford lost his job.[7]

During the fall of 1932, Ford returned to challenge the man who had fired him earlier. Right from the start, the election coverage centered almost completely on Burke's campaign. Virtually every newspaper account of the election rallies focused on the words and achievements of the incumbent and offered only passing coverage of his opponent, John Joe Ford. For his part, Ford had little to offer. He spoke proudly of his perfect attendance record while serving on the old city council, and he asserted that his years working in all the branches of the health and charities department made him "thoroughly qualified to handle the position." He promised to improve refuse collection and disposal, and he also appealed to the senior citizens by promising to have their old age pension checks sent to their homes. "At present men and women at the age of seventy go down to city hall and have to stand in line for hours sometimes, and get little money, seven or eight dollars. I will change this."[8]

Most of his public pronouncements, however, centered on the Municipal home. "If I am elected, I promise to improve conditions in the City Home and to give the patients there better treatment . . . They are getting pretty good treatment there now, but it could be better. I will also have a registered nurse on day duty and a registered nurse on night duty at the City Home."[9]

Burke's campaign strategy was to take the high road. Stressing his hard work and accomplishments despite limited resources, he proudly spoke of his compassion while making the hard decisions that come with his office. He stayed away from direct confrontation with candidate Ford. In light of the overwhelming support he had from local newspapers, he did not need to attack his opponent. The papers did all the work for him. "I have conducted a clean campaign and have said nothing about my opponent . . . But if I had anything to say about my opponent, I would come up here and say it myself."[10] With great frequency following the primary, the press reminded voters that John Joe Ford was "an alleged aide-de-camp in the famous organization of Ex-Alderman John W. McCarthy. The story is abroad that very much the identical element which made McCarthy the spending champ of all times in city affairs is with Ford. . . . We cite only what insiders say about the old McCarthy crowd that is gathering about him . . . John Joseph Ford has been promising all kinds of jobs to people in return for their support which means an enormous expense for the city and the taxpayers."[11]

The day before the election, Burke was assumed by the pundits to be a landslide winner over his opponent. Such overconfidence and an election day snowstorm, however, proved to be Burke's undoing. He lost to Ford by just 180 votes of the 26,764 votes cast. In the two years that followed, Commissioner Ford lived up to his promises, but the results of the 1932 election set the stage for the rematch that would come during the fall of 1934.

Among the dozen candidates seeking the health and charities seat that year, Burke again seemed to be the early frontrunner along with incumbent Ford and James L. Carney. At the traditional school rallies, Ford was subjected to the verbal blows from the many contenders who accused him of surrounding himself with poor advisors and of mishandling the Muncipal Home, the dump, and the collection of ashes. He offered little in the way of rebuttal, however. As the *Lawrence Telegram* reported, incumbent Ford "made no attempt to defend his administration. He played upon the emotional side of his listeners with stories of his kind deeds. He characterized himself as the man with the human heart."[12]

Despite Peter's poem of support and Ford's efforts to improve conditions at the Municipal Home, he failed to win one of the two primary slots for the December election. Burke's defeat two years earlier was on the minds of his many supporters and he received the largest vote tally of everyone in the race. James Carney narrowly defeated Ford for the second spot on the December ballot by just three votes. In the general election held on December 12, 1934, Burke defeated Carney by about 1,400 votes. Shortly thereafter, Peter's son-in-law, Edgar Blanchette, lost the job he had been given two years earlier by Ford—a serious blow given the ongoing Depression. Burke served successfully as director of public charities for several more terms. During 1936 and 1937, the city hospital and home were remodeled and renamed the Bessie M. Burke Memorial Hospital after Alderman Burke's deceased wife, who had served as a volunteer for many years before her death in September of 1934. Although Peter backed Ford in 1934, Dave Burke attended Peter's funeral in 1938.[13]

As the Depression dragged on, Peter continued to lament the troubles men like himself had finding work. In his poems "Over Forty-Five" and the "War Time Vet," he returned to the theme that he so often wrote about. Ever since his poem about the Shanty Pond Sewer in 1899, Peter had recognized the importance of work for a man or a woman, and he still hoped to find a job that would pull him and Maggie through these difficult times. Although many were able to get jobs and bring home paychecks, others could not. After losing his city job, Edgar Blanchette was able to secure work through the Public Works Administration (PWA), the agency created by the Emergency Relief Act (ERA), as an activities coordinator at the Riley Park playground. He also tended bar at Bateman's Saloon on South Broadway.

But Peter was an old man now, in his early seventies, and not as fortunate as his son-in-law. Some federal jobs programs set maximum age limitations for those seeking work and the continuation of the Veterans Preference Act favored veterans for available jobs. These restrictions compounded the problem of older men and women in need of work. They were over forty-five and not veterans of World War I. Still a proud man and not quite ready to admit his limitations, Peter became frustrated by his inability to get work. His loyalty toward veterans was tested. So he picked up his pencil to lament his plight and that of his friends, who wanted work but simply could not find it.

Over Forty-Five

Old timer, can you tell me, what are we going to do.
While we have depression? There's no work for me and you.
Our old age is against us, no matter how we strive,
We may look and seek, but there's no work for men o'er forty-five.

We may as well stay at home; there's no job we can get,
If they want to hire help, they'll give preference to the vet.
If all those men that lie over there should have come home alive,
While the winds do blow, there's no show for men over forty-five.

Our city jobs are like the mill. You and I remember when
A youngster wouldn't work the streets, 'twas left to the old men.
He wouldn't be seen shovel'n into a team, he was ashamed or shy;
Along came big pay, then they held sway, o'er men of forty-five.

'Twas then the sheik came to work on the street, necktie and silk shirt;
He liked the pay he got each day; he didn't like the work.
If he saw his girlfriend on the street he'd run away and hide—
He didn't want her to know how he got his dough—and under forty-five.

The woman that's working in the mill on her feet all day,
O'er frame or loom in those hot rooms—no wonder she turns gray.
When the boss sees that first gray hair, then he begins to connive;
What to do; have her through. She's over forty-five.

Let us all be cheerful as long as we may live.
We will all be equal when buried in the grave.
Our worries will be done 'til kingdom come; then once more alive.
But our age will stop in that hallowed lot, though we're over forty-five.

War Time Vet

We are waiting for you, prosperity; why make you such delay?
Depression had been with us so long, it seems it's going to stay.
The nation and state can build their roads, no job a civilian can get,
When for work we apply, "No" is the reply, "you're not a war time vet."

When this country came into war, it's true I was no kid,
I was too old then to enlist, but I had two sons that did.
They both now sleep in Flanders fields; none have returned as yet—
Let the poppies wave o'er heroes' graves, they're only war time vets.

All honor to our soldier boys who fought there with the French,
And those that fell midst shot and shell or died in gas-filled trench.
Though many ne'er crossed the seas, e'en them we'll ne'er forget,
They stayed this side, but we take pride in each grand war time vet.

Depression, we'd like to see you go, tho' it looks as if staying here,
We'll be watching around the corner when prosperity must appear.
We'll be waiting, watching, for she may come to us yet,
Trust in God, we'll get a job, and not as a war time vet.

At the age of seventy-four, Peter did his best to remain active and involved in the Irish community. He would walk down to South Broadway to attend church, visit with friends at Tiger Three, or pay his respects at one of the many South Side taverns. It took an old man much longer, however, to walk the half mile to South Broadway. The trip home took even more time. In spite of his age, he was not shy about heading across the O'Leary Bridge into North Lawrence to spend time at one of his favorite establishments, the Wayfarer Tavern. On many a night, his daughter Frances would sit by the window as darkness set in, wondering whether Peter would be able to safely navigate his way home from the saloons. On one occasion, my father, Joseph, recalled sitting with her as Peter drifted up Everett Street and unexpectedly lurched out in front of a passing car. Seeing only the headlights, Frances thought he had been hit. But a moment later, out of the dusky shadows, Peter continued on his journey home.

Unemployed and physically frail, Peter was becoming less mobile. More and more, he spent his free time at home at 53 Everett Street, where he had lived for over a decade. He had come to enjoy leisurely walks into the large wooded fields behind the house, an area very familiar to him. Ever since the Irish first settled along Shanty Pond in the late 1840s, the western shore of the pond was always seen as a favorite recreation site. Where the pond and the Merrimack River met stood a large stand of pine trees that attracted residents from throughout Lawrence for family picnics, church outings, and romantic strolls. Farther west beyond the Pines, as they were called, was a much larger field shaded by a scattering of trees and known as the Grove.

After the turn of the century, children leaving the 8:30 Mass at St. Patrick's on Sunday morning would head down Salem Street to play in the Pines and the Grove. Some played sporting games, others played cards, and the older kids played games of chance until someone spotted the priests or nuns coming down to check up on everyone. Most any Sunday afternoon during the latter part of the nineteenth century, one would see hundreds and sometimes thousands of people engaged in a wide range of activities in and around this area. They watched boat races on the river, played baseball, ate and drank, attended political rallies, and enjoyed traveling zoos. On the northern edge of the Grove, bordering the Merrimack River, was a large hill known as Cushing Hill or Hurricane Run. (Later generations called it Bum's Hill.) During the winter months young and old would race toboggans and bobsleds down Hurricane Run into the Grove. A local businessman built a wooden starting ramp to increase speed and charged a nickel per trip. Still others just went down the side of the hill and out onto the frozen river.

Frances Cassidy Blanchette, her son Buddy and her niece Caroline cut wood behind the house on Everett Street. The South Side Grove is in the background. Fall 1938. Courtesy the Cassidy Collection.

In the mid-1930s, during the height of the Depression, Peter wrote another poem that took a nostalgic look back at the days he so loved. "The South Side Grove" offers a glimpse into the sights and experiences enjoyed by so many from Shanty Pond and from throughout Lawrence decades earlier. In fact, the Cassidy's unofficial backyard on Everett Street was made up of these forty or more acres of undeveloped land belonging to the Essex Company. Peter would live on Everett Street until his death. For the remaining years of his life he frequently spent time enjoying the activities that took place in the South Side Grove. For this old man, now savoring his final years, it was clear that there was no better place to spend a weekend afternoon than in the

Grove. During the winter months of the Depression, when finding money to buy heating fuel was a challenge for most families, Peter was known to head out the back door and make his way up Cushing Hill to the old toboggan ramp. There he would strip its wooden boards and framing timbers to burn as firewood in the boiler back home. Without work, it was difficult to do many things, including keeping the house warm.

The South Side Grove

Some folks they like to travel, they always want to roam,
To city, beach and country scenes, which we have here at home.
In any clime at any time no matter where they roam,
Where e're they've been they saw no scenes to match the South Side Grove.

You can sit beneath the tall oaks, the elms, the spruce, the pines,
Or stroll along the high grass, the golden rod and vines.
It's there the pussy willows in their spring abundance grow,
With the clover, daisies, buttercups in the South Side Grove.

Now to find this beautiful place I'll tell you how to go;
Off Broadway turn down Shattuck Street, 'twill bring you down to Rowe.
When you pass the swimming pool, keep to the river road,
You will see the children's playground in the South Side Grove.

When you see the old chutes you will think of other days,
There is only a reminder left, its almost all taken away.
When the nights were cold for young and old and there was lots of snow,
Then they would go tobogganing in the South Side Grove.

When you've seen this once, 'twill bring your memories back,
Just keep on to the top of the hill and see the beautiful Merrimack.
See the sailboats, rowboats and canoes moving to and fro—
This is one of the beauty scenes in the South Side Grove.

It's a grand place in the summertime to spend an afternoon,
You can stay till the sun goes down and the rising of the moon.
Then wait until the little stars come out, to twinkle up above,
On such a night it's a delight in the South Side Grove.

There were good time in it long ago when they held the picnics there,
The people came from all around—they came from everywhere.
They came to view Tom Burns' zoo; how the woods did give echo,
To the music, dance and laughter in the South Side Grove.

One of Peter's last pieces of writing was written during the late summer of 1935. It's unusual because it is the only narrative piece of his writing that has been preserved. Everything else that remains is written in verse with rhyme. At that time he sent this letter to the Phoenix Bridge Company, he was recovering from a heart attack he had suffered a year or so earlier. His letter is at times funny, at times sad. It offers poignant insight into both the Depression and Peter's final years. The original copy of this letter is filled with misspellings, absent many capital letters, and strewn with numerous punctuation errors. It's likely that he was too proud to share it with daughter Frances first, knowing that both she and her husband were working very hard to provide for all those living at Everett Street. Peter still was unable to secure work of any kind and was too embarrassed to be asking for help. He was proud, however, that he and his wife still were able to "buy their own feed."

August 11, 1935
Lawrence, Mass.

Phoenix Bridge Co.

Sirs,

On July 27th, while crossing the O'Leary Bridge that your company has been working on taking the iron from the old bridge that was in the river, you had the cement side of the bridge, or what you might call the rail, protected with boards on top of the rail, or what you might call it. I hope you know what I mean. There were clamps holding these boards. So while crossing from the north side over to the south side, on the east side, my shirt sleeve got caught on one of the clamps and gave it such a tear that it could not be repaired.

I hope you will not think it rude of me to ask you for a shirt or the price of one. I would not stoop so low but the God's honest truth is I can't afford to buy one. I was trying to sell it to a one armed man, a friend of mine, but it was no go. He had the wrong arm gone or I must have the wrong sleeve torn. When I say I can't afford to buy a shirt, I want to explain that I have not worked for over a year. Me and my wife is living with my daughter. Her husband is working 3 days on the

E.R.A. and I can't get a job on the E.R.A. because they say I have only a wife. I have no dependents and they won't give me work.

Perhaps you might think how me and me wife gets along. Well, we get our room free, but we buy our own feed. My wife gets $5.00 a week old age pension and we live the best we can. The shirt costs $1.35 cents when I bought it, but I see them in the stores for a $1.00 just as good. I ask that you forgive me for asking this favor from your company.

P.S. If you think I am trying to extort something, you just write to the Mayor or our City Marshall.

> *Yours,*
> *Peter Cassidy*
> *53 Everett Street*

Up until the end of his life, Peter remained true to Irish roots and traditions. He gathered a collection of all his songs, a lifetime of work, carefully pasted them into a ledger book, and asked a trusted friend from the Moose lodge to care for it. On March 20, 1937, he brought a touch of the Irish and the well-known Cassidy wit into the city's courtroom. The following short newspaper account paints the picture of a frail old Irishman spreading goodwill on St. Patrick's Day.

> Peter F. Cassidy, Lawrence's Shanty Pond Poet, is as Irish as Irish can be. At the present, he is serving on jury duty in the local courthouse. Wednesday, he brought a couple of dozen shamrocks and distributed them to his fellow jurymen, court attaches and to the judges sitting here. As a result, there was hardly a lapel in the courthouse that did not sport a tribute to the Emerald Isle's famous saint.[14]

Peter celebrated just one more St. Patrick's Day. On Thursday evening, May 12, 1938, he died at his home at the age of seventy-seven. As was the custom, a wake was held on Everett Street, and he was laid out in front of the window with the view of the steeple at St. Patrick's Church and Shanty Pond. Over the next several days, hundreds of his Irish friends and family paid their last respects at a typical Irish wake. Seen more as a time for celebration than mourning, visitors offered up their prayers and shared libation and scores of humorous stories about "Old Pete." Peter's obituary read in part, "Peter Cassidy, a well-known and esteemed resident of this city for many years, died early last night. . . . He was a well-known parodist, having written many parodies and songs, and his work along that line made him known as the

Shanty Pond Poet."[15] The following Monday a high requiem Mass was celebrated at St. Patrick's Church, and later he was buried at the Immaculate Conception Cemetery. At long last, Peter met his God.

On one of the last pages of his scrapbook Peter penciled in the following poem and signed his name. No published copy exists. Though this first draft is not one of his better works, it offered the reflective thoughts of an old man who knew that he was approaching the end of his life and took comfort in his faith.

Laddie Boy

A lone farewell dear laddie boy, from you I now must take,
Since first we met, you've been my friend,
I know friends will take care of you, if it's only for my sake.
Our parting now must come to an end,
Happy hours we have had together, just only you and me.
Alas those pleasures for us are no more.
I'm going to my Creator, He's called me to his throne,
Where my sorrows and my troubles will be o'er.

Peter F. Cassidy

Two years after Peter's death, Maggie Cassidy, his wife of over fifty years, joined him on November 29, 1940. On June 29, 1942, his youngest daughter, Frances Cassidy Blanchette, died after a sudden illness. Shortly after their mother's death, Peter's grandsons, Joe and Buddy Blanchette, went off to fight in World War II. Upon returning from the war, Joe married Nancy Hyland and later purchased the Cassidy home on Everett Street from his aunt, Margaret Coughlin. He lived there and raised his family with his wife until 1982. Margaret Coughlin used the proceeds from the sale to buy a cottage at Hampton Beach, New Hampshire. She named it the "Frances Patricia" in honor of her stepsister.

Epilogue

At the close of the twentieth century, few know of the existence of the pond that was surrounded by the Irish shanties, or the community known as Shanty Pond. Along South Broadway, St. Patrick's Church continues to stand proudly, having recently celebrated its 125th anniversary. While cherishing its Irish heritage, the parish now ministers to a diverse ethnic congregation. All of the apartments where Peter lived at the four corners of Shattuck and South Broadway have been destroyed, but the Tiger Three Fire Station still stands nearby. In addition to his Everett Street home, only his apartment building at 134 South Broadway remains today. Riley Park on Everett Street (the location of the Grove, the Pines, and Cushing Hill) underwent a major renovation in the early 1990s, but a small plaque recalls the memory of Smiling Phil Riley.

Across the river in North Lawrence, much has also changed. The Central Fire Station is gone as is the original Hibernian Hall on the Plains, O'Sullivan Park and the Immaculate Conception Church. Were one now to attend Mass at St. Mary's Church, once the center of the Irish community, one would hear the priest conducting services in Spanish rather than with a thick Irish brogue. The fourth great wave of immigration into Lawrence occurred during the final decades of the twentieth century. Spanish-speaking people from Latin America, Puerto Rico, and the Dominican Republic flooded into the city, much the same way the Irish, the French Canadians, and the Italians did over a century earlier. In each of the former Irish enclaves, the Plains, "across the Spicket," and Shanty Pond, Spanish-speaking immigrants are beginning the same journey the Irish began one hundred and fifty years ago. The obstacles are essentially the same, but the opportunities are still great.

In the decades following Peter's death, men and women of Irish descent continued to hold the mayor's office and many of the seats on the city council. But, reminiscent of the 1870s, political change is once again afoot. Residents with Hispanic names are serving on the police and fire forces, teaching in the schools, and working at city hall. Scores of small businesses with Spanish names have sprung up throughout the city. With each election more Hispanic candidates are found on election ballots, and some are winning seats in state and local government.

One hundred years after Peter settled down on South Broadway, the view from Shanty Pond has changed in many ways. The colors, dress, dialects, foods, and the music are all different. But little else. Peter wrote of the Irish immigrant's desire for a good job, food on the table, a nice home, and an afternoon at the ballfield. His poems described Irish faithfulness to God, country, heritage, and friends. In this respect, the view from Shanty Pond today is much the way it was.

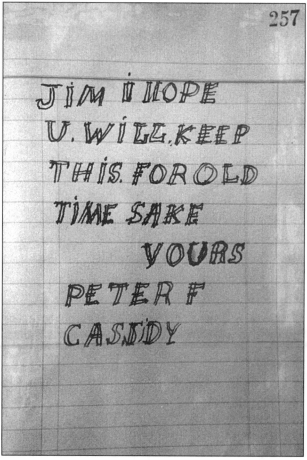

Peter Cassidy's note to Jim Johnstone Sr., asking his longtime friend to preserve for posterity the record of his life's work. Courtesy the Cassidy Collection.

Chapter Notes

Chapter 1: The Making of an Immigrant Family

[1] Peter Grey, *The Irish Famine*, Harry N. Abrams Inc., New York, 1995, p. 68.

[2] P. Berrerford. Ellis, *History of the Irish Working Class*, Pluot Press, London & Chicago, 1996, p. 111.

[3] Donald B. Cole, *Immigrant City, Lawrence, Massachusetts, 1845-1921*, University of North Carolina Press, Chapel Hill, NC, p. 30.

[4] Aaron Robert Morrill, "Life and Work for the Early Irish Laborer of Lawrence Massachusetts," (Bachelors thesis), State University of New York, 1982, p. 10.

[5] Donald B. Cole, *Immigrant City, Lawrence, Massachusetts, 1845-1921*, University of North Carolina Press, Chapel Hill, NC, p. 29.

[6] Maurice B. Dorgan, *Lawrence Yesterday and Today, 1845-1918*, Dick and Trumpold Publishers, Lawrence, Massachusetts, 1918, p. 32.

[7] In 1999 this region would generally encompass land bordering present day South Broadway (called the Turnpike at the time), west along Kingston Street to Emmett Street (which bordered the river inlet called Shanty Pond), north to Rowe Streets, and then east along Rowe and Shattuck until returning to South Broadway. Further to the south, along the Turnpike, lived one of the city's major figures, Daniel Saunders, who was a very large landowner along the Turnpike and Andover Street.

[8] Dover Street was later renamed Salem Street. Today this block is directly across from St. Patrick's Church.

[9] Residents of the Patch described its boundries as being South Broadway on the east, the railroad tracks to the south, Newton Street to the west, and Durham Street to the north.

Chapter 2: Coming Over

[1] *Irish Immigration to the U.S.: What It Has Been and What It Is.*, Rev. Stephen Bryne, O.S.D., New York Catholic Publishing Society, New York, 1873

[2] The Fenians were a militant organization based in the United States and Ireland. Founded in 1858 and known in Ireland as the Irish Republican Brotherhood, its objective was the armed overthrow of British influence in Ireland.

[3] Donald B. Cole, *Immigrant City, Lawrence, Massachusetts, 1845-1921*, University of North Carolina Press, Chapel Hill, NC, pp. 71-72.

[4] *The Lawrence Daily American*, March 17, 1874.

[5] *The Lawrence Daily American*, March 18, 1880.

[6] *The Lawrence Daily American*, March 1, 1884.

[7] *The Lawrence Daily American,* March 18, 1871.

[8] *The Lawrence Daily American,* March 18, 1878.

Chapter 3: Returning Home: A Sense of Place

[1] It is important to consider carefully the context in which the term "Shanty Pond" is being presented. The term was first used to refer to a body of water on the South Side of the river, and later to identify the area east of that body of water or pond where the Irish built their shanties and lived for decades. Long after the Irish vacated their shanties for more permanent homes the area continued to be known as Shanty Pond, even after the pond itself was filled-in. Initially, the Shanty Pond district was most narrowly defined as that area between present day Kingston Street to Shattuck and Rowe Streets. Its western boundary was the pond itself and its eastern boundary generally ran along present day Newton Street from Kingston Street and angling northeast to Shattuck Street. By the turn of the nineteenth century, the Shanty Pond community ran to the B&M railroad tracks, just east of South Broadway, and depending upon the source, the southern border of the Shanty Pond district followed the spur of the B&M that paralleled Andover Street.

[2] Some of these early property holders were William Hart, Michael Driscoll, Timothy Driscoll, Patrick Collins, John Dinneen, Morris Breen, Daniel Donovan, Patrick O'Sullivan, William Murphy, Peter McDowell, Ann O'Leary and Mary Moriarty.

[3] Board of Health Report, *Lawrence City Documents*, 1891.

[4] Board of Health Report, *Lawrence City Documents*, 1892, 1893.

[5] *Lawrence City Documents,* 1894-1895

[6] *Lawrence City Documents*, 1989-1900, pp. 273-275.

Chapter 4: The Irish Political Ascendancy

[1] *Lawrence American*, November 15, 1856.

[2] Thomas P. McKieran, "The Story of the Irish People in Lawrence," Supplement to the *The Sunday Star*, March 15, 1936.

[3] One of John Breen's great achievements as mayor was said to have been the straightening of the Spicket River that ran through the Plains. After leaving the mayor's office, Breen remained politically and socially active for the rest of his life. John Breen was a member of the Knights of Columbus and the Ancient Order of Hibernians and was the quartermaster to the Ninth Regiment of the local militia during the 1890s, an organization in which Peter Cassidy also served at this time. The ex-mayor also served on the school committee from 1889 to 1910. John Breen died on December 21, 1910, and was survived by his wife Mary Jane Brackett and four daughters.

[4] *Evening Tribune*, January 2, 1899.

[5] *Evening Tribune*, January 2, 1899.

[6] The sewer committee was made up of Mayor Eaton, Alderman Cornelius Lynch and Alderman Hugo Dick. The remaining members of the Board of Alderman that year were Andrew Caffrey, Henry Lane, Narcisse Miville, Louis Lynch, and Louis Matthes.

[7] Donald B. Cole, *Immigrant City, Lawrence, Massachusetts, 1845-1921,* University of North Carolina Press, Chapel Hill, NC, p. 72.

[8] For example, eight Democrats and two Republicans could enter the primary for the director of engineering seat. After the primary vote, or caucus as it was sometimes called, was held in early November, the two candidates with the most votes would faceoff in the December election, even if both happened to be Republican.

[9] Born on Elm Street on January 15, 1853, Paul Hannagan attended St. Mary's parochial school as well as the public schools. At the age of ten, however, he went to work in the Everett Mills and later the Pacific Mills in order to bring additional income into his home. Soon afterward, he took up and mastered bricklaying, and later he held a job as a plasterer. Then he started several businesses, including the Ballardvale Spring Water Plant in 1898 and the Brightwood Mills in North Andover.

[10] *Lawrence Weekly Journal,* December 19, 1896.

[11] *Lawrence Telegram,* November 12, 1914.

[12] *Lawrence Telegram,* April 13, 1914.

[13] *The Leader,* November 7, 1915.

[14] *The Leader,* December 12, 1915.

[15] *Evening Tribune,* May 11, 1915.

[16] *The Leader,* July 15, 1915.

[17] *Lawrence Telegram,* December 10, 1915.

[18] *Evening Tribune,* December 10, 1915.

[19] *Evening Tribune,* November 27, 1917, and *Lawrence Telegram,* December 7, 1917.

[20] Jim Cadogan went back to the police force for a short time, but resigned on January 5, 1919. As a young man he was known as an outstanding athlete in baseball and track, and he later played baseball in the policeman's league. He was a member of the Lawrence Lodge 65, BPOE and lived at 53 Osgood Street. He died at the Burke Hospital following a short illness on April 9, 1966, at the age of 95.

[21] The other figure mentioned in "The Central Fire Station," Fire Chief Dennis Carey, was born in Lawrence in 1869. He was appointed a "call man" to the fire department in 1891, given a permanent position in 1993, and became captain in 1902. He assumed the role of fire chief in 1912 and held the post until 1918 when he left the department and entered the real estate and insurance business. He later ran unsuccessful campaigns for the commissioner of public safety post. Former Chief Carey died on August 16, 1933, as a result of serious injuries suffered when his roadster crashed into another car near Rockingham Park.

[22] *Evening Tribune,* November 28, 1938.

[23] *Evening Tribune,* October 26, 1931.

[24] *Evening Tribune,* December 7, 1931.

[25] *Evening Tribune*, December 6, 1927.

[26] Peter Carr was a member of many organizations including the Fr. Mathew Temperance Society, the Knights of Columbus, Ancient Order of Hibernians, Division 8, Lodge 440 of the Moose, and the Eagles and Elks clubs. He lived at 636 Lowell Street with his wife, Mary Scanlon. They had no children.

[27] *Lawrence Directory*, 1930, p. 202.

[28] *Lawrence Telegram*, May 6, 1914.

[29] *Evening Tribune*, May 20, 1913.

[30] *Evening Tribune*, May 20, 1913.

[31] *Lawrence Telegram*, Jan 26, 1921.

[32] Peter Cassidy Collection.

.

Chapter 5: Icons of an Irish Community

[1] Peter Cassidy Scrapbook.

[2] *Lawrence Telegram*, February 3, 1914.

[3] Maurice B. Dorgan, *Lawrence Yesterday and Today, 1845-1918*, Dick and Trumpold Publishers, Lawrence, Massachusetts, p. 231.

[4] *The Leader*, June 30, 1912.

[5] *The Leader*, February 3, 1914.

[6] *Evening Tribune*, February 14, 1914.

[7] *The Leader*, February 9, 1914.

[8] *The Leader*, February 15, 1914.

[9] *The Leader*, May 3, 1914.

[10] Peter Cassidy Collection.

[11] James Louis Davey was born in Salem, Massachusetts, on February 12, 1896. He received a BA from Boston College and was ordained into the priesthood on May 25, 1921. His first assignment was in Charlestown at St. Mary's Parish from 1922 until 1929. That same year he was sent to St. Patrick's where he served until the fall of 1933. Sadly, several years after being transferred to St. Ann's Church in Quincy, he became ill and died in 1937. He was forty-one years old.

[12] William J. Carty was born on February 4, 1901, in Roxbury, Massachusetts, and like Father Davey, he studied for the priesthood at St. John's Seminary. He was ordained in 1928 and sent for a short time to St. Edward's Church in Brockton. The following year, at the age of twenty-nine, he was assigned to St. Patrick's Parish. Upon leaving St. Patrick's, he went to St. Cecilia's in Boston where he remained for nine years. He served as a chaplain in the army from 1941 to 1946 and then returned to parish life until ill health forced him to retire in September of 1964. Just five months later, on February 4, 1965, Father Carty died on his birthday.

[13] Unidentified Caffrey family newspaper clipping.

[14] *Evening Tribune*, March, 1937.

[15] *Evening Tribune*, November 22, 1937.

[16] William Caffrey lived at 16 Royal Street with his wife Catherine at the time of his death.

[17] *Evening Tribune*, March 3, 1919.

[18] *Evening Tribune*, March 3, 1919.

[19] *Lawrence Telegram*, July 10, 1922.

[20] *Lawrence Telegram.* August 14, 1922.

[21] Maurice B. Dorgan, *Lawrence Yesterday and Today, 1845-1918,* Dick and Trumpold Publishers, Lawrence, Massachusetts, 1918.

[22] In 1915, the organization's leaders at St. Patrick's were High Chief Ranger Harry Rooney, Vice-Chief Ranger John Carney, Finance Secretary James T. O'Dowd, Recording Secretary Joseph A. Carbury, and Treasurer John W. McCarthy.

[23] Officers in 1915 were High Chief John J. Sullivan, Vice Chief Peter W. McGuire, Treasurer Patrick Judge, Financial Secretary Martin Casey, and Financial Secretary Michael McCarthy.

[24] The Lawrence chapter of the Moose had its organizational meeting on Sunday afternoon, January 15, 1911, at city hall. One hundred and eight candidates were initiated into the lodge by a degree team from a Boston Moose Lodge, and the first officers of the Moose in Lawrence were elected and installed. They were: Dictator Michael A. Scanlon; Past Dictator Robert S. Maloney; Vice-Dictator Walter Cantwell; Prelate John W. Dennison; Secretary Charles S. Tivnan; Sargeant-at-Arms Thomas F. Raidy; Inner Guard W. S. Gillespie; Outer Guard Michael Mulcahy; Physician Dr. John Bannon, and Trustees John P. O'Brien, Peter McGrun, and Luciano Delgrandes. The Moose met on the second and fourth Thursday of each month at the Moose Temple at 573 Common Street near Broadway.

[25] *Evening Tribune*, December 6, 1913.

[26] The list included Joseph Walsh, Walter Higgins, John Scanlon, George Coleburn, Patrick Brennah, Omer Gagnon, Patrick Boyle, James Connell, Maurice Conkley, John Cahill, Magloire Bernardin, Maurice Walsh, Joe St. Cyr, Cornelius Sheelian, and the former mayor and past dictator, Michael A. Scanlon.

[27] *Evening Tribune*, April 12, 1915.

[28] *Evening Tribune*, May 9, 1914.

[29] Peter Cassidy Collection.

[30] Phil Riley was the last of five children born to Philip Riley and Mary Brady.

[31] *Evening Tribune*, April 14, 1919.

[32] *Evening Tribune*, April 14, 1919.

[33] *Evening Tribune*, April 14, 1919.

[34] *Evening Tribune*, April 14, 1919.

[35] *Evening Tribune*, April 30, 1919.

[36] *The Leader*, December 5, 1915.

Chapter 6: The Irish Go to War

[1] Maurice B. Dorgan, *History of Lawrence, Massachusetts*, publisher Maurice B. Dorgan, Lawrence, Massachusetts, 1924, p. 206.

[2] *Evening Tribune*, August 2, 1918.

[3] Born in South Lawrence on July, 18, 1890, Francis Leahy was the son of John Leahy and Mary McNamara. After graduating from grammar school in 1904 Francis Leahy attended the Lawrence Commercial School for a year. In June of 1907 he enlisted in the U.S. Army and was assigned to duty in the Philippines where he served with distinction. Upon his return he worked for the Bay State Street Railway Company before reenlisting in the army in 1910. In the summer of 1916, then Lieutenant Leahy went to Mexico for five months with Company F of the Lawrence National Guard unit. He was very popular among the members of Company F and later played a key role in recruiting men for service when the company needed added strength in 1917. He was promoted to captain in France by General Pershing in February 1918, but died just five months later.

[4] *Evening Tribune*, December 24, 1917.

[5] *Evening Tribune*, January 19, 1918.

[6] Maurice B. Dorgan, *History of Lawrence, Massachusetts*, publisher Maurice B. Dorgan, Lawrence, Massachusetts, 1924, p. 207; *Lawrence Telegram*, April 16, 1919; Edward Sirois and William McGinnis, revised by John Hogan, *Smashing Through "The World War" with Fighting Battery C*, , The Meek Press, Salem, MA, 1919. pp. iv, 172.

[7] *Lawrence Telegram*, Jan 17, 1918.

[8] *Evening Tribune,* May 1, 1917.

[9] *Evening Tribune*, February 13, 1919.

[10] *Evening Tribune*, February 13, 1919.

[11] Peter Cassidy Collection.

Chapter 7: Baseball and Boxing

[1] In 1922 a partial list of the leagues included the Mill, Eastern, Police, Industrial, City, Church, Amateur,and Playground leagues. Examples of team names included the Tower Hill Stars, the Micks, the Owls, the Ramblers Athletic Club, the Tremonts, the Buffaloes, the Legion, the Tribune Newsboys, the Ex-Ball Stars, St. Annes, the Dentists, the Spicket Stars, Pacific Mills, CYMA, Smith & Dove, K of C, and the Independents.

[2] Members included Peggy Burns, Veronica Burke, Helen Curtin, Elizabeth Carter, Helen McLaughlin, Catherine Gildea, Verna Minahan, Gert Drew, and Florida Jacques.

[3] Carolyn Thornton, "Making a Difference: Lizzie Murphy (1894-1964)," *The Providence Journal*, 1998.

[4] *Evening Tribune*, June 20, 1922.

[5] *Lawrence Telegram*, June 20, 1922.

[6] *Evening Tribune*, June 21, 1922.

[7] *Lawrence Telegram*, July 10, 1922.

[8] Lizzie Murphy retired from baseball in 1935 at the age of forty. Shortly thereafter, she married a Warren, Rhode Island mill superintendent named Walter Larivee. She became a widow several years after their marriage, and spent the rest of her life working in the mills or on oyster boats. It was said that she soured on baseball in her later years, rarely talking about her glory days on the ballfields and never accepted invitations to speak or receive a public honor. She died on July 27, 1964, at the age of seventy.

[9] Born to Mr. and Mrs. Frank McDonough in 1899, Billie was a thin and frail young boy whose physical condition always worried family and friends when he was growing up. He attended the Packard Grammar School and graduated from Cannon's Commercial School. In June of 1917 he left his job as a clerk at the Lawrence Dye Works and signed up to fight the Germans in France. Like many of his buddies, Billie joined Lawrence's famed Battery C of the 102nd Field Artillery. He had just turned nineteen at the time and was reported to have been one of the youngest men to enlist in Battery C.

[10] *Lawrence Telegram*, August 10, 1922.

[11] In the years that followed, baseball continued to be a favorite of city residents. One of the more popular teams to form after McDonough's death was called "the Millionaires." On Saturday, May 3, Billie McDonough's body was borne on a caisson to St. Mary's Church where a funeral Mass was celebrated. His closest friends from Battery C served as his bearers: William Howe, William Hart, Frank Haley, Timothy Barry, William Coughlin and Edgar Blanchette. Kloby Corcoran was an honorary bearer, along with fellow boxer Arthur Flynn and Frank Kennedy, part owner of the Independents. Billie McDonough was a member of Lodge 65 of the Lawrence Elks Club, the American Legion, and the Veterans of Foreign Wars. Prior to the war McDonough lived in the Tower Hill section of Lawrence at 64 Oregon Street. Later, he lived in South Lawrence. He was buried in a family plot in St. Augustine's Cemetery in Andover, Massachusetts.

[12] *Kelly's Heroes: The Irish Brigade at Gettysburg,* T. L. Murphy, Farnsworth House Military Impressions, Gettysbugh, PA, 1997, p. 6.

[13] *The Leader,* May 25, 1915.

[14] Peter Cassidy Collection. No author attributed to the newspaper clipping.

[15] Born on November 9, 1888, in Keyesville, New York, Thomas "Kloby" Corcoran took up residence in Lawrence where he began his amateur boxing career.

[16] At the time of his death Kloby Corcoran resided in Reading, Massachusetts with wife, Anna (Connelly) Corcoran.

Chapter 8: The Struggle for Irish Freedom

[1] *Evening Tribune*, December 13, 1919.

[2] *Evening Tribune*, April 25, 1919.

[3] *Evening Tribune*, June 28, 1919.

[4] *The Pilot*, July 5, 1919.

[5] Peter Cassidy Collection. Source of newsclipping not attributed.

[6] *Evening Tribune*, July 1, 1919.

[7] *Evening Tribune*, June 16 and July 1, 1919.

[8] *Evening Tribune*, October 25, 1920.

[9] *Evening Tribune*, March 18, 1912.

[10] *Evening Tribune*, March 18, 1915.

[11] Peter Cassidy Collection. Newspaper source and the critic's name are unkown.

Chapter 9: Politics and Patronage

[1] *Lawrence Telegram*, December 15, 1920.

[2] *Lawrence Telegram*, January 6, 1921.

[3] *Lawrence Telegram*, January 19, 1921.

[4] *Evening Tribune*, January 5, 1921.

[5] *Lawrence Telegram*, March 5, 1921.

[6] Edward Callahan was born in County Limerick on April 4, 1874, and came to the United States in 1886 after the death of his parents. Upon his arrival in Lawrence in 1888, he lived at 22 Stearns Avenue, attended St. Mary's Church, and later married Catherine O'Hare. He first entered politics in 1898 when he successfully ran for the common council. In 1904, 1905, and 1906, he was elected representative to the state legislature and was elected state senator in 1918. For a ten-year period, he also worked for the water department. He died on February 14, 1951, at the age of seventy-six. He had been a member of Division 8 of the Ancient Order of Hibernians and the Holy Name Society.

[7] Mike Scanlon was born on Chestnut Street in Lawrence to William and Elizabeth Scanlon on December 11, 1867. Shortly thereafter, his family moved to 51 Oak Street, also in the Plains. For a time he attended St. Mary's School and at the age of seventeen went into the carpentry trade and later the construction business, which he practiced for most of his life. Once married, he and his wife Sarah McCarter moved to the northernmost section of Lawrence, across the Spicket, to reside at 87 Avon Street. He began his political career as a member of the school board in 1900. In 1907 he served as alderman from Ward Two under the old city charter. He was Grand Knight of the Knights of Columbus and past president of both the Fr. Mathew Temperance Society and the Lawrence Nest of Owls. He was also a member of the Elks, the Eagles, the Friends of Irish Freedom, Ancient Order of Hibernians, Division 8. On St. Patrick's Day 1952, Mike Scanlon suffered a serious fall that fractured his skull. He was taken to the Bessie Burke Hospital in grave condition, but little could be done to save the eighty-four-year-old Scanlon. He died one week later on March 24, 1952. After a solemn high requiem Mass at St. Mary's Church, he was buried at the Immaculate Conception cemetery. He resided at 22 Arlington Street at the time of his death.

[8] *Evening Tribune*, December 1, 1923.

[9] *Lawrence Telegram*, November 10, 1925.

[10] *Evening Tribune*, February 11, 1925.

[11] *Evening Tribune*, December 8, 1927.

[12] *Evening Tribune*, December 9, 1927.

[13] *Evening Tribune*, December 8, 1927.

[14] Born in 1873, Pat McNulty spent much of his early adult life as a brick mason. Prior to his election, he served as a construction foreman for a large contracting firm. During this tenure, more permanent roads were surfaced and more miles of sewer built than in any prior six-year period. One of his proudest achievements was the construction of a new and larger water filtering system, something he had fought four years to have installed. Pat and his wife Catherine lived at 117 and later 119 Tremont Street in North Lawrence where he died on Friday, December 31, 1943, at the age of seventy. His funeral was held at St. Mary's Church on January 4, 1944. He was a member of Division 8, Ancient Order of Hibernians.

[15] *Lawrence Sunday News*, November 17, 1929.

[16] *Lawrence Sunday News*, November 8, 1929.

[17] John McCarthy was born in the city on June 17, 1877, to Charles McCarthy and Mary Goggin. He remained in the city throughout his life where he and his wife, Anna Donovan, raised their five children at 21 Garfield Street. As a youngster he attended St. Mary's School until the age of fourteen.

[18] *Lawrence Sunday News*, December 9, 1929.

[19] *Lawrence Telegram*, September 28, 1931.

[20] *Lawrence Telegram*, October 15, 1931.

[21] *Lawrence Sunday News*, October 25, 1931.

[22] *Evening Tribune*, December 7, 1933; December 8, 1933.

[23] *Evening Tribune*, December 9, 1933.

[24] In his later years, John W. McCarthy continued his membership in St. Patrick's Parish, the Bon Secours Hospital Guild, the Holy Name Society, and the Battery C Veterans Association. On October 19, 1952, John W. McCarthy died at the age of seventy-five. A funeral Mass was celebrated at St. Patrick's Church, after which he was buried at the Immaculate Conception Cemetery.

Chapter 10: The Wets vs. the Drys

[1] Alice L. Walsh, *Sketch of the Life of the Rev. James T. O'Reilly, O.S.A.*, Free Press Printing Company, Lawrence Maassachusetts, 1924. pp. 7,8.

[2] *Lawrence Telegram*, December 6, 1897.

[3] *Lawrence Telegram*, January 17, 1920.

[4] *Lawrence Telegram*, October 28, 1920.

[5] *Evening Tribune*, January 8, 1921.

[6] *Lawrence Telegram*, February 23, 1921.

[7] *Evening Tribune*, January 15, 1921.

[8] *Lawrence Telegram*, January 3, 1925.

[9] *Evening Tribune*, September 8, 1925.

[10] *Evening Tribune*, February 5, 1925.

[11] Born in Ireland in 1872, Pat O'Connor emigrated to Lawrence in 1892 and lived on the Plains at 147 Oak Street.

[12] *Lawrence Sunday News*, November 15, 1925.

[13] *Lawrence Telegram*, November 16, 1925.

[14] *Lawrence Telegram*, November 10, 1925.

[15] Along with his wife, Nora Coakley, Pat O'Connor raised seven daughters and frequently spoke of them during the campaign. He was a member of the Ancient Order of Hibernians, Division 8, the Knights of Columbus, the Lawrence Liquor Dealers Association, and a prominent member of the Lawrence Elks Lodge.

[16] *Lawrence Sunday News*, May 14, 1933.

[17] For most of his adult life, Patsy O'Connor lived in North Lawrence, at 59 and later 24 Avon Street. For a short time, from 1914 to 1916, he resided at 64 Bigelow Street, the Carletonville area of South Lawrence, where he probably came to know Peter Cassidy. Pat O'Connor died at his home on 24 Avon Street on Sunday evening, July 16, 1944 at the age of seventy-one. His wife had died several months earlier on November 18, 1943. Both were active members of St. Laurence's Church and were buried at Immaculate Conception Cemetery.

[18] *Lawrence Sunday News*, February 1, 1931.

[19] *Lawrence Sunday News*, February 1, 1931.

Chapter 11: The World Closes In

[1] Peter Cassidy Collection. No source attributed.

[2] They included Anna M. Neversky of 41 Mechanic Street, Anna Kobos of 5 East Street, Catherine Ahearn of 8 Swan Street, Margaret Bronson of 279 Lawrence Street, Josephine Frederick of 27 Clarke Street, and head nurse, a "tall good looking blond" named Mary R. McCarthy, of 12 Greenfield Street.

[3] Fifty of the 250 residents of whom were medical patients. Private hospitals provided over 200 available beds to residents of the Lawrence-Methuen area; the Lawrence General, 150 beds, the Clover Hill, 31 beds; and the Barr Sanitarium with 24 beds.

[4] *Lawrence Sunday News*, December 11, 1927.

[5] Born in 1889, David J. Burke was the son of David and Susan (O'Neil) Burke and he attended St. Mary's school as a boy. After first learning the steamfitters' trade, Dave went on to be an agent for the John Hancock Insurance Company and then the owner of the Postoffice Bowling Alleys and Dave's Diner. In his later years he worked as a salesman for Merrimack Valley Distributing Company.

[6] *Lawrence Telegram*, November 21, 1932.

[7] John Joseph Ford was born on December 1, 1881, to Patrick Ford and Ellen (Monohan) Ford who lived at 175 Lowell Street with their eight children. Like Mr. Burke, "John Joe" attended St. Mary's parochial school but family finances forced him to drop out at a young age. He started working for a meat and grocery store owned by James McAvoy at the corner of Valley and Hampshire Streets. Reaching manhood he went to work for Ford Brothers, a liquor distributor, and later started his own trucking and moving business.

[8] *Lawrence Telegram*, December 9, 1932.

[9] *Lawrence Telegram*, December 9, 1932.

[10] *Lawrence Telegram*, December 10, 1932.

[11] *Lawrence Sunday News*, November 27 and December 4, 1932.

[12] *Lawrence Telegram*, November 14, 1934.

[13] Dave Burke died on March 3, 1954 at the age of sixty-five while at the McGowen Hospital. After losing his reelection bid in 1934, John Joe Ford later served as a local WPA administrator and was member of the city housing authority until he retired in 1951. He attended St. Patrick's Church for much of his adult life where he was a member of the Holy Name Society. On February 7, 1964, following a long illness, John Joseph Ford died at the Bessie M. Burke Memorial Home. After a funeral Mass at St. Mary's Church, he was laid to rest at St. Mary's Cemetery.

[14] Peter Cassidy Collection. Author unknown.

[15] *Evening Tribune*, May 13, 1938.

Selected Bibliography

Author's Note: This biographical listing is not intended to include all of the resources I consulted in creating this book, but only those most helpful to understand and convey the events at the turn of the twentieth century. It should be noted that the vast majority of the information used to write this book came from my research of the local newspapers and official city records published during the covered time period. These include:

Lawrence City Documents, 1889-1900
Lawrence City Directories, 1846-1938
The Lawrence Daily American, 1869-1914
The Lawrence Daily Journal, 1860-1862
The (Lawrence) Evening Tribune, 1890-1938
The Lawrence Sentinel, 1861-1887
The Lawrence Sunday News, 1925-1933
The Lawrence Telegram, 1996-1937
The Lawrence Weekly Journal, 1896-1898
The Leader, 1903-1917
The Pilot, 1915-1925
The Sunday Star, 1935

Other sources include:

Cole, Donald B. *Immigrant City, Lawrence, Massachusetts, 1845-1921.* University of North Carolina Press, Chapel Hill, NC, 1963.

Coogan, Tim Pat. *The IRA, A History.* Roberts Rhinehart Publishers, Niwot, CO, 1994.

Connolly, S. J., Editor. *The Oxford Companion to Irish History.* Oxford University Press. Oxford, England & New York, NY, 1998.

Dengler, Eartha, Katherine Khalife, and Kenneth Skulski. *Images of America, Lawrence, Massachusetts, Vol I.* Arcadia Press, Dover, NH, 1995.

Dorgan, Maurice B. *Lawrence, Yesterday and Today, 1845-1918.* Dick and Trumpold Publishers, Lawrence, MA, 1918.

————. *History of Lawrence, Massachusetts.* Publisher Maurice Dorgan, Lawrence, MA, 1924.

Ellis, P. Berresford. *A History of the Irish Working Class.* 1985 Edition. Pluto Press Limited. London, England, 1985.

Foster, R. F. *Modern Ireland 1600-1972.* 2nd Edition. Penguin Books. New York, NY, 1989.

Grey, Peter. *The Irish Famine.* Harry N. Abrams Inc. New York, NY, 1995.

Hoobler, Dorothy and Thomas. *The Irish American Family Album.* Oxford University Press, New York, NY, 1995.

MacManus, Seamas. *The Story of the Irish Race, a Popular History of Ireland.* 4th Edition, The Devin-Adair Company, New York, NY, 1944.

McCaffrey, Lawrence J. *Textures of Irish America.* Syracuse University Press, Syracuse, NY, 1992.

————. *The Irish Catholic Diaspora in America.* 3rd Edition. The Catholic University of America Press, Washington, D.C., 1997.

McKiernan, Thomas P.. "The Story of the Irish People in Lawrence." Supplement to *The Sunday Star,* 1936.

Miller, Kerby and Wagner, Paul. *Out of Ireland, The Story of Irish Emigration to America.* Elliot & Clark Publishing, Washington, D.C., 1994.

Moody, T. M. and Martin, F. X., Editors. *The Course of Irish History,* 3rd Edition. Roberts Rinehart Publishers, Boulder, CO, 1995.

Morrill, Aaron Robert. "Life and Work for the Early Irish Laborer in Lawrence, Massachusetts. (Bachelors thesis), State University of New York, 1982.

Morison, Samuel Eliot. *The Oxford History of the American People, Vol. 3.* The New American Library, Inc., New York, NY, 1972.

O'Mahoney, Katherine A. O'Keeffe, *Sketch of Catholicity in Lawrence and Vacinity.* Sentinel Steam Printing, Lawrence, MA, 1882.

Woodham-Smith, Cecil, Editor. *The Great Hunger, Ireland 1845-1849.* 7th Edition. Old Town Books, New York, NY, 1989.

Sirois, Edward D. and McGinnis, William. Revised by John Hogan. *Smashing Through "The World War" with Fighting Battery C.* The Meek Press, Salem, MA, 1919.

Skulski, Kenneth. *Images of America, Lawrence, Massachusetts, Vol II.* Arcadia Publishing, Dover, NH, 1997.

Walsh, Alice L. *Sketch of the Life of Rev. James T. O'Reilly, O.S.A.* Free Press Printing, Lawrence, MA, 1924.

Index

ORDER FORM

Why not share *The View...?*

Thank you for purchasing a copy of *The View From Shanty Pond*. Why not give a little Irish nostalgia to family and friends? It makes a great gift: holiday, birthday, St. Patrick's Day ... or anytime. They'll love *The View*.

Web Site: www.shantypondpress.com
Toll Free Telephone: 1-877-853-2459
E-Mail: orders@shantypondpress.com
Fax Orders: 1-802-425-2030
Postal Orders: Shanty Pond Press
                    Dept. 222
                    350 North Pasture Lane
                    Charlotte, Vermont 05445 USA

Please send me _____ **copies of** *The View From Shanty Pond*.
I understand that I may return my book purchase for a full refund if I am not satisfied. No questions asked. We do not refund shipping costs.

Price list: 1 copy: $24.95
                 2-10 copies: $19.95 each

Please ship my book(s) to: *(Please print)*
    Name: _____
    Address: _____
    City:_____ State:_____ Zip:_____

Shipping & Handling (USA): $4.00 for first book, $2.00 for each additional book.
Sales Tax: Please add 5% for books shipped to Vermont.

Payment Method: *(No cash, please)*
❑ Check or Money Order
Credit card: ❑ Visa ❑ MasterCard
    Card Number: _____
    Name on Card: _____ Exp. Date: _____
    Signature: _____

Call Toll Free and Order Now!
1-877-853-2459

ORDER FORM
(See reverse side)